# FELLOW TRAVELER

A Memoir of a Twentieth Century American Life

BY ESTHER ROWLAND

Fellow Traveler: A Memoir of a Twentieth Century American Life

By Esther Rowland

ISBN: 9781483552453

Cover design by Cameron Rowland

# DEDICATION AND ACKNOWLEDGEMENTS

This book is dedicated to my husband and life partner, Lewis Phillip Rowland, MD, whose father, upon hearing the fancy name his wife had chosen, renamed him Bud on the day he was born. Without Bud, and without our three children, Andy, Steve and Joy, this book could not have been written. That also holds true of my mother, my father and my brother Jack.

I also acknowledge the encouragement and appreciation I have received from my grandchildren: Mikaela and Liam Luttrell-Rowland, Cameron and Mariel Rowland, Zuri Ray-Alladice and Christopher Lee; my children's spouses, Kathy Wayland, Sharon Lee, Makanda McIntyre, and Darryl Alladice; and my grandchildren's spouses or significant others, Jesús Soto Cóndor, Rachel Lewis, and Emmy Levitas. Others who have helped me along the way include my niece, Amy Edelman, my writing group: Sarah Key, Hanna Griff, Jennifer Wortham, Emily Socolov, and Marissa Piesman; my other friends: Carmel Berkson, Elinor Blank, Vilma Bornemann Caralay, Constance Brown, Joan Burstyn, Julia Chase-Brand, Mary Marshall Clark, Charlotte Fahn, Billi DiMauro, Mindy Thompson Fullilove, Ruth Gainer, Sheila Hayes, Martha Katz, William Landau, Marta Petrusewicz, Helen and Donald Price, Robin Roy, Julie Ruben, Flora Schiminovitch, Timea Szell, Gerta Vrbova, and Ellen Weiss. In addition, I am most grateful to my professional writing instructors, Patricia Bosworth, Hettie Cohen Jones, and most of all Gerry Albarelli, who taught me the best way to tell a story and encouraged me to publish this book. And with the publication of this Bookbaby book I greet another baby, my great-grandson Jacob Bernard (Cobi) Cóndor, who has also arrived at just this time.

We are a family of people who like to write, much thanks to Bud. He was editor of *Neurology* for ten years, and of *Merritt's Textbook of Neurology* for eight editions, and he has been honored by the neurological community for correcting manuscripts with a red pencil, before the days of computerized text tracking. His colleagues actually formalized his contribution by giving him a "Red Pencil Award" in 1987 when his term as editor of *Neurology* was completed. At the ceremony, and ever since, many who have described their astonishment at what he had done to their articles, almost always end up saying, "I am eternally grateful to Bud; he taught me how to write." Bud helps us all with our manuscripts, with the red pencil at the ready. My son, Steve, my daughter, Joy and my grandson, Cameron have also edited, proofed, and turned this manuscript into a book. It's great to have built in copy editors, especially ones who love to do it. So if you find a mistake in this book, you'll know whom to blame.

Bud Carrying The Red Pencil Award 1987

# INTRODUCTION TO FELLOW TRAVELER: A TWENTIETH CENTURY LIFE

"But who would want to read my book?" I asked Gerta as we were walking together in the lobby of the Hilton Hotel in Istanbul. Gerta Vrbova, Professor of Physiology at the University of London, was in Istanbul for the meeting of the World Congress of Neurology. I was there accompanying my husband, Bud Rowland, Professor of Neurology at Columbia University. Gerta and I, both born in 1926, were talking about the second memoir she was writing. She was happy to hear that I too was writing about my life. She had completed one book about escaping from the Nazi invaders in Slovakia and Hungary, and was working on a sequel about fleeing from the Communist government in the post-war period in Czechoslovakia. My life was not so dramatic. There was no Nazi genocide in the United States, no Soviet takeover, and we were spared the agony of having our country invaded and dominated by a treacherous enemy. With Gerta's memoir as an example of a personal story that was worth reading, I asked my question. And she answered instantly, and without hesitation. "I love to read about normal lives. It is what keeps me sane."

Although I never wished that I had been born in the Europe of the twenties and thirties, as a child I often wished that I had been born poor or in need of crutches or at least braces on my teeth. Or maybe born really rich, with parents who had tons of money and then lost it all in the Great Depression. As a young adult in the forties, when I met children of workers, I wished that my mom and dad had been in the working class and struggling against oppression. I wished that we lived in one of those great workers' housing projects in New York, like the "Coops" or the Amalgamated, where everyone one was a trade unionist, or a Socialist or Communist or a labor-Zionist, and lived as a community with shared values and shared common spaces for classrooms, and libraries. Instead, my story is of a white, middle class girl who grew up on the Grand Concourse, in the West Bronx, in a family of two kids and a mom and a dad; and the dad ran a small business and weathered the Depression with relative ease. Fortunately for my self-image, we were also Jewish and victims of the quota system, which made it difficult to go to certain schools or to rent certain apartments. Furthermore, even if my parents were comfortable as adults, they grew up poor and their parents had suffered through the experience of Czarist Russia, the pogroms, and the difficult move from one continent to another. So there is complexity in my background and it has been enhanced by our non-observant but Jewish sensibility that requires us to commit ourselves to social justice and compassion for the "other."

In 1932, my Uncle Izzy handed me a campaign button with a picture of Franklin D. Roosevelt. "He's a good man," my uncle said. "He will fight for all the poor and hungry people and get them jobs." I wore my button with pride until the great day when FDR was elected. A few years later, haunted by the pictures in *Life Magazine*, which arrived weekly, bringing the suffering of the Ethiopians and later of the Spanish Loyalists right into our home, my interest in righting wrongs was cemented. Since that time, in the role of a concerned-citizen, I have lived through and participated in the struggles for justice in the United States. It has been a period of rapid social change in American history, from the twenties to the beginning of the current century.

I have identified most of the characters in this book by their real names. However a few names have been changed, especially those belonging to people who have done or said foolish things.

In the digital version of my book I have added easily accessible links, mostly to the sounds of the times and the people I have written about. In the print version I have noted these links for the reader to connect to on the internet.

The title I have chosen, "Fellow Traveler," alludes to three things. First, it refers to the journey through life that my husband, Bud Rowland, and I have taken since we met and married in 1952. Second, it is the name of the political path we have followed as members of the non-communist left in the United States. Although in this context "fellow traveler" is usually a term of opprobrium, I am proud to be in the company of such fellows as Columbia Professor Franz Neumann; I.F.Stone, the journalist; Leo

Huberman and Harry Magdoff, editors of the Marxist magazine, *Monthly Review*; and the British historians, Edward and Dorothy Thompson. They were all great human beings as well as advocates for social justice, despite being labeled "pro-communist." The third meaning of "Fellow Traveler" is, of course, the literal one. Bud and I have traveled together all over the world, usually to medical meetings and to invited lectureships related to his job and to his prominence in the worldwide neurological community.

# CONTENTS

## Travels

# BEFORE THE BRONX—1926-1933

I was born Esther Edelman on April 12, 1926 in Lenox Hill Hospital in New York City. My family consisted of my mother, Ida Shifrin Edelman, my father, Abraham Simon Edelman, and my brother, Jacob Aaron Edelman (Jack) who was 3 years old at the time of my birth. We lived in an apartment on West 86th Street in Manhattan. My father worked as a fur merchant in his own business on West 30th Street, just a short subway ride from home. My mother also worked in the business, as bookkeeper, secretary, and consultant. She had flexible hours and usually left the house at about ten in the morning and returned home in the late afternoon. A young German man, Otto Munch, was my father's assistant in the business, and Otto's sisters, first, Gudren, then Suzie, and later Anna, lived with us, took care of the house, cooked the meals, and watched over Jackie and me. My brother spoke German before he spoke English and I spoke English with a heavy German accent. My mom later told me that when I was asked about Jackie, my reply was "Chockie hiss ha goot poy.'"

Esther and Jack in Central Park, 1929

Central Park was just two blocks away from our apartment and it was a favorite place for our nurses to take Jackie and me. There were small hills to climb, a lake where Jackie could sail his little boat, water fountains, trees, and grass that we could tumble on. On a wintry day, when I was four, our nurse was holding my left had and Jackie's right as we crossed Columbus Avenue, a busy street, on the way back from the park. A street-car was approaching but we had the green light. The motorman applied the brakes but skidded on the icy tracks, and knocked me down. A policeman saw what happened, grabbed my outstretched arm and pulled me along the tracks before the wheels of the trolley could run over me. The story made *The Daily News* and showed a picture of me on the lap of the policeman and wearing his cap. "Cop Cheats Death" ran the headline. I do not remember being hit. What I do remember was the ambulance ride, which took me to a local drug store (the place for outpatient emergencies in those days), where I was given a pelvic examination. That evening, *The Daily News* held a photo session in my house. The policeman who saved my life was George Wandling, who several years before had saved someone else and was the proud possessor of a silver-plated pistol, his reward for heroism. Not only was he a twice-recognized hero, he had also been voted the Adonis of the NYPD because of his build and his handsome face.

My parents were obviously grateful to him and kept the friendship for several years. They were also deeply affected by the accident and the near miss. I think I became even more precious to my Dad from that time on. My father adored me and he thought there was almost nothing that I could do wrong; I was his favorite. My mother, too, was very loving and had the remarkable ability to convince my brother and me that each of us was her favorite.

**Policeman Keeps Pace With Car, Holds Girl From Death Beneath It**

Running beside a moving south-bound Columbus Avenue car, Patrolman George Wandling at the West 68th Street Station, gradually drew Esther Edelman, four, of No. 11 West 68th Street, daughter of a wealthy clothing manufacturer, from the front of the trucks yesterday afternoon and saved her from being dragged under the wheels at 77th Street.

The child was torn from the grasp of her nurse, Miss Judrun Hanson, and wedged between the fendguard and the top of the trucks when crossing 77th Street.

Miss Hanson was knocked down. A few minutes after the car had struck a taxicab at the crossing. Wandling saw the child slipping and above

to Dennis Cunno, the motorman, who was unable to stop on the slippery rails.

Wandling grasped the child's hands and, as the car slid along, began dragging her closer to him. The car went fifteen feet over the crossing before it stopped, with Wandling jammed against an elevated railroad pillar, with the child in his arms. The girl, Wandling and Miss Hanson were treated for cuts and bruises by an ambulance surgeon, Walter Hatch, driver of the cab, was not hurt.

Despite his plea that he was unable to stop at the crossing and was forced to continue against the lights, Cunno received a summons. Charles Wandling, on every traffic signal, a Wandling known as the "Beau Brummel" of the department, remained on duty.

COP CHEATS DEATH—Esther Edelman, 4, was saved from death beneath surface car's wheels at Columbus ave. and 77th st. by Policeman George Wandling, with whom she's shown. Officer ran along, dragging girl, until motorman stopped car.

DAILY NEWS, WEDNESDAY, JANUARY 29, 1930.

After our German childhood nurses left, my mother had difficulty replacing them. When I was five years old, a new housekeeper was in charge of us one evening when my parents were out. She was a young, thin Irish woman who wore a large crucifix around her neck, dangling on top of the white apron she wore over her gray uniform. She gave Jackie and me dinner and allowed us to listen to one radio program and then said, "Go to bed." I replied, "Go to bed yourself." Her thin face froze into a scowl. She grabbed me and forced me to the floor, made me get on my knees to pray to God to forgive me for talking back to her. I cried myself to sleep but the next morning I told my mom what happened, and the woman was sent on her way.

I am the child in the middle

I went to public school in Manhattan where I started pre-school at the age of four-and-a-half. My mother had persuaded the local public school to accept me into their small kindergarten class. Kindergarten was not popular in those days (1930), or at least not in our neighborhood. The class comprised just six five-year-old children when the school accepted my mother's request to allow me to join. I stayed in kindergarten for a year and a half, until I was old enough to enter first grade, all at P.S. 166.

My first-grade teacher, Miss McGhee, a tall lady with grey hair that was tied in a bun, used her wooden pointer to smack the children on their backsides if they displeased her. One day we were learning to read from big flash cards, which she held up one at a time. The first card had "TWO" printed on it, with the number 1 in the lower left corner. She said, "Esther, come to the front and read the number written on this card." I said "1." She looked at me, puzzled, said nothing about my response, and then held up the next card on which "ONE" was printed and a small 2 in the lower left hand corner. "Read the number on this card," she said. I said "2" and the pointer came smashing down on me! "I know you can read" she shouted, "and I expected more from you." "But you said, 'Read the number,'" I sobbed. "Sit down, Esther, and stop crying!"

Another time, she found a small puddle on the floor. "Who did this?" she screeched. Silence. "I want the child who did this to come forward!" More silence. "All right. Line up in a large circle!" And we did, and she walked around the circle feeling every child's pants. I prayed that I wouldn't peepee in fright.

The most significant global event of my early childhood was the Great Depression, which hit the U.S. in 1929 when I was 3 years old. My father kept his business but would have downgraded our living situation if he had had the choice. Unfortunately, he had just signed a three-year lease on our apartment and, even though people had lost fortunes and Broadway was filled with apple carts and vendors begging for sales just to make a few pennies on each, the landlord held us to the full rent ($200 per month) for the duration of the lease. When we were free of the contract in 1932, the landlord begged to renegotiate, but my father would not deal with him again. So, we moved to a much simpler apartment -- smaller and without a doorman or elevator man and in Flushing, Queens rather than in Manhattan. This time my brother and I shared a room. Empty wooded lots surrounded our building. For us it was like living in the country.

A month before we moved, my mother took Jackie and me to enroll in P.S. 20, a large public school that was five blocks away from the new home. On that visit, the principal, a friendly man who greeted us with a big smile, asked my mother and Jack to have a seat at a table in his office and then motioned to me to join him at his desk.

"So, Esther," he said, "welcome to our school. We are glad to have you." He pointed to a chair for me to sit in while he too sat down and reached for a pen and some papers on his desk. "What grade are you in?"

"1B," I told him, and he started to write something. "But I would like to be in 2A."

(In those days school classes were organized on a six-month rather than a yearly basis and were willing to let children skip a term if their teachers thought they could handle the work of the next class.)

I turned to look at my mother to see if she agreed with me. She looked a bit surprised but shrugged her shoulders, as if to say "why not?" The principal looked at me with a half smile as he put down his pen. "Well, I might consider the change, but first I want to give you a little test." He had a pile of crayons on his desk and asked me to give him a few. "Few" sounded like "two" so I gave him two. Then he asked me to give him several. That sounded like seven, so I gave him seven. Satisfied, he then said, "All right, but let me see you write in script, which the second grade children have learned already." I did not know script except for my name, which the doorman on 86th St. had taught me. So I wrote my name for the principal and he assigned me to second grade.

On a bright October morning in 1933, Jackie and I walked together to our first day of school in Flushing. When lunchtime came I looked for Jackie who was supposed to take me home, where my mother was waiting to feed us and to find out if all went well. My brother was nowhere to be found. Feeling quite certain that I knew the way, I proceeded to walk by myself. After about ten minutes of walking and finding nothing familiar in sight, I asked a man who was eating his lunch, leaning on his pick-up truck, "Mister, could you tell me where is 140-30 Ash Ave." He replied, "Walk about five blocks back to the school and then turn left and walk five more." Knowing that I would never make it on time for both lunch and the return to school, I asked, "Could you please take me there in your truck?" He looked surprised but said, "Let me finish my sandwich and then I'll take you. Hop into the front seat." Within minutes we pulled up to the apartment house where my mother was fixed to the window and practically frantic. When I proudly told her that I had convinced the truck driver to give me the ride, she replied in a stern voice, "Esther, look at me and listen. I do not want you to ever do that again. There was a look of fear in her eyes as she said, "Never, never! You do not ask strangers for rides." The Lindbergh child had been kidnapped and murdered just a half a year earlier and it was still causing national nightmares.

Jackie and I spent most Saturdays at the movies. We lived in walking distance of Main Street in Flushing and would find out what was playing at the local theater as we approached it and read the marquee. One Saturday Jack got really excited. "It's a triple feature: a Charlie Chan, a Chandu the Magician, and a Fu Manchu!" I was excited because he was excited. What I really liked at the movies was the lottery. Each ticket had a number and we were told to hold on to it. Between the major features, the lights would go on and a man would come onto the stage with a load of toys. He would announce the lucky winner's number and the winner would come up and choose the prize. That Saturday, the man put his hand into a big glass bowl pulled out a number and called it out loud. It was the same as the one on my ticket. I showed it to Jackie. "You won, you won!" he said as he made way for me to get into the aisle to walk up to the stage. I knew exactly what toy I wanted--a tiny electric stove that ran on a battery and worked as a hot plate. Jackie was proud of me too, but I thought he would have liked me to pick something like a dump truck instead.

I was happy in my new second grade class, although my self-taught handwriting was terrible and I got my lowest grades in penmanship. But the teacher still thought I was smart and reliable. One day she had yard duty and she had to leave the classroom ten minutes before we completed our quizzes. "Esther," she said, "when you finish your test, please place it here on my desk. When the bell rings, I want you to collect all the papers and put them into one pile. Then, children," and she turned to address the whole class, "after you have handed in your papers, line up. Esther will lead you to the stairs and down to the yard where I will be waiting. Is that clear?" She then came to my seat and gave me some further instructions: "Esther, I want you to go down the stairs on that side of the building," she said as she pointed to the window-side of the classroom. Unfortunately, she was also pointing in the direction of the fire escape. When the test was done and the bell rang, I collected the papers, lined the children up and escorted them through the fire escape door, down a flight of stairs, right into the yard where the teacher was waiting for us with the most horrified look on her face.

One Monday in February, my mother, knowing that neither she nor a household helper would be at home for lunch the following day, asked me to find out if I could have lunch at school. I was told that for 50 cents I could buy a lunch ticket for a whole week. I was excited about this new adventure. Perhaps I would do it often and thus save myself from the long, wintry walks to and from home at lunchtime. The next morning was icy cold and I wore my little muskrat coat, which had been given to me by one of my Dad's furrier friends, who had remodeled it from an old coat of my mother's. When I walked into the lunchroom I suddenly became the center of attention. All of the children were staring at me. And then they rose from their chairs and crowded around. "Ooh can I touch it?" "No, I want to touch it." "No, me first." Everyone wanted to stroke my fur coat. I was mortified, and also frightened. The kids were dressed in old clothes and they looked poor and hungry. When I told my mother what had happened she realized her mistake; this was a federally sponsored lunch program for the children of the unemployed. I never went back to the lunchroom and I never again wore that muskrat coat to school.

In September of 1933, just before my family left Flushing, all the children from PS 20 marched down Main Street in a parade to celebrate President Roosevelt's National Recovery Act (the NRA). The boys wore white shirts and dark pants; we girls wore white dresses, and the teachers tied sashes diagonally across our chests. They were red, white, and blue, with the NRA logo, a blue eagle, in the center. We marched, ten abreast, in the street, right through the center of town. No one had told us what the NRA stood for. The teachers just seemed to regard the parade as a disruptive necessity that had been ordered from above. I remember feeling uncomfortable about marching, and especially about marching in straight lines: "Eyes Forward," "Keep in Step." It would have been better to look at the onlookers as they looked at us.

After one year in Flushing, my parents decided to move out of Queens, which my father, who had sinus trouble, considered "low and swampy," to the Bronx, which was "high and hilly." There they found a big apartment on the seventh floor in a building that had two elevators that were driven by elevator men and a private garden, just for the tenants, in the adjacent lot. Our rent was $90 a month. We stayed there for eighteen years.

# THE MURIEL ARMS

We moved to the Grand Concourse in the Bronx in 1933 when I was seven years old. The Grand Concourse, although not nearly as pretentious as its name, was a wide boulevard, more than four miles long, lined with trees and apartment houses on both sides. Our building was ten stories high, towering over all the neighboring buildings that were the traditional six-stories. The empty lot next door had been converted into a garden, complete with paths and a gazebo and reserved for the building's tenants, many who owned small businesses, like my father. We hardly knew our neighbors and had only one set of friends in the building: the Jacobs clan, father, mother, children, aunt and uncle, who lived in two apartments on the second floor.

We children were supposed to play in the garden, safely protected from the street traffic and the outsiders who did not have access to this private space. But, of course, we all preferred playing on the sidewalk, and even in traffic on the street. One of my favorite games was one my brother engineered, using me as his helper. He carved a row of little arch-shaped holes in a balsa wood strip, which he then leaned up against the curb, in the service road in front of our house. The size of the holes ranged from the exact size of a small marble, called an "immy," to one five times larger. There were five holes and they were numbered 1,3,5,7,10; 10 was the smallest. The player provided his own immy and could choose the hole he was aiming for, and reap a reward ranging from 1 to 10 immies if he got it into the proper hole. If the immy hit the wood and did not make it into a hole, Jackie kept it. And since almost every player aimed for the tiny #10 hole and missed, Jackie would be loaded with immies at the end of the session. Later he would sell them back to his customers for a price that was much lower than the price in the toy stores. My job was to collect the loose marbles from the street as fast as they were rolled. Sometimes I would be in charge of the whole operation, if Jackie decided to take a break. Occasionally a car would come, the driver, peering through his small windshield, would toot his horn and we scattered, only to start up again as soon as he passed.

Our apartment house, at 2665 Grand Concourse was called the "Muriel Arms." Sam Minskoff, the owner of the building, named it to honor his daughter, Muriel, who was at that time a pretty twelve-year old. To me, she was a real live princess, who actually lived in a duplex apartment on the fourth and fifth floors, with her parents, Sam and Esther, and her brothers, Henry, Jerry, Myron and Walter. They were like an imperial family. Their chauffeured limousine awaited them at the front door, taking the father and oldest brothers to their successful real estate business, Muriel, Myron and Walter to their private schools, and Esther to her household errands. Once I was bouncing a tennis ball in the lobby when Mr. Sam Minskoff, himself, emerged from the elevator. Instead of yelling at me, as I expected a landlord would, he was extremely friendly, with an avuncular interest in me. He asked my name, what apartment I lived in and then, satisfied with my presentation, he asked what kind of toy I would like him to buy for me. I was stunned and embarrassed and simply replied, "Whatever you like." Thereafter, whenever I saw him, he would repeat the question, get my mumbled and embarrassed response: "I don't know" or "Whatever you like," and we would go our separate ways. A few years after we moved in, the Minskoff family, by then, millionaires, moved to yet another Minskoff building on Park Avenue. I never got the toy.

Our apartment, 7B, had a good view above the neighboring buildings and was quietly secluded from the noises of the street. I used to love to give my apartment number when asked my address, for living on the seventh floor meant living in a luxury building.

(Many years later, I found out that the building code in the twenties, when the Concourse and all of those apartment houses were built, required fireproofing if the building was higher than six stories. As far as I know, only two buildings above 170th St. were taller. I finally understood why our home was the equivalent of luxury housing of those days. Not only did we have a great view from all of our windows, we were also protected from fire.)

Basically, it was a nice apartment, light and airy, with three exposures, one facing the Concourse, one facing the garden, and one facing the courtyard. Even more important, we had two bathrooms and three bedrooms. The D train on the IND subway line had just been opened and the Kingsbridge Road station was on our corner, just in front of the house.

My favorite room was my brother Jackie's. The previous tenants had carved it out of a large dining room by adding a dividing wall. They had used it as a den, and my parents furnished it with bookcases, a desk and a studio couch. The absence of a door, and Jackie's inherent good nature, made it a place where any of us in the family could enter. The living room had the big Philco radio, the size of a large low chest, and Jackie had a small one that sat on a table. At about five o'clock, after coming home from playing each afternoon, I used to plop down on Jackie's couch to hear the daily line-up of radio serials that he had chosen for us. We started with *Jack Armstrong, The All American Boy*, then, *Buck Rogers in the Twenty First Century*. During these time slots, my friends were listening to *Uncle Don* and *The Singing Lady*, programs that were a bit more appropriate for my age, but I was thrilled to be allowed to listen with my big brother and it never even occurred to me to use the radio in the living room for a different set of shows. After dinner we returned to Jackie's room for such weeklies as *The Lone Ranger* and *The Shadow*.

On the other hand, I remember listening in the living room with my mother and dad to the Monday night *Lux Radio Theater*, sponsored by the Lux toilet soap company. It was an hour-long drama, an adaptation of a Broadway play or a Hollywood movie, featuring the original actors. Once a week, it was a "must" in our house.

We also listened to the news, often in the form of *The Five Star Final*, a drama with actors depicting the plights of real people and the awful things that happened to them like drowning in a well or burning up in a house fire. These were the scary programs, but I felt protected by listening with grownups.

Jackie's room and mine shared a common wall, so when he was deeply immersed in reading *The Count of Monte Cristo*, he decided to imitate Alexander Dumas' hero and carve a hole between our two rooms. Night after night Jackie used his penknife to scrape, and scooped up the bits of telltale plaster to hide it from the prison guards (in this case our parents). Finally one evening I heard his voice in the hollow. The link was completed and we were then supposed to hook up our "telephone": two paper cups attached to a string. After the first night we never used the tunnel again and just forgot about it until a house painter discovered it a few years later.

When Jackie was thirteen, he persuaded our parents to buy a record player for his room. They agreed and gave him full reign to select the machine and to buy our first records. He chose an RCA Victor model, which fit nicely on the top of his bureau. The bonus that came with the set was $50 worth of free classical records and he busily set about making the selection. Records were expensive in those days and, since we had none at all in the house, Jackie tried to make our collection as representative as possible within the confines of his own developing taste for classical music. He chose several singles in the form of overtures. There were two by Rossini: the lively *Barber of Seville* and the *William Tell* (selected because it included the theme music for the *Lone Ranger*). He chose Tchaikovsky's *1812 Overture,* with its live cannons in the concluding bars and also the *Fifth Symphony*, which included "Moon Love," a popular tune of the time. We listened to everything over and over again. Then one day he came home with another purchase, this time using his own money. It was an album of seven inch rather than twelve inch 78s and it was called: *Six Songs for Democracy*. These were the songs of the International Brigades who were fighting in Spain against the fascists and for the Spanish Republic. The album was mostly in German and sung by Ernst Busch who was a soldier in the Thaelmann Column. They were German anti-Nazis who had managed to get to Spain and who named their group after the leader of the outlawed German Communist Party. When I saw Jackie's proud purchase and asked how much he had spent, (something like $6.00) I thought he had made a big mistake. But after listening to it and reading the text that came with it, I was won over. Thereafter I learned every song by heart, sung in the same German accent as Ernst Busch, to the extent that when I came forth with a chorus of my favorite "Freiheit" years later, my friend Bob, who heard me, wanted to know how I had learned to pronounce German so well since I had never studied it in school. "Die Heimat ist weit/ Doch wir sind bereit/ wir kempfen und seigen fur dich/ Freiheit!." ("Our Homeland is Far/ But We Are Ready/ We're Fighting and Winning For You/ Freedom!")

"The Thaelmann Column" Ernst Busch
http://www.youtube.com/watch?v=2CZgXSAAhis

The apartment was furnished with well-constructed English reproductions that came from a large furniture store on Grand Street on the lower East Side. Most of it had been bought when I was too small to remember. What I liked the most were the draperies in the dining room and living room, especially the summer ones which were made of linen and block-printed with birds of paradise. I used to love sitting on the radiator in front of the windowsill, with the drapery back-ties unhooked, playing with an imaginary friend and hidden from view.

My room had twin beds, one for me and one for the sleep-in housekeeper. It was also the room with the fire escape. I remember one maid, Pauline, who looked like the actress, Paulette Goddard and seemed so out of place doing domestic work. She loved to wear high heel shoes and looked really gorgeous in her fitted coat with a blue fox collar that my mother had originally bought for herself but had given, or sold very cheaply, to

Pauline. One night Pauline, coming home from a day off very late, and having left her key at home, entered the apartment through the fire escape. My mother, who had found the forgotten key, was waiting up for Pauline to let her in, and heard her come through the window of my room. Mommy told me later that she had scolded Pauline for stupidly walking down the fire escape, all the way from the roof, in high heels and past the neighbors' windows. "Why didn't she call me to leave the door open or to leave the key under the mat?" my mother asked. She never told me what Pauline's response was, but I'm sure she must have mumbled that she was afraid to wake up the family once she discovered that she did not have the key. Poor Pauline was fired the next day, which upset me greatly. "Don't you believe in giving people a second-chance?" I asked my mother. "Look, Darling," she replied, " I am not happy with her to begin with and this stupid behavior—walking down a fire escape, and in high heels, is the last straw!" I protested: "You always tell me that working people have rights, so why not Pauline?" My mother reached out to stroke my face and she seemed to appreciate my argument. After all, I was just quoting her. But Pauline had already left and my mother did not change her mind. Furthermore, after Pauline was gone, my mother decided to hire day help instead, and from then on I had a room of my own.

# GROWING UP ON THE GRAND CONCOURSE

The move to the Bronx from Flushing had many advantages. Not only did we have a much larger and grander apartment, but also there was much more for us kids to do within a short walking distance. There were several movie houses for our Saturday afternoons; there was the soda fountain almost next door to the theaters, and we were in a bustling neighborhood with a department store, lots of markets, parks. No more empty lots.

The Grand Concourse was designed to be a Champs-Élysée lookalike; it had a main road five lanes wide and then a pair of two-lane side roads separated from the center by a barrier of grass and trees on each of the two sides. And that is where the comparison to the Champs-Élysée ended. The name, Grand Concourse, might have made some folks believe that it was more than just a wide boulevard. We dwellers, on the other hand, called it "The **Con**course." Grand or not, walking up and down the sidewalks that abutted this busy street was a fun thing to do for kids on Saturdays.

J.S. Krum was the store that made candies and featured a gigantic soda fountain where we gathered nearly every Saturday afternoon, after the movies, and spent the remainder of our twenty-five cent movie-and-treat budget on either a twelve-cent ice cream soda or a fifteen-cent ice cream sundae. Occasionally we would choose instead a street-sold, ten-cent Charlotte Russe, a mound of whipped cream that covered a chunk of sponge cake and was sold in a paper cone and topped with a maraschino cherry. But my favorite was the "Black and White," a chocolate soda with vanilla ice cream, at Krum's.

J.S. Krum's in the thirties when unemployed men were hired as temps to advertise

Ten cents was the price of a child's movie ticket, a child being age twelve or under. I remember the dilemma we faced when each of us, myself, and my friends Rhoda and Ruth, turned thirteen. We all did so at about the same time, in the spring of 1939. For about six months we had no problem simply asking for children's tickets. After all we had not noticeably changed in a few weeks or even a few months. What should we do, however, the following fall, when we were back from a long summer of growth, with menstrual periods, and wearing bras? I decided that the best strategy was to lie up front. Ask at the booth: "Do we have to pay adult prices when our thirteenth birthdays are coming next week?" "Oh no dear, of course not" was the answer. "And I wish you a happy birthday." We got away with variations of this ploy a few times. I was proud of myself for engineering such a sophisticated strategy. In contrast, however, I remembered the day of my fifth birthday when my Dad took me on the subway. As we reached the bottom of the stairs, he motioned to me to crawl under the turnstile as I had always done in the past, while he stopped at the cashier's booth to get some nickels in change to pay his own fare. "Daddy, don't you remember that today is my birthday and I am five. You've got to pay for me," I said loudly and proudly. My poor Dad was caught in the deception and threw up his hands.

On the other side of the Concourse, a few blocks south of Krum's, there was an Art Deco theater called the Ascot. This was our hangout when we were in high school and could not get enough of the great foreign movies they showed. I especially remember *The Baker's Wife,* a French classic, and my all-time favorite actor, Jean Gabin, in *Pepe Le Moko, The Lower Depths*, and best of all, *Grand Illusion.* In summer camp, when all the girls had pinups of Robert Taylor and Tyrone Power, my bed was framed with pictures of Jean Gabin, upon whom I lovingly gazed as I woke up each morning. Unlike the Hollywood beauties, he had a heavy, dark and pock-marked face, which sported a perpetual scowl. I loved him.

Jean Gabin

The *Loew's Paradise,* just a few blocks north of the Ascot, still stands as a Concourse landmark. It was one of the famous movie palaces of the period, with golden cherubs, floating clouds on the ceiling, and a lavish interior with dark red upholstered seats and lots of gold fleck. I never felt that it was the place that dreams are made of—the place where poor people went to forget their own shabby surroundings, although that might have been true for some. Rather, I thought of it as a kitschy rendition of an over decorated imitation of a French chateau. Furthermore, I remember it as a place where we girls had to constantly change our seats when dirty old men sat next to us and tried to feel us up.

In the thirties and the forties, my New York was filled with sex fiends who loved the crowded subways so they could freely grab onto some girl's behind. Because the perverts also hung out at movies, the theaters eventually had to restrict children from going in without adults. At that point we asked adult strangers who were buying tickets to "take us in." Once inside, we children bolted and sat where we pleased. The authorities looked the other way. Later, fearing the loss of a huge Saturday afternoon business from the kids, the theaters provided employees whom they called "matrons" to supervise a section of the theater where all the children were herded.

Alexander's Department Store stood on the corner of Fordham Road and the Concourse, a haven for shoppers seeking good stuff at lower prices. "Meet me in front of Alexander's," was a familiar Bronx call, vying with "Meet me at the Biltmore Clock," the motto of the rich kids of Westchester.

Poe Park, just across the street from the Muriel Arms, was a favorite hangout where my girlfriends and I used to sit on the benches and talk, or jump rope on the paved paths. When we needed a bathroom break, we would use the one in the Poe Cottage, the place where Edgar Allan Poe had written "The Raven." Inside, there was an enormous, scary replica of a raven, which we had to pass on each visit to the toilet.

Far to the west down Kingsbridge Road, was Citarella fish market, the place where the now famous Citarella had its humble start. It was where young Grace Citarella and her husband opened their first business, and also the first non-kosher fish market in our heavily Jewish neighborhood. Even though we were Jewish, my parents were non-observers and not kosher, so there was no reason for us not to eat shellfish except that there was no place to buy it. Monday night was fish night in our house, and I dreaded it until Citarella came into our lives in the early 1940s. My mother discovered it one day and walked into a world of lobsters in the tank and oysters, crabs, shrimp all laid out in glass cases sitting on huge beds of ice. Intrigued by the display, my mom was tempted to buy but hesitated because she had no idea how to cook any of this exotic stuff. Grace, a short, slightly plump woman, about thirty-five years old, with black hair carefully folded into a net, and lively brown eyes, told her exactly how it should be done. "Peel the shrimp and put them in water with a little vinegar and cook them until they turn pink." That night we had shrimp for dinner and from then on we were loyal customers. Grace, wearing her long white starched apron, with a belt tied twice around her waist, opened the oysters for us. I remember how, at dinnertime, they slid down my throat, rich with the salty taste of the sea. Grace cooked the lobsters just in time for us to pick them up and serve them at our dining table. All we had to do was melt the butter. Jack and I loved to shop at Citarella, gladly offering to unburden Mom from this chore so we could learn how to cook seafood. *(Years later when we returned to New York, we rediscovered Citarella on the upper west side of Manhattan, but Grace had retired.)*

On Kingsbridge Road we had two favorite hangouts: the Jewish delicatessen, and the Jewish candy store. The deli was the place Jackie and I would go for an occasional lunch or dinner, if no one was at home to feed us. They specialized in soup and sandwiches. At lunchtime it was filled with house painters, called "paintners," dressed in their cotton jackets, pants, and caps, smeared with pink, blue, and yellow paint, the colors of the apartment walls. They were Jewish and hungry, slurping huge bowls of soup and the free side order of half a loaf of fresh rye bread for dipping. For our lunch, my brother and I always chose a sandwich, usually corned beef or pastrami piled high. We ate it with a Dr. Brown's Cream Soda or Root Beer, our favorites.

The "Jewish" candy store was the place for a two-cent egg cream, a chocolate flavored soda that was made with milk and seltzer, or huge ice cream sodas, served in giant glasses that had three curves, one for each scoop of ice-cream. One day I dropped my glass filled with a brand new ice cream soda and it smashed to bits. The candy store man, seeing how sorry I was that I broke his glass and that I lost my delicious soda, immediately made me another. "No charge," he said. "Enjoy."

On our way back to P.S. 46 after lunch, I would stop at a different kind of candy store near the school. They sold chocolates from a box. The price was a penny apiece, but if you got one with a green (pistachio) center, you won a penny and could try again. Or if you had another penny you could also try again. We tried until our pennies ran out.

# FORWARD MARCH!

All was working out well in our move from Flushing to the Bronx, all except P.S. 46, the local public school closest to our home. It was a school where the children were mostly Jewish and the teachers were mostly Irish single women who had graduated from normal school, a two-year teacher-training program that they had entered directly from high school. The hiring agent was the principal: Dr. John D. Haney, who sat in an inner office, which in turn was guarded by an outer office where his administrative assistant sat. Outside of both sat a rotating student-guard. The guards were members of the eighth grade class who took turns monitoring the hallways, the staircases, and the bathrooms. I know because, when I reached eighth grade, it was my job to arrange the staffing of these guards—at least for the girls.

If you pass an old public school building in New York City you might notice some faded lettering embedded in the brick outside wall that says "Girls Entrance" or "Boys Entrance." In the old days, which were my days, the children were divided by gender for several activities. For example, boys were taught science and shop, while we girls were taught cooking and sewing. I don't know what went on in the science class, but in cooking, we made toast on the gas stove, even though most families had electric toasters by then. We mostly watched as the cooking teacher demonstrated the more complicated recipes, such as eggs and cookies. Best of all, we ended the class by eating whatever the teacher had made. In sewing, we learned all the stitches and made our cooking aprons and even a dress. Jack brought home a lamp he had made in shop. It was made of metal and it worked.

Another division of the boys and the girls was the separation of the schoolyard into two areas, each having its own entry into the building. Every morning we girls gathered in front of the "Girls" doorway and lined up according to our grade and our homeroom class. And we stood there until a bell rang, whereupon, the Captain of the Guards, a unique post held by the most popular eighth grade girl, stepped up to a podium and yelled: "Forward March!" And into the doorway and up the stairs we filed. When

I was about to enter eighth grade the election for the most popular girl took place. The secret ballots, counted by Miss Gaffney, my homeroom teacher, placed me second to Dorothy Capell, a tall blonde, who was then deemed Captain and I, the runner-up, became First Lieutenant.

The job of the Captain was to say "Forward March." The job of the First Lieutenant was to work out the duty assignments for each monitor each day of the week and to present the list to each of them on the appropriate day, and to find substitutes at the last minute if one was absent. I was honored to be First Lieutenant, as opposed to Second Lieutenant or Third Lieutenant. Neither of them had any specific jobs other than to walk up and down the long queues of pupils, shushing them as they waited to enter the building. I worked hard at my job and successfully staffed all of the guard positions each hour of the day, making sure that none of the guards was assigned during her major subject classes. I was satisfied. But after I graduated, I met a girl who had been a class ahead of me at '46, who told me that she was present when Miss Gaffney had rigged the election in favor of Dorothy Capell because I was Jewish. I couldn't believe what I was hearing, but of course, it made sense. Some of our Irish teachers were anti-Semitic. Even though I had no proof that she tampered with the election, I have kept my grudge against Miss Gaffney for allegedly depriving me of the title "Captain" and of the opportunity to stand on a pedestal every morning and shout: "Forward March!"

Every week we had an assembly at P.S. 46 when either the lower school or the upper school gathered in the large auditorium and Dr. Haney officiated. I remember one such gathering when I was in fourth grade when Dr. Haney chose the American flag as his topic of the day. In his stentorian voice, he called on us to "observe Old Glory in its splendor." He then pointed his finger at us and shook it up and down, saying, "If there is anyone in this room who does not believe in the American flag, I call upon you to stand up now and show your face!" I remember myself grabbing tightly on to my seat to prevent myself from accidentally rising and thereby incurring his wrath.

I remember another assembly when one of my fellow fifth graders, Gerhard Hepner, sent around a note to those of us he identified as fellow Jews. "If you are Jewish do not sing 'Holy, Holy, Holy'. It's a Christian song. Just keep your lips closed." It was with great satisfaction that we showed this defiance, even if no one appeared to have noticed.

Even in this potentially hostile environment, I was a good student and well liked by most of my teachers. Others in the class were less fortunate. In fourth grade, one of my classmates, a small boy who fidgeted a lot, spent much of his time sitting beside the teacher—in the lower drawer of her desk. Little Stephen Spinner seemed miserable but uncomplaining, with his behind deep in the drawer and his legs dangling over the edge. The teacher claimed that this was the only way she could conduct the class and keep her eyes on this small, but wiry, possible troublemaker.

In fifth grade I had a teacher who liked me a lot. Our class had been chosen to present the Christmas play, with the whole school as our audience. Miss Hill chose me to be Mrs. Santa Claus, one of the two main parts. I had done some acting in camp and I was so happy to have been chosen. But just before rehearsals started, Miss Hill, who had not auditioned us before, decided that she had to know what our singing voices were like because the play was a musical. First, she asked the boy she had chosen to be Santa to sing, "Go Down Moses," the song she had chosen for the test. He did well. Next it was my turn. "When Israel was in Egypt land," so far pretty good. "Let my people go," I bellowed. But when it came to "Way down in Egypt land, tell old Pharaoh..." I was so off tune that the class started to laugh. "Esther," said Miss Hill, "I'm afraid that the part will be too difficult for you. May I have another volunteer?" she asked, as I sat stunned, with tears starting to form in my eyes. Another girl sang beautifully, got the part, and I was placed in a non-singing and non-speaking role as a green balloon, one of many, in a dance number. Miss Hill complimented me on how graceful I was. It didn't help.

In seventh grade we began to move out of homeroom into specialized classes and, from this experience we realized that our homeroom teachers, as bad as some were, were usually better than the others. For geography, for example, we had a middle-age woman, Miss Holden, who loved to travel, and used every sabbatical to do so. In those dark Depression days, only the rich, the businessmen, and the public school teachers who were entitled to sabbaticals every seven years, traveled abroad. Her trips to Mexico and to Spain had left a deep impression on her and we were constantly reminded about the evils of socialism: the Mexican threats to the international oil companies (her brother was an oil executive), and the Spanish Loyalists' threats to the Church. The worst part of the class, however, was that she had no lesson plan, and geography, for her, was just talking about her travels and her strong opinions about what she saw. If it happened to be a wintry day outside, Miss Holden, a skinny lady in her sixties, would rub her arms and say to Honora Weinberger, one of her favorites, "Honora, get me my fur." Whereupon Honora would jump up, run to the closet and fetch a ragged fox boa, claws and all, which Miss Holden then tied around her shoulders. She loved Honora because she loved her name. "What a wonderful name!" she would exclaim, "Don't ever let anyone call you Nora!" A day later she would rub her arms and say "Nora, I feel chilly, get me my fur!"

Our history teacher that year was just as bad. A plump, blonde woman who wore flowery dresses and enough perfume to make the entire classroom reek of sweet gardenias. She conducted each lesson by writing notes on all of the blackboards in the room, front, side, and back, and then having us copy them into our own notebooks. By then the class was over.

# MY MOTHER'S STYLE

My mother was always years ahead of her time, but she was also deeply rooted in and affected by her past. She was a woman of simple but elegant taste; she liked soft, loose clothing, knits, formless hats, all stuff that became available after the Second World War, but not in the 30s and early 40s. Black was one of her favorite colors, much to the shock of her sisters and her friends from the shtetl who thought black was an old-world color, not that of a modern New Yorker.

My mother hated to be regimented and she applied this rule to corsets, girdles, garter belts, sanitary belts, shoulder pads, hats with a shape of their own, and, as often as possible, to bras. Without having concerned herself with the fashion industry's on-going battle for and against the "natural look," she was a living example of it. We lived on the Grand Concourse, but my mother's shopping habits were different from any other woman of her age who lived in the Bronx. She had started her married life on the Upper West Side of Manhattan, went to business on West 30th Street, and shopped in Lord and Taylor, Bonwit Teller, Saks Fifth Avenue and Macy's Little Shop. She had charge accounts everywhere and was in the habit of buying, charging, sending, returning, and then starting all over again. The UPS guys knew us well, for they were forever delivering and then picking up the same packages.

My mother's problem was that she knew exactly what she wanted, but it was impossible to find. On a typical Saturday she would announce that she had nothing to wear, which was close to the truth, and downtown she would go, but never alone. My Saturdays were subject to her command. She might have liked to take my father and my brother as well as me, but she never even dared suggest it. Rather, she chose just me. What was a daughter for, after all, if not to be her mother's companion and consultant and aide-de-camp in this great shopping war? Daddy and Jackie would be the final judges, but she and I were the scouts.

Such Saturdays would start by putting me on alert and, as soon as she finished her morning chores, we would descend into the subway for a forty-minute ride on the D train and a walk to Fifth Avenue. My mother's plan was to avoid all sales ladies if possible. She preferred to snoop around the racks herself. Unfortunately, in most of the stores she had chosen as acceptable, this was hardly possible. The sales crew would be out in full force with their fake smiles, ready to pounce. Usually middle-aged, dressed fashionably, with heavy lipstick and coiffed hair, these women were more than a match for my mother. Her only hope was that the stores would be busy and that she, who, by definition, was still wearing last year's clothes, would be overlooked if there were a more promising customer. She would then be left to her own devices, to browse and if nothing looked good, we would be off to another store. But if she landed in the hands of a sales lady, we surely had a battle ahead. "Madam, let me take you to a comfortable dressing room where I can bring you a number of dresses and you can try them on." And off we would go. I liked that idea because I could at least sit on a chair. The sales lady would bring out several items and my mother would refuse them all. This would happen again and again until my mother would weaken and decide that something was worth considering. She would try it and conclude that she hated it, but the sales lady would inevitably say: "But Madame, once you put on your girdle and a better-fitting bra, the dress will be perfect for you." My mother would just sneer at her, pass me a knowing glance, and move on to the next dress, if there was one. Finally, I would get so tired of this that if something had the slightest possibility, I would blurt out that I liked it very much. Then the sales lady, seeing that there might be a chink in the armor, would join me in praise of the item. Together we would chant that this one was the best by far and she should definitely take it. Two powerful voices against my worn-down mother would usually clinch the sale.

Little did the sales lady know that my mother would rearm after the item was delivered. There were still two more obstacles to overcome. The first was my mother's mood at the time she tried on the dress at home. More often than not she would decide that the belt was too stiff or that a bulge was revealed in her corset-less figure. If that were the case, she would take it off in no time flat, fold it back into the box, re-paste the sticky tape with her own saliva, grab a postcard and write to the store ordering a next-day pick-up, something the stores did at no charge in those days. If, by chance, she rather liked the dress she would confront the second obstacle and model it for the two would-be stand up comics in the house, my father and my brother. "Very nice," one of them would say, "it reminds me of a flowerpot." They never liked prints. Or, "Does it come with anti-toxin?" my brother might ask if he spotted a bit of snakeskin on the belt trim. You name it; they said it and she believed it. At that moment I would rush out of the room hating them all as I saw one more Saturday wasted and another coming up.

Shopping for food, on the other hand, was, for my mother, a simple phone call. As a working woman with a telephone on hand, my mother never set foot in a grocery store or a butcher shop, but rather did all her marketing by phone, for delivery. But one Saturday night, on the way home from a visit to Uncle Sam and Aunt Becky, my mother remembered that she needed some meat for the next day. The kosher butcher opened after sundown on Saturdays. My mother and I entered the store, where we actually appeared in person, for the first time. The butcher, a middle-aged man, wearing a yarmulke and a long white coat, was behind the counter and my mother addressed him with a questioning "Mr. Rubin?"

"Yes," he said, "May I help you? "

"Mr. Rubin, I am Mrs. Edelman."

"Oh my God, Mrs, Aydelmann," he cried, "I recognize your voice." He ran around the counter to where my mom was standing and gave her a hug. "And this must be your big girl," he said as he patted me on the head. "One of my best customers," he proclaimed loudly to all the people in the store, who were by that time gaping at us. "Mrs. Aydelmann, I'm so happy to meet you!"

My mother used her business acumen to compensate for her lack of domestic skills. In sewing class at P.S. 46, we girls were required to make a dress and wear it to school. We had to choose a fabric, choose a pattern and sew. There were no sewing machines at school. The children were, however permitted to use the sewing machines they had at home. No one mentioned whether or not the mothers were permitted to help. When I confronted my mother with my dilemma, that I was probably the only one in the class who did not have access to a sewing machine or a mother who knew how to sew, she smiled her knowing smile and said, "Don't worry, Ketzel, we have Mr. Gelfand to help us." Mr. Gelfand was the tailor who owned the dry cleaning store on Kingsbridge Road, just around the corner from the Muriel Arms. "Oh, Mommy," I responded, "that wouldn't be fair." "Why not?" she asked. "You don't think the other girls are going to do it by themselves, do you?" I decided to wait a bit and see how much progress I could make sewing the dress by hand. The seams were lumpy and not secure. I had visions of wearing the dress to school and having it fall apart, right in the classroom, where all the boys would be ogling and all the girls would be giggling. In the end, Mr. Gelfand sewed the dress on his machine. The seams were secure. I wore the dress to school on the appointed day, got a passing grade, and never wore it again.

For the first eleven years of my life, my mother had long dark brown wavy hair, tied into a bun that framed her rounded face and deep brown eyes. It made her look like the sweet, old-fashioned moms that showed up in the storybooks. She went to a beauty parlor every week to have her nails done, first with pink and later with colorless nail polish. And she also had her beautifully shaped eyebrows trimmed. I loved the way she looked in her bun and so did my best friend at summer camp whose mother had bobbed and dyed hair. "I love the way your mother looks," said Jeannie, much to my surprise. "She looks like a real mother!" I was surprised because Jeannie and most of the girls in my bunk were very rich and I assumed they basked in their parents' stylishness. But after Jeannie's comment, I was proud that my mom, who went to work when their moms stayed home, was deep down the "real mother." But, the following winter, I was playing in front of our apartment house and I watched my mother emerge from the subway with her hair cut short.

"What happened to your hair?" I shrieked.

"Don't you like it?" she replied. "When I went for my manicure in that little beauty parlor across from Macy's, the girls decided that I should look more up-to-date, so we cut it. Don't you like it?" she asked again. I didn't like it for weeks after, but I gradually adjusted to her haircut. As years went by she cut it even shorter, washed it every day and fluffed it with her fingers. She never had it set or dyed and used the professionals only for further cutting.

My mother never stopped her manicures, however. When we talked about it, she would think back to her own mother, whom she adored, whose hands were rough and chafed and cracked, the markings of poverty and the unbelievably difficult life of poor immigrant women on the lower East Side of New York. My mother was determined that neither she nor I would ever live like, or look like that.

# MY EXTENDED FAMILY: ON MY MOTHER'S SIDE: DOTTIE AND IZZY

My mother liked to talk about her arrival in the United States in 1902. She was nine years old when she landed in New York with her mother and two sisters, Bessie and Dottie. My mother was the oldest of the three girls. She was born after her mother had lost two other babies in their infancy. To "prevent" this from reoccurring, the rabbi had recommended that my mother, whose name was to be Sarah, be called Chaya Sarah instead, thus adding the word for "life" for good luck. In addition, she had to wear only white clothes for the first three years of her life. My grandparents obeyed the rabbi and my mother survived.

The family, part of a large Shifrin clan, resided in the village of Zembin in Belarus. My grandfather and my mother's older half-brother, Izzy, left the "old country" at the turn of the twentieth century without my grandmother and the three girls. Once settled, with an apartment in the lower east side of Manhattan and a small store where they sold herring and smoked fish and groceries, they called for the rest of the family to join them.

My mother was proud of the fact that they had enough money to buy second-class tickets on a ship, *The Amsterdam*, which they boarded in Holland. Thus they were spared from the crowding and the discomforts experienced by those in the steerage. Nevertheless, when they arrived at Ellis Island, they were herded into a room, examined, questioned and treated with what my mother perceived as scorn. Years later when we all went to see the Charlie Chaplin movie, *The Immigrant*, my mother laughed aloud as we were shown a boatful of immigrants arriving in the harbor and the title reading "Land of the Free." Thereupon, the crowd of eager passengers is lassoed together by a huge encircling rope. My mother formed her opinions quickly and firmly. She thought that the interrogators at Ellis Island were heartless.

Through the vast network of family connections, my grandparents found tenement apartments on Hester Street, and later, Cherry Street; they were cramped and lightless. Large families squeezed into small rooms, with shared bathrooms at the end of long public hallways. My mother's greatest disappointment, however, was being bullied by the children they had as neighbors. Thrilled to go to a playground one day, she climbed onto a swing only to get pushed off and onto the ground by the local American-Jewish children who taunted her with their chant: "Greenhorn, Popcorn, Five cents apiece." She cried as she ran home and she often described the incident to me when I asked her: "Mommy, what was it like when you were a little girl and came to America?" She never forgot the hurt of that day and it influenced the way she felt about "The Promised Land."

After school each day she would walk past the street vendors who were selling everything from food to clothing to pots and pans from their pushcarts, and the icemen carrying the huge blocks of ice in giant pincers. From Hester Street, she would go to Allen Street, then over to East Broadway, where the Education Alliance had its after-school classes and clubs. Having come from Russia in 1902, as a nine-year-old whose only language was Yiddish, she worked hard to learn English, well and quickly. At the Education Alliance, a Settlement House where new Jewish immigrants gained an extracurricular education, she joined the writers' club where she perfected her English under the tutelage of Elias Lieberman, a renowned educator and poet, who served as the creative writing instructor.

My mother loved music and gleefully described the entry, through a window of their apartment on Hester Street, of a piano that could not fit into the doorway or the narrow staircase. "All the neighbors gathered as the piano was lifted off the truck and hoisted up," she told us. "And you should see the neighbors, cheering. 'Mazel tov' they shouted as the piano, swaying from side to side and rocking back and forth, finally slid into the apartment window." She took lessons and played it constantly.

My mother's middle sister, Bessie, was seven when they arrived. She had a large scar above one eye, the result of the kick from a Cossack's horse. According to the story told later by her daughter Ruth, Bessie, then age six, ran after the Cossacks who had just raped her mother and was felled by the kick. Bessie developed epilepsy that plagued her for the rest of her life.

I never heard this story from my mother and was shocked to hear it from my cousin Ruth long after our mothers had died.

Dottie, the baby of the family, was the opposite of my mother. Blue-eyed and forever smiling, when five-year old Dottie arrived in the United States she loved everyone on sight and was eternally grateful for all the blessings sent her way. She adored the rich ladies, the German Jews, who came down to the Lower East Side from their homes in Manhattan's good neighborhoods, to teach the immigrant Jewish ruffians how not to smell bad, how not to tear at their food, how not to argue in loud voices, how not to join the Socialist Party, and how not to embarrass their rich Jewish counterparts who lived uptown. My mother thought these women were snobs who pretended concern for the plight of the immigrants but were really distressed at the behavior of their fellow Jews. Her sister Dottie thought they were remarkably generous, giving their time and money to help the newcomers assimilate.

The sisters grew up. My mother enrolled in Washington Irving High School and stayed there only long enough to become a skilled typist and bookkeeper. She left school when she got a job in the business office of a fur manufacturer. When she was in her mid twenties, my father, a successful fur merchant and business associate of my mother's boss, met her and fell in love with her beautiful face, her sharp mind, and her old fashioned simplicity, which she combined with a feminist modernity. She was inspired by heroines like Emma Goldman, the anarchist who was considered to be a troublemaker and thus deported back to Russia by the United States government.

Bessie was the intellectual of the family who wanted to apply to college only to be prohibited by her father from doing so. She went to work, had a nervous breakdown and married a chemist who had a college degree. When I graduated from high school and all the other relatives gave me money or jewelry, this Aunt Bessie gave me the three-volume biography of Abraham Lincoln by Carl Sandburg. I treasured it.

Sister Dottie remained in her parents' home, taking care of them and helping out in their appetizing store, where they sold herring, pickles, and smoked fish, all Jewish favorites. She was married briefly to a musician, whom my mother considered unworthy, but he died of pneumonia in the first year of the marriage. She had a baby who was born just after her husband died, and the baby also died a few months later. Dottie continued to live with her parents until they died in the mid-nineteen thirties. For a short period after that she had a good office job, a Christian boyfriend, and the life of a career woman, with vacations in Havana and many friends. Then she met Morris Hirsch, a carpenter, a Jewish immigrant from Romania. Morris loved the country life and chose the "Jewish Catskills" to be his home. Once he and Dottie were married, they pooled their resources and bought a property in Monticello, New York, where he renovated a row of bungalows to be rented out each summer to Jewish families from Brooklyn or the Bronx.

The "Jewish Catskills," and the bungalow colonies within, became a haven for the Jewish factory workers and small businessmen who dwelled in the City and hankered for the fresh air of the countryside. Hearkening back to the country life of the shtetl, to the agrarian ideal of the intrinsic value of trees and grass and land, to the utopian model of shared housekeeping and community living, the bungalow colony with its shared kitchen, called the "kokhaleyn," was appealing. The rents were low, the wives and children could have an entire summer away from the city, with the husbands visiting on weekends. Mothers watched out for each other's kids, shared food and kitchen chores, enjoyed a restful vacation for themselves and a wonderful social life for their children who were free to roam, and to play in the fields.

When Mama and I visited Dottie and Morris in Monticello in the 1950s, my mother would comment, "This is not a life." Nevertheless, it was clear that Dottie and Morris were successful summer landlords. Sweet Dottie ran a small convenience store for the immediate daily needs of the moms and the children. She developed a system of charge accounts for those housewives who only had money when their husbands showed up on the weekends. The children were permitted to charge their candy bars and soda pop and ice cream and with great affection would call Dottie and Morris "Mr. And Mrs. Hershey Bar." Morris was the ever-ready plumber and electrician, garbage collector and driver. He chauffeured the residents to the market in town, to the movies, to the hairdresser. He entertained the children with the story of his false teeth. "Look at this," he would say to the little ones as they ate their Good Humor ice cream bars on the stoop in front of the store. "See this perfect set of teeth," and he removed them for all to see. "I measured my mouth myself, something only an expert carpenter like me could do. I sent the measurements in the mail to the company and they sent the teeth back a few weeks later. And look how well they fit." He then popped them back into his mouth and smiled as the children's eyes grew wider and as their moms groaned.

Dottie and Morris worked twenty-hour days in the summer and she had little to do in the winter. Thinking about this, as we sat in our warm apartment, my mother would say: "She had such a good existence as an office worker, when she lived in that charming apartment in Brooklyn Heights. And now? Now she's living in half-built houses in freezing winters." And she stood up from her chair and walked over to the window to shut it.

My mother also had an older half-brother, my grandfather's son from his first marriage. A tall and chubby man with a light complexion, blue eyes, and ruddy cheeks, Uncle Izzy loved books and the outdoors. He was a socialist and an early environmentalist. His favorite newspaper was the socialist newspaper written in Yiddish: *The Jewish Daily Forward*. His favorite book was Thoreau's *Walden Pond*.

Izzy was miserable working at his job behind the counter in the family appetizing store. He lived with my grandparents and his sister Dottie in an apartment in Brooklyn and was cared for by my grandmother, whom he loved. But after my grandmother died in 1937, Izzy, feeling hopelessly abandoned, tried to commit suicide. Discovered in time to save his life by Dottie, he was admitted to the psychiatric ward at Bellevue, diagnosed as schizophrenic, and ultimately transferred to Creedmore, a state hospital for the mentally ill in Queens. And there he stayed for the remainder of his life.

My mother visited him once a month and she usually took me along. We would spend the first half-hour looking for him or waiting for him to arrive at the reception desk. Seeing the other patients, many who were toothless, and wearing ill-fitting and shabby overcoats, carrying bundles, looking frail, and talking gibberish, made me want to get out of there fast. But when Izzy arrived, he was jolly and full of smiles and so happy to see us. We would take him to a nearby diner and he would order a big meal and eat it with relish, talking between bites about how lucky he was to be at Creedmore. In between visits, my mother would send him a check for his incidental expenses. In response, she would receive a penny postcard, written in large letters, in green ink, with a message for all to see. The cards were almost all the same.

*"Dear Ida. I rec'd your check and thank you for it. Today I ate well because I am now assigned to the kitchen crew. I am so lucky to be here. The Capitalist System is cruel. It exploits the workers and benefits only the rich. Thank God for Creedmore, where I can live in peace and read my books and wander on the grounds in my free time and hear the birds sing. Yours Truly, Bro. Isidor.*

My mother was a loyal sister who kept in touch with her siblings, provided them with money if needed, and visited them (by phone daily with her sisters and by traveling, at least once a month, to where Izzy was housed.) But she was a "business woman," with a different life style and different tastes from theirs. She prided herself on her modernity and her ability to have assimilated well into American culture, even though she, like they, was born in a small Russian village. Her separation from her past, and from her sisters, contributed to the loneliness she experienced as Jackie and I became more independent.

# MY FATHER

My father, Abraham Simon Edelman, was born in Russia in the village of Shklov, in the province of Mogilev, in Belarus. He loved to talk about his birthplace. He used to repeat a little saying he had learned as a boy: "I'm from Shklov, Mogilev, Starji Bychev, Rogachev---on the Dnieper." He pronounced the Russian words with relish, and added "on the Dnieper" after a short pause. So did I, chiming in, as a small child, as I sat on his lap and listened to tales of his boyhood. He told me about his dog, Pyus (with the accent on the second syllable). Pyus was a Russian wolfhound who accompanied my Dad wherever he went. "One night," he said, "my father sent me to the shul to douse the lights. So Pyus and I went. And, in the dark, we made our way back home through the forest. Suddenly, in the distance we heard the howl of wolves. I was so frightened but Pyus led me home safely." My father smiled as he remembered how Pyus had protected him. But his voice saddened as he finished the story, "And then one day, Pyus was dead. A neighbor poisoned him. Pyus had probably stolen some food." I hugged my Daddy and cried for poor Pyus.

The family moved to New York in 1908, when my father was sixteen. He had one older brother, Sam, who had to leave Russia or be drafted into the Russian army. He also had three older sisters, Jenny, Bessie and Rosie. They came to New York with their mother, Rachel, but not Jacob, their father. I never knew whether Jacob had already died, or was ill, or was waiting to come later and died before that happened. When Sam arrived in America, he was ready to work in the fur business where he found a job for himself and one for his younger brother. They had little formal schooling, learned English at night, and adapted well. My father's job was that of a traveling buyer. He used to comb the New England farms in search of trapped muskrats. In the process he befriended a farm family, the Tiltons of New Hampshire. Mr. Tilton, my father told me, was a graduate of Exeter Academy, but he was also a working farmer. He and his wife liked my father, who was probably the first Jew they had ever met. My father, even as a young man just starting out in business, was a legendary "honest Abe." He offered them good prices for their trapped muskrats; he paid his bills on time as he told them about life in Russia and in New York City. He became a friend whom they often invited to dinner in their home. Daddy described eating fish chowder that was filled with fish heads, Mrs. Tilton's rendering of tasteless Yankee cooking. He managed to eat the soup but even twenty years later he remembered how difficult it was to keep it down. And as he said this, he cupped his hand tightly over his mouth, rolled his eyes and jerked forward. Then he broke out into a laugh.

Roaming the American countryside was an educational experience for an immigrant boy. My father always had an easy time meeting new people and people liked him right away. He also fell in love with country life and dreamed of buying a log cabin as a second home. That never happened. The relationship with the Tiltons lasted many years. I remember visiting them when Jackie and I were still in grammar school. Jack says he too recalls the nauseating fish soup, but I have no recollection of that and I think he was just retelling one of our Dad's vivid stories, as if it had happened to him. What I remember is how impressed I was that there is a town in New Hampshire called Tilton. I had never before known people whose town was named for their family.

In 1918, when my father married my mother, he was an established businessman with a good income. By the mid-twenties, my dad and his older brother Sam were both flourishing. Sam owned a large house in the Bronx, a big car, driven by a chauffeur, and a solid manufacturing business. My father preferred to remain a merchant, buying and selling luxury furs, especially mink and sable, living in an apartment in Manhattan, and driving his own car.

Coming to America at the age of sixteen meant that my father was too old to lose his accent, unlike my mother who came at nine and worked hard to speak perfect English. I was embarrassed when my father spoke in a setting where the others were native born. I also was embarrassed by his baldness, something that had happened in his early twenties. He looked older than he was. At my brother's Bar Mitzvah, when Daddy went up to the Bema, wearing his fedora, I suddenly saw how handsome he was. Actually, he was an elegant dresser; he wore three-piece suits, well-laundered shirts, ties from Sulka, and dark grey fedoras from Dobbs. On Sundays, however, he would put on his "leisure" jacket, a loose tweed jacket that was popular in those days, and also called a "bagel jacket." Around the house he was hatless, tieless, comfortable, and very bald. If any of us commented about his baldness, his ready answer was: "grass does not grow on a busy street." And then he would chuckle in triumph.

The Edelman family laughs a lot. They love jokes and they indulge in what they believe is good-humored mockery, which other people call insults. My father used to tell the story of a scene in the family living room when he was a young man, sitting with two of his sisters, when the third sister appeared with a boyfriend she was bringing home to introduce to the family. Whatever the stranger would say would result in first, a few snickers, and then uproarious laughter from the family members. Needless to say, all of the sisters married late, and despite the careful pruning, none of them had good marriages. As for jokes, I remember one of my father's favorites: "Hello Ginsberg," a man shouted as he sharply whacked the back of the man in front of him as they walked down the street. The man who had been whacked turned around and said, "I'm not Ginsberg! But even if I was, why did you slap me so hard?" At which point the first guy sniffed, raised his eyebrows and said: "And who, may I ask, are *you* to speak for Ginsberg?"

My father was gregarious. He enjoyed playing cards with friends from his business and lunching with his business associates where deals were made and jokes were swapped. As a fur merchant, my father traveled to fur auctions, mostly in Canada, by train, but occasionally to Europe, by ocean liner. Once airplanes became available to business travelers, he was an avid fan. My mother rarely accompanied him.

When my grandmother was dying, my mother wanted to have as much time as possible to be with her at her home in Brooklyn. My father, who was about to leave for Montreal by train to attend a fur auction, decided at the last minute to travel instead by car and take Jack and me and Otto, his assistant, with him. Jack was fourteen and I was eleven. We had to stop at a hotel on the way and when I awoke in the morning I realized that I could not manage my braids by myself and Mommy was not there. Daddy was at a loss but Otto came to the rescue. He had seen his sisters in Germany braid their hair and in no time he was able to reconstruct the process. He became the official braider for the rest of the journey.

When we arrived in Montreal, Daddy and Otto went to the auction and Jackie and I were left to fend for ourselves. On the first day we explored Mount Royal, at the top of which Jack, who was then an amateur photographer and an avid stamp collector, insisted on taking my picture, a close-up of me with the city in the background. "It will be just like a Canadian postage stamp," he said. "Only instead of King George, it will be you."

Esther on top of Mt Royal with Montreal in background, 1937

The second and last day we decided to explore the racetrack. Someone had given my father two free tickets, which he could not use and he was happy to give them to us. "You can watch the horses race," he said. So off we went. We found our seats, got our programs and loved sitting outdoors amidst the crowd of grownups, men and women, who were either marking their cards or loudly cheering. Either he looked older than thirteen, or his age made no difference, but no one stopped Jackie from also placing bets on the horses. Before each race we would leave the stands, go to the betting windows, and Jack would make the selection. He would glance at the sheets, check out the odds, and then decide, with me egging him on, which horse should be chosen for win or place or show. My choices were based on the horse's name. His choices were based on the odds. Then we ran back to our seats to cheer for our picks. If we had a winner, we would run back to collect our money and then place another bet. We left with a bit more money than we had brought with us and demanded that we go again, to another track, when we stopped in Saratoga on the way home.

"Please, Daddy, let us go," I pleaded."

"Okay, my little gamblers. Maybe you'll win enough to buy me lunch."

Daddy loved to give gifts. He came back from his trips with exotic purchases. One of his and our favorites was smoked goldeye, a fish that was indigenous to the lakes of Manitoba. He would buy it by the case and distribute it to his customers and friends upon his return. At Christmas time he bought about twenty ties at Sulka, an upscale men's clothing store. Jack and I were delegated to carry the selection to the twenty furriers he had chosen to receive them. We laid the ties on a showroom table and watched as the furrier made his choice. And we were the ones who got thanked.

For years, every Sunday afternoon, just after lunch, my father would walk the five blocks to the garage he had chosen for his Chevy and drive it back to take the rest of us on our weekly fifteen mile ride to suburban Westchester. He found a spot in Irvington, where we could park the car and either sit on the grass or walk around the reservoir. He loved being in the "country." On the way home we would often stop for gas at the Gulf Station, where he would get a free copy of a Gulf newspaper designed to keep cranky children busy with the comics. Invariably, after that stop, I would become nauseated, provoked by the smell of gasoline that pervaded the filling station and the Gulf newspaper. I hated those rides, but we were not given a choice.

I used to talk to my Dad about "big topics," and with my mother about my clothes, my daily activities, my schoolwork, my friends. As I became a teenager, Daddy and I talked about my choice of college and about politics and about the war in Europe that looked like it would soon include the United States. If the country were to go to war, he was worried that his business would fail. He extrapolated from his own psychology: "Who, after all, would want to buy a mink coat when her son was fighting in some far off place?" But he was wrong on that score. American business did well during the war and there was so much black market money around that luxury businesses boomed.

My father was basically a peaceful man. But one day, when I was about ten, I had had a terrible fight with my brother and was threatening to destroy his model airplane; whereupon, Jackie grabbed my arm, smacked me, and pulled the plane away. When my dad arrived home from work, I greeted him by running into his arms and sobbing, "Jackie hit me." Exasperated, my father grabbed my brother, and actually removed his own belt and held it tightly in his hand, ready to smash down on my brother's backside. I cried, "Don't you dare hit my brother!" At that point my father dropped the belt, threw up his hands, and gave me a look of dismay that usually accompanies the saying "What do women want?"

During the war years, when *The New York Times* was delivered each morning, Daddy, Jack and I engaged in conversations at the breakfast table. My father did not like communism one bit, but my brother was an adamant defender of the Soviet Union. And I was always on Jackie's side. "Your pal Stalin signed a pact with Hitler," my father would shout. The discussions were heated in that period starting just after the German invasion of Poland in September of 1939. Britain and France had declared war on Germany but there were no battles. It was the period of the "phony war." The signing of the Nazi-Soviet pact in 1939, and the Russian invasion of Finland that same year, became divisive moments in our household. My father would scream that the Russians were no better than the Germans and my brother would scream back that the Allies were preparing to side with Hitler against the Soviet Union. The arguments ended on June 22 of 1941, when Germany invaded Russia. After that my father became a Russian nationalist. He followed the daily reports in the *Times* and the maps showing the progress of the invasion. And when his beloved Mogeliev was in the news, he would proudly repeat the ditty about Shklov, Mogeliev, Starji Bychev, Rogechev—on the Dniepr.

# MY EXTENDED FAMILY: ON MY FATHER'S SIDE: THREE COUSINS

Lou, who lived in Boston, became one of my three favorite cousins. He was handsome and charming and very smart. Lou loved my parents and visited us as often as possible, even spending one summer with us at a beach-house that my parents rented in the Rockaways in 1928. Twelve years older than Jack, (and fifteen years older than me), he took on the role of a big brother at first and, as we grew up, he became a good friend and an important influence on both of us. Although accepted by Harvard as a commuting student (Harvard's way of filling the Jewish quota and keeping them off campus as much as possible), he chose Clark University in Worcester so that he could live away from home and avert the overly watchful eye of his mother, my father's sister Bessie. Despite this, Aunt Bessie made a habit of weekly visits to Worcester, to bring home-cooked food to her darling zoonia (son). As soon as she arrived with the roasted chicken, Lou would divide it up so that all of his housemates had a piece. This drove Aunt Bessie crazy: "Let their mothers send them food. I spend money and time buying and cooking your food. Why do you give it away?" But Lou would never back down.

Lou met Pearl in Boston when he was still an undergraduate at Clark, and she, a graduate student at Radcliffe. Aunt Bessie, who pronounced "Pearl" as "Peril," tried her best to talk him out of marrying her. But Lou and Pearl, like many other students in the depression days, passionately believed in the Communist Party and their alliance was sealed by a shared political view. Pearl was skinny, nervous, a chain smoker, who eschewed makeup or an interest in clothes. She had short, dark, curly hair, and she scratched her head delicately with her pointer finger as she talked and smoked. It was as if she were waking her brain to provide the information that had been approved by the Party to support her arguments. She was dedicated to her scholarly work and to the Party and little else. Lou, by contrast, took an interest in everything. He laughed a lot and he loved us and my mom and dad, even though we were part of the bourgeoisie. After college, Lou and Pearl moved to New York and Jack and I visited them regularly. At first they lived in a basement apartment of a luxurious brownstone in Brooklyn Heights, owned by Pearl's wealthy sister. When their child, David was born, Pearl, who had a PhD in Psychology, decided to place the baby on a rigid feeding schedule according to the clock, rather than "on demand." This was the trendy notion of the time but it turned out to be a disaster. Invariably, when we arrived for our visit, David would be screaming and Lou would be pacing up and down with him, but forbidden to give him a bottle until the required four-hour period between feedings was reached.

My brother and I always talked politics with Lou and Pearl, and they intensified our awareness of the problems of the poor and the oppressed. And, although we also learned these sensibilities at home, being close to Communists was an education of a different magnitude. Pearl was an avid reader and always had facts and figures at the ready. She was, however, humorless and doctrinaire. If I suggested there might be some truth in the findings of the Dewey Commission, that the confessions of treasonous behavior by the most important original Bolsheviks had been extracted by threats or torture, she would reply, "Esther, you are so naïve. John Dewey is a liberal," she said disdainfully, "who has been set up by Trotsky to conduct the so-called investigation. Those men were traitors." And then she would scratch her head even more fervently than usual. I learned not to question her judgments. The ideal setting would be a discussion with Lou alone. But that did not happen until much later when Lou would join Jack and me on occasional summer weekend trips. Although she was always invited, Pearl had no interest in coming with us to play tennis and swim and have fun in a hotel in the mountains.

The cousin whom Jack and I saw most often was Arthur, Uncle Sam's son. He was two years younger than my brother and one year older than me. We visited him on Saturday nights, when the men played poker and we children played penny poker in the basement playroom of Uncle Sam's enormous house in the East Bronx. Arthur loved playing games and telling jokes and hanging out in his neighborhood, which was filled with poor Jews who had escaped from the lower East side but had not yet made it to the Concourse. His best friend was Lawrence, whom Arthur renamed Lala. The two boys hung out in Lala's father's candy store where Arthur, laughing, would call out, "Mach me ha malted." Arthur was a head taller than most of us, something his mother proudly attributed to the substitution of cream when the doctor told her, "Drink plenty of milk during your pregnancy." And she replied, to herself, "If milk is good, cream is better."

Sam was my father's older brother, a fur manufacturer who, starting from scratch, ran a successful business in the twenties. He built a huge house just across the street from Tremont Park. Sam had a big grey Peerless, with big white tires. At first he also had a driver who was separated from the back seat by a glass window. Five people could fit into the back seat, three on the bench and two more in jump seats. After the stock market crash, Sam got rid of the driver but kept the car. We loved taking rides in it, sitting on the jump seats, opening the glass window to tell Uncle Sam something and then closing it again for privacy.

Uncle Sam married Aunt Becky, an old fashioned woman whose mission in life was to make a comfortable home for her husband and her children and to be sure that everyone was fed amply. Sam loved how Becky cooked and how she frugally shopped for meat and vegetables, touching and smelling each item to make certain that it was fresh and then bargaining for the price she was willing to pay.

After Arthur, their last child, was born, a few years before the stock market crash, they built and moved into the big house. In 1930, Becky decided to rent out at least two of the rooms. So the children grew up with the strangers who shared their dining table for meals and occasionally asked for favors. "Sonny, here's a nickel. Go, darlink and get me a Daily Vorker," was one of the requests made of Arthur, who loved to imitate this reclusive boarder. Becky found a woman named Sadie to help with the cleaning, the boarders, and the children. Sadie lived in the house, in a tiny attic room, for twenty years. From time to time something in the house would be missing—a silver spoon or a candlestick, or perhaps an earring. And Sadie would be the most ardent searcher, looking behind the furniture, under the carpet, in the garbage. When Sadie died, the family finally went into her room to clear it and discovered all of the missing items in a hatbox in the closet. They could not believe what they saw.

Arthur's sister, Ruth, another favorite cousin, married George Kleinsinger, a composer, and lived the glamorous life of a bohemian in Greenwich Village. When her husband-to-be was courting her, he decided to speak to Uncle Sam about the possibility of marriage. Sam was afraid that George would never be able to support a family. George loved to repeat the conversation he had with Sam, using his best imitation of the way Sam spoke: "Vat is your immediate plan?" Sam asked George.

"Well, I am hoping to get on relief."

"My God, what kind of ambition is dat!"

"Oh," George replied. "Then I will be eligible for the WPA Arts Program and get paid just for composing music."

And that is exactly what happened. Those were the days when the government supported the arts.

Jack and I loved to visit Ruth and George. We were proud of the one celebrity in the family and loved to play and replay the recordings of George's *Tubby the Tuba* and his *Baseball Cantata*, which was written when the Brooklyn Dodgers played in the World Series against the New York Yankees. Another favorite of ours was his *I Hear America Singing*, which was based on the poems of Walt Whitman. But best of all, they lived in a fourth floor walk-up apartment on Bleecker Street in Greenwich Village, with artists and writers and musicians and people of many nationalities and social classes. It was an inspiration for us to liberate ourselves from the Bronx as soon as we could.

"Tubby the Tuba," Danny Kaye

https://www.youtube.com/watch?v=udpVpF0uxMs

"The Baseball Cantata"

https://www.youtube.com/watch?v=J-vyRkeUm5M

After the three older children were married, Sam and Becky decided to move with Arthur to a much smaller space, in the West Bronx, right on the Grand Concourse just across the street and down the block from us. From their living room they could see my brother's window, and Sam, noting that Jackie's light was shining late at night, would say to Arthur, "Jackie's studying, and look at you, listening to junk on the radio." *(Unless it was the night before his final exams, Jack was not studying!)*

Cousins Arthur and Lou circa 1990

# REGULAR GALS:
## WALTON HIGH SCHOOL (1939)

In January 1939 I was graduated from P.S. 46 Bronx, and placed in an honors section at Walton High School, the class that was reserved for the top student or students from each of the feeding lower schools. On the first day of high school I was shocked to find myself in my new homeroom without any friends, or even acquaintances, from P.S. 46, even though many of the other girls knew each other from their previous schools. My search for a new friend lasted until the very first lunch recess when I found myself staring at a girl who was also quite alone and was also staring at me. The reason we were staring at each other transcended the fact that each of us was alone. Rather, it was as if we were looking into a mirror. We were the same height, same build, same hair color, and pretty much the same face. "Could we have lunch?" I started to ask her. "Yes, let's have lunch together," she replied.

This was the beginning of a short but very dear friendship of two girls from opposite backgrounds. I was a Jewish girl from the West Bronx who lived in a fancy apartment on the Grand Concourse. We had a maid who came every weekday to clean and cook and to be an adult presence in a household where both parents worked outside the home. I spent every summer from the age of five through fifteen at a sleep-away camp in the Poconos, and, during the school year, took piano lessons on our Steinway Grand, dance lessons at the nearby Jewish Community Center, and elocution lessons in Greenwich Village. Our family always had a car. We lived well by 1939 standards.

Marion Frick lived on 149th St and Third Avenue in the Bronx. Her neighborhood was a mixture of people with the common denominator of poverty. Marion was Catholic, of German background, but both her parents were American-born. Her father had been murdered just a year before I met her, the victim of a numbers racketeer to whom he owed a substantial amount of money. When she told me that a man in a bar in her neighborhood had shot and killed her dad, I felt sick. I tried to imagine what it would be like if something like that happened to my dad. Marion lived with her mom, and her sister who was a few years older and had quit high school to get a secretarial job. I visited them a few months after I met Marion. Her sister, a pretty brunette who looked like Marion (and me), was spending that Saturday at home, helping clean the house. Marion's mother, a skinny woman who wore a flowered housedress and slippers, greeted me with a limp handshake and a half-smile that revealed a missing tooth. Walking through their apartment, I realized, for the first time, that a railroad flat was so named because you had to walk from one room to another the way you walk in railroad cars. Each room led into the next and hallways and vestibules were absent.

Lunch with Marion became a regular. We would sit in a small alcove in the cafeteria, pretty much by ourselves, talking about school and about our families, and eating. Once or twice a week my mother would make me a triple-decker cream cheese on date-and-nut bread sandwich, an exact replica of the one served at Schrafft's, an upscale restaurant chain that was popular at that time. Marion, as usual, would bring her huge sandwich of ham or liverwurst on German rye bread and a container of pickles and another of homemade potato salad. On one of those days Marion looked envious as I opened the package that held my sandwich. "Could I have a taste?" she asked. "Here," I replied as I pushed the cream cheese mound in her direction. "Would you like to taste mine?" she suggested. "I would love that," I replied without hesitating. And we switched lunches and continued to do so on all the cream cheese on dated-nut-bread-days. She just adored the triple-decker, which my Mom would cut into four triangles, and I gobbled down the delicious German feast.

At one of our lunches, Marion talked about the student guard whom we had just passed as we descended the stairs to enter the lunchroom. "Stop talking when you're walking," she had just scolded in her screechy voice. "I really hate her," Marion said. "Me too," I agreed. "Good," said Marion with a glint in her eye. "I dare you to pull her hair." "Sure." I replied. And she came up with a plan, relishing every detail as she conjured it up. "Esther," she said, "You'll walk up to her saying 'What's that in your hair?' And then you'll pull her hair. Then you and I will continue up the steps quickly."

Stuffed with my ham sandwich, feeling guilty about the unequal exchange, but mostly wanting to take my place as a regular girl and not just a goody-goody teacher's pet, I left the lunchroom with an excited Marion. We went up the stairs, met the guard who was telling us as usual to slow down or keep right, or whatever. I went up to her, grabbed her hair as I said: "Oh my God, what's that in your hair?" and gave it a good yank. She started to scream, "You pulled my hair" and grabbed my arm. "What's your name and class? I'm going to report this." "My name is Esther Edelman and I am in 9CA. Go ahead and report me but I did nothing wrong."

A few days later I received a note from our class's guidance counselor to come to her office. I arrived, knocked, and was waved in by a heavy-set woman, whom I did not know but had seen around. She was seated at her desk, with an open folder in her hands. "Esther," she said, pulling off her glasses, as she raised her head above the papers she had been reading. "You have such a fine record and glowing reports from all of your teachers, I can hardly believe that you would pull a staircase-guard's hair. What's the meaning of this?"

"I thought I saw a bug. I am really sorry if I hurt her."

"Well, next time I hope you would be polite enough to tell her you saw something amiss and let her take care of it. I am glad you have said you are sorry. You may go now."

I left the room feeling queasy that I had lied blatantly and gotten away with it. I will never forget that silly little incident. But had I told the whole truth, I would have had to tell about the dare, and about how I wanted to be a "regular girl" and thus involve Marion.

Marion had never been to my house; I had never invited her, and she had never asked to visit. I really did not want her to see how different my life on the Concourse was from hers in the South Bronx, and I suspect that she preferred to hang out with her neighborhood pals and her family on the weekends, rather than do the movie and ice cream soda routine with me and my friends. She and I did spend one Saturday afternoon going downtown to the Loew's Paramount to see a movie and a live stage show that featured Frank Sinatra, who was then a seventeen-year old crooner who had become all the rage. Even I, who was only a lukewarm fan of popular music, was dying to see him in person. The theater was packed and we had to stand on a huge line in a waiting area in the theater lobby. We were huddled together tightly, with hardly any space between us. Marion was behind me. Suddenly I heard her shout, "Get your filthy hands offa me!" as she turned around to confront the guy who was standing behind her, her face flushed with anger. I was astonished and embarrassed to hear her outburst, which caused everyone on the line to turn to look at her, but I also deeply admired her bravery. It worked. The guy wormed his way out of the line and disappeared.

That summer of our freshman year at Walton, Marion and I managed to pull another fast one on the authorities. However, this time I was proud of our deception. It was the summer of the World's Fair in New York City and my family had bought me a season pass, which I was unable to use when I went away to camp. I gave it to Marion for July and August, and I had hoped it would provide an escape from her neighborhood into an exhibition of what the world was coming to: modern highways, and long distance telephones, and gadgets of all kinds to make life easier. There were free samples of all 57 products made by the Heinz Company, and hot dogs to buy, and roller coaster rides, and exhibits and people from all over the world. She used the pass a few times and later told me that she hated to go alone and her friends couldn't afford to join her. But when she used it, no one ever doubted that she was Esther Edelman as she flashed the card with its picture ID at the admission gate.

When school started again in September, Marion and I rarely saw each other. We were completely separated by Walton's tracking system. I remained in the so-called "Classical Honors" group and shared no classes or lunch periods with Marion who had decided to pursue a commercial diploma. And when the Fair returned in the spring of 1940, much of the fun and the fantasy were gone. Many countries that had large exhibits in

1939 had withdrawn in 1940. They were preoccupied with a life and death struggle that preempted their desire to sell their wares or to lure tourists. The Second World War had arrived

# HIGH SCHOOL IS THE TIME FOR CRUSHES
## (1939-43)

Walton High School was, in the 1940s, a huge school of nearly 8000 students. It was open to all Bronx residents provided they were girls and it appealed to those seeking a single-sex education, not uncommon at the time. The girls did not have to compete for the attention of boys, and parents could be reassured that education was the primary goal of the school. There was an elaborate tracking system, subdividing those who were college-bound from the others and, within each group, separations that were determined by academic ability. I was placed in the honors group of the college-bound, a class called CA for Classical Academic. We were all supposed to study Latin, but because the country was at war, the need for living languages took precedence over the Latin requirement and we were allowed to choose French or Spanish, if we so desired. I had watched my brother struggle with Latin and quickly chose to substitute four years of French. I fell in love with the language and dreamed of going to Paris where I would speak perfect French and spend my time on the Left Bank chatting with friends in an outdoor café, a dream that could not possibly come true until the war ended. Meanwhile, Mrs. Garabedian, our teacher, who began each period with us singing "Sur le Pont d'Avignon" or "Frère Jacques" or "Le Marseilleaise," enchanted those of us who had chosen French. Once, she invited us to her home on Riverside Drive where she served us madeleines and pôt au chocolat. We spoke only in French and pretended that we were in Paris. I loved it!

There were other memorable teachers, but the first whom I really adored and who singled me out to make me into a personal friend was Mrs. McCracken in the History Department. I had her for only one class, Civics, in my sophomore year. It was my first course in what was later, in college, to be called Government or Political Science, the subject I would choose as my major. In Civics, we talked about social policy, about equity, about how government could make things work for people but often, because of corporate interference, chose to favor the few over the majority. I remember one day when the class was about to be dismissed, I asked a question that showed that I had been thinking hard. It had to do with a specific housing policy that was being promulgated by the New York City Council, which on the surface seemed to promote equality, but actually would in effect just serve the best interests of the landlords. Mrs. McCracken nodded her head vigorously and said: "You are absolutely right." She asked me to stay after class so that we could talk; she invited me to her home for dinner; she wanted me to meet her husband. She wanted me to join a small and select group of "Anne's favorites," girls she had chosen as special, the kind of girls she would have liked as daughters, if she herself had children. I was proud to be a McCracken girl.

Mrs. McCracken was a master teacher. She was smart, verbal, and enthusiastic about her work. When I met her, she was about thirty years old, a slim and energetic woman who looked older than she was. She dressed like most of the women teachers her age in conservative dark print dresses, fastened with a slim leather belt, and low heeled, comfortable pumps. Her dark brown hair was straight and cut chin-length, her face was lively but not pretty. She had a hooked nose, a darkish complexion and crooked teeth. Her beauty lay in her outgoing personality and her quick wit. A year before I met her she was still single and had taken her class to the World's Fair where she was assigned an official guide to escort her group. As the day wore on, Haveling McCracken, the young guide, chatted and laughed and flirted with Anne. Haveling, who had just graduated from Lafayette College in Easton, Pennsylvania, was in search of work as a writer in New York City and had taken the temporary job at the Fair, as a first step. He was large and handsome with an Orson Wellesian big body and boyish look, and an encyclopedic knowledge of literature and music. To Anne, he represented a world apart. He was someone she would have been unlikely to meet through her normal circle of friends, most of whom were New York Jews of immigrant backgrounds. He wooed her and she quickly fell in love, and they were married soon after. When I met Anne in 1941, she was actually a newlywed. Before that, she had been a plain Jane spinster, one with a secure job. She adored Haveling and did all she could to please him, including bringing home her "girls." To help her husband find work, Anne also invited the parents of her girls to her home, hoping thereby to introduce

Haveling to some business people who might be in a position to offer him an opportunity. I remember one such evening when Haveling had a long conversation with my father and talked with him about the possibility of a loan to start a venture. "If you, or someone you knew were to give me the money," he said, "I could offer all of these first editions as collateral." He proceeded to remove book after book from his shelves, showing that each was a first edition of prized American literature. My father said nothing. That same evening, when the conversation turned to my parents interest in the weekly Metropolitan Opera broadcasts, Haveling played recordings of several arias from Don Giovanni. I remember it because it was my first encounter with "Madamina" (Lepporello's listing of the Don's conquests). I was impressed with Haveling's knowledge of opera. He was a charmer, like Don Giovanni. And we, Anne's students, developed crushes on him, something he clearly enjoyed.

By the end of my junior year my friendship with the McCrackens had gradually diminished, and I was not in touch with them once I started college. Anne had either found new favorites or had lost interest in the home visits. In 1949, when I returned from my job at Mt.Holyoke, I called on the McCrackens and borrowed a book as I left their apartment. It was a novel by Louis Auchincloss, which Anne had just read and liked a lot. "Take it, Esther. You'll like it. You can return it after you finish it." I barely got into it, was not interested, kept it too long, and, after I mailed it back to her, I called a few days later to see if she had received it. "This is the last time I will ever lend you anything. What nerve you have to send it back to me with a torn dust cover!" I was so shocked by her response, all I could say was that I was sorry and I hung up, resolved not to contact her again. I heard that Anne died an early death from cancer just a few years later. (*Only now do I realize that she may have been ill already when I called, and the dust cover that I never considered to have any significance could have affected the value of that book, had it been a first edition.*)

In the beginning of my junior year my Biology teacher was Esther Schlanger, a perky woman, probably in her early forties, with a pretty face and a warm smile. She was a political progressive and added a social science component to the Biology syllabus. It was so refreshing for me to see that a science course also had social implications. We had several debates in class on issues that were being discussed in the world at large at that time. One, for example, concerned the crisis in agriculture and the oversupply of food that remained unsold. The question was: "Should the farmers destroy the excess crops and get paid by the government for the loss? Or was there a better way of dealing with this problem since a large part of the population was still suffering from the effects of the Depression and going hungry?" I remember arguing for a national food bank, keeping the crops, and distributing them to the hungry.

A second social issue we debated in class was the question of eugenics, which was a popular movement at that time, one supported by many intellectuals and progressive thinkers including Harold Laski, a renowned left-wing political scientist and professor at the London School of Economics. I spoke defending forced sterilization: "After all," I said smugly as I stood in front of the class arguing my position, "is it not foolhardy to allow mentally deficient people to have babies and thus add more mentally ill people to the population?" I really believed that. But no sooner had I finished my presentation, one of my classmates, a girl who was poor, judging from the clothes she wore, stood up and shouted, "What right have you," she asked angrily, "to tell me or anyone else not to have a baby? If I bring a baby into the world and love that baby and care for that baby, I have a right to have him. Don't you have a heart?" I was stunned. I returned to my seat and thought and thought about what I had been saying. And I finally concluded that it was indeed heartless. (*Later I learned that not only was eugenics heartless, it was racist, and used by the Nazis to justify killing the mentally ill and the Jews.*)

In my sixth term at Walton, I had another crush. This one was on my English teacher, Mr. John Cocks. His course was an elective in journalism and his knowledge of newspaper writing style indicated that he himself had once been a working reporter, making him even more glamorous to a classroom of teen-age girls.

Mr. Cocks was a tall, athletically built man, with reddish blonde hair and the fair skin that was common to his Scotch-Irish background. He dressed immaculately; he always wore a suit, usually tan in color, a silk, patterned tie, and a starched white shirt. He was probably in his early forties and his attitude as a teacher was that of a kind authority figure, rather than a friend. Because he had been a working journalist, he had more panache than just an English teacher. His extracurricular job was faculty advisor to the *Walton Log*, our weekly newspaper. I joined the *Log* staff that term and he chose me to be the sports editor, giving me the name Eddi Edelman as my byline. I looked forward to our daily English period and then working in the *Log* office as many afternoons as necessary to get the paper out. He liked me and often complimented me on what I was wearing—a brown tweed riding-jacket was my favorite that spring—and I wore it as often as possible, knowing that he liked it too.

Mr. Cocks knew a lot about the English language and he taught us to write with precision and style. He spoke with elegance, in a deep voice and without a trace of a regional accent. He taught us to savor the language, to avoid shibboleths, to speak and write succinctly and clearly. But he did not know a lot about social science or about New York City. One day he went around the room asking each of us to report on a book we were reading other than for homework. When my turn came I announced that I was reading "Toward Freedom" by Jahwaharlal Nehru. Actually, I wasn't really reading it but my family owned the book and I knew a little about the Indian freedom movement. "Would you please spell that name?" he said. And then: "Who is this Nehru?" I felt embarrassed for him, and a bit guilty that I claimed to have read the book and thus unnecessarily had put him on the spot.

Later that spring, Mr. Cocks had volunteered the services of our class to work on the rationing system that had just been installed in the United States. We had to go to a training session at the Office of Price Administration in Manhattan and learn how to issue ration books for sugar. He had made a date for us to meet him at an address on Fifth Avenue, and then added that it was in the Fred F. French Building, "wherever that is." I immediately raised my hand. "I know the building and it's on the southeast corner of 45th Street and Fifth Avenue." "Thanks, Esther," he said. "I'll meet the group there tomorrow at one o'clock." When I arrived, he and many of the girls were already there and he was fuming. "Esther, this building does not have an OPA office. How could you have misled us so badly and with such certainty?" he demanded, with clenched teeth and his face redder than usual. The address he had, 521 Fifth Avenue, was definitely a few blocks away, but as we were about to proceed further downtown I pointed to the outside of the wrong building where, engraved in the marble front, were the words Fred F. French Building. Once again, without really meaning to, I had embarrassed him.

A few weeks before the end of the term, I wrote a long, funny poem about him and I handed it to him as I was leaving at the end of class one day, feeling proud of my piece, and hoping he would call me into his office and congratulate me—or even better, read it aloud to the class. It was written in the style of a Norman Corwin radio script. (*Corwin was one of the popular radio-script writers of the era. His scripts were witty, topical, and rhyming- and so was mine.*) It was the story of the trial of Miss CA (the Classical Academic girl) who was accused of being a snob and brought to court accordingly. I never made a copy for myself, and can only vaguely remember the refrain which referred to "the handsome, the amazing, the dreamy John Cocks, the guy who only wore white woolen socks." He never returned it to me; he never said a word about it. But my final grade that semester in his class was 98, the highest he gave. I never knew whether the poem contributed to his assessment of my work.

I was eagerly looking forward to my second semester of the senior year when I would become Editor-in-Chief of the *Log* and work even more closely with him. But he left Walton High School before my last term began. He had either been transferred or had asked for a transfer, I never knew which. And, in his place, the new advisor was a mousy lady whom I disliked and who, I am sure, disliked me. When the new advisor and the outgoing editorial staff voted, I came in second —Editor of Page 1, rather than Editor-in-Chief. When I wrote a liberal editorial, Miss Mouse rejected it as unsuitable, and I had to rewrite it according to her likes. The final blow to me was the comment chosen about me in the senior yearbook. Next to my picture and my name, the yearbook editor, who was also the *Log* Editor-in-Chief, had submitted the epithet: "Esther's a Cog in the Wheels of the *Log*." When I saw it, before it went to press my heart sunk—did I want to be remembered just as a cog in a wheel? I thought it was demeaning and I protested. Gloria Asch, the editor, replied: "I don't see what's wrong with it. But if you don't like it just write your own, and do it right now." In haste, I referred back to a comment made about me in our summer camp paper: "Esther's a Girl Who's Pretty and Tall, In Character and Leadership She Beats Us All." They printed it, and when I saw it next to my picture, I wished that I could tear it out of every book. What a pompous thing to say about myself, and it doesn't even rhyme properly.

Mr. Cocks had a simple wife (whom I met once briefly when I went to his apartment to pick up something we needed for our class). I think he liked Walton and he really seemed to like those of us who were worldly and clever, but I sensed that he did not feel comfortable with us. I remember one day when I met him in the hall and stopped to say hello. He was talking to Barbara Levy, a tall blue-eyed blonde with long wavy hair, whom I knew as a younger member of our *Log* staff. We three chatted for a moment just as Mrs. McAuliffe, the principal, came clacking by in her brown and white Spectator heels and determined walk. She was a prissy woman in her forties who had just gotten married, to the disbelief of all the girls who had pegged her as a quintessential "Old Maid." Seizing the moment, Barbara, another smart-ass fan of Mr. Cocks, said in a loud voice, "John, wipe the lipstick off your face." His face turned bright red, almost as red as the so-called lipstick Barbara lied about. I envied her brazenness and thought what she said was really funny, but in retrospect, I think we were all a little too much for Mr. Cocks.

# MY BROTHER JACK

"Bill Dickey, Lefty Gomez, Lou Gehrig, Tony Lazzeri, Red Rolfe, Joe DiMaggio, Dixie Walker." I would pipe up with these names as soon as my brother Jackie asked me to name the Yankee lineup. As a little girl, I loved dolls and dress-up and the things a little girl was supposed to like. But my live-in companion was a boy, three years older than me, with black wavy hair, rosy cheeks, a few freckles on his nose and a mischievous twinkle in his brown eyes. My brother Jackie liked all the things a little boy was supposed to like: building models, playing chess, exploring new places in the city, and teaching his little sister to memorize stuff like the Yankee lineup and The Passover Four Questions in Hebrew.

Because my mother went to the office every day, there was almost always a housekeeper at home to give us lunch and make dinner, and to be the adult presence in the house. But my mother assigned Jackie the task of minding me in those hours after school before she arrived home. He took me with him even when we lived on 86th Street in Manhattan. One day, when he was eight and I was five, he was whacking me for something I said or did and a woman who was passing by scolded, "Little boy, stop that at once! You should not hit a little girl!" And Jack replied: "She's my sister and I can do what I want to her." Once we moved to the Bronx, I was on my own in the afternoons, but if I did not have a girlfriend from school to play with, or if Beulah Jacobs, who lived in Apartment 2B in the Muriel Arms, was not around, I hung out with Jackie, who would allow me to watch whatever he and his friends were doing. I was proud to be included in the big boys' games, even if I wasn't allowed to play.

Jackie did not crave center-stage, and discovered early that he could use me as his mouthpiece. He went to Hebrew School and learned how to read the Hebrew alphabet and therefore was the designated child to ask the four questions at the Passover Seder. But rather than accept that exalted position, he decided that I was the youngest child present at the service, so it was my job and not his. I did not read Hebrew, so he taught me the passages to say by heart. He would read them to me over and over and I would learn the pronunciation and the accompanying melodious lilting; "Ma nish tah nah halai- lah hazeh-eh, mi chol ha lai-lo-os," I would chant. And when the grownups at the Seder beamed their enthusiasm at my performance, Jackie's face was the proudest of all. He was pleased with his teaching skills and my performance, but especially proud that he had figured out a way of passing the onerous burden from himself to me.

Had we had a dog, which almost none of the apartment dwellers in those days would even think of having, Jackie might have spent his time teaching the animal new tricks. But instead, he practiced on me. When visitors came he would entertain them by asking me to recite the Yankee lineup, and when he abandoned the Yanks for the Dodgers, of course I became a Brooklyn fan. When I was enrolled in Sunday school at Tremont Temple, the teacher offered a Hershey bar to the child who read the assigned Hebrew passage the fastest. So each Saturday night Jack would read my passage to me, have me commit it to memory, and the next day I would be the fastest, and win the candy, which I shared with my brother at Sunday lunch.

As we grew older, Jack was still my teacher of the things that I was not to learn in school. He was becoming more and more interested in the political events of the day: Mussolini's war in Ethiopia, the Civil War in Spain, and the rise of the Nazi Party in Germany. My parents subscribed to *Life Magazine*, which carried graphic photographs of these events. Cousins Lou and Pearl influenced the way we thought about politics, and the pictures and captions in *Life* kept our anti-fascist sensibilities passionately alive. Jack joined the "left-leaning" American Students Union in high school and when he entered City College he identified with the pro-Soviet group in a campus that was so finely tuned into left politics, that there were three major Socialist-leaning factions: the Socialists, the Trotskyists, and those whom others called "Stalinists." They spent all their free time in the cafeteria that was located in the alcoves of the basement room of Shepard Hall on the Uptown campus. Each group carved out its own space. Alcove1was claimed by the Socialists and Trotskyists; Alcove 2, by the pro-Soviets.

Political agitation became a huge part of the City College education in the liberal arts school.

And through my brother, I was also politically engaged, although none of my girl friends was interested in talking about world events. Talking about boys and clothes was more fun. So until I entered college I led a double life: politics at home, girl-talk with friends, and a combination of both at school, depending on the class.

Jack was drafted into the Air Force in 1943, when I was a freshman at the downtown branch of City College, the business school, which had no alcoves. It was a sad day for us, especially, for my father who, every time the imminent deployment was mentioned would shake his head as and say, "I don't believe that this is happening." A few weeks before the day set for his departure, Jack was given the option of appealing the decision. He was reluctant to ask for a request for deferment to complete his college degree because it looked cowardly and also there was little chance that a deferment for that reason would be granted. But my father, who agonized over the possibility that his son would be harmed, asked, "Why not try?" And my mother added, "They will either say yes or no." And I said, "Try Jackie, please try." Jack did request an extension but to no avail.

Once the appeal was turned down, my mother managed to contain her fears and just kept busy with everyday life, shopping, cooking, and working downtown. And I knew that I would miss my brother but never believed that anything bad would happen to him. Where would he go? What would he be doing? It was a time when all the young men were being drafted. I had already gone to two engagement parties of high school classmates. They were marrying their boyfriends just before the husbands-to-be were being sent overseas. The war was viewed as a struggle between the forces of good and evil, and every family was caught in its sweep, some more than others. My father, however, never stopped worrying.

The night before Jack was to report to his deployment center, I organized "A Farewell Party For Jack and Artie." Arthur Gelb, a friend from City College, was slated to go at the same time. About a dozen classmates and friends showed up. Jewel Lubin was there, and Dick Jacobson. Both were friends of Jack's from the American Student Union. We gathered in the living room, turned on the phonograph for Glenn Miller's Band music: "In The Mood," "Pennsylvania 6-5000," "Moonlight Serenade," were our favorites. On the hour we would switch to the radio to hear the news: It was the time of the battle of Naples, the battle of the Solomon Islands and the Russians fighting to regain their losses in the Ukraine. The war was raging on all fronts, and there were signs of victory too. The party was a mixture of bravado and apprehension. No one knew where Jack and Artie would be going or what would happen to them. We drank beer and cream soda, ate corned beef and pastrami sandwiches from the Jewish Deli, and hugged each other good night when it was time to go home.

"In the Mood"

https://www.youtube.com/watch?v=_CI-0E_jses

The next day, Jack and Artie appeared at the center together; Jack was taken and Artie turned away for a physical disability that marked him "4F" and not eligible to serve. Rather than returning home triumphantly, Artie suffered. He never returned to City College, took a job instead, and then transferred to NYU. (In the end he lucked into a career as reporter, City Editor, and finally National Editor of *The New York Times*.)

Jack was assigned to the Air Force and sent to basic training in Miami. One day, three months later, my father came home from work with train tickets in his hand. He was going to Miami to see Jack just as he was finishing his training there and before he was to be sent to "God knows where?"

Jack and Dad in front of Muriel Arms, 1943

# MY LANDLADY: MADISON, WISCONSIN (1944-1946)

In the spring of 1944, it became clear to me that I had no future at City College. I had gone there for a year and a half, hoping that the rules would change and that women would be allowed to major in the liberal arts. This did not happen. I told my parents at dinner one evening that I had to transfer and that I was considering schools that were out of town. "I wish you could stay at home," said my father. "I will miss you." My mother leaned over to me and stroked my hand. "But you must do what you have to do, unless you can find a way to stay in New York," my Dad continued. I was determined to leave home and excited about my new venture. I chose a few schools, all co-ed, all out-of-town, all with good social science programs, for I knew that was my calling. The University of Wisconsin accepted me, and I was set.

I worried a bit about moving from New York, the overpopulated city loaded with East European immigrants, to a relatively small city in the Middle West. On the other hand, there were many New Yorkers in Madison at the time I went there. I knew that Wisconsin was a strongly liberal state, the home of the La Follettes, father and son, both senators and leaders in the progressive movement in the United States.

Once accepted, I called the Housing Office to ask for a space in one of the dorms. "Sorry, Miss Edelman," I was told, "The war is on; the dorms are full; soldiers and sailors are living on campus. But we can provide you with a list of off-campus houses. You'll have to negotiate your own lease. Come a few days before the term begins."

I turned to my mom who was listening to the call.

"They say I have to find my own room. I have to go early."

"I'm coming with you," my mother declared.

I was surprised because my mother was not a big traveler, but I knew that she was a mother who wanted to know exactly where and how I was going to live away from home. She feared that I would be tempted to choose housing that was cheap and unsafe, or coed, things that mothers worried about.

A few weeks before the term began my mom and I were at Penn Station, boarding the Trailblazer to Chicago, in the search for my home for the next few years. After we arrived in Madison, it did not take long. We had a few listings close to the campus, a major factor for both of us. The first was a home with a room for rent at $5.00 a week. It looked okay to me but my mother's sharp eye noticed that the family who owned it had had a beer delivery that day and there was a case of six-packs on the porch. She vetoed it before we even looked inside. Our remaining choice was equally close to the campus. It was a small white cottage, two stories high, with a peaked roof and a small white fence around the property. I rang the bell and a plump woman in her thirties, with a ruddy face and straggly blond hair, opened the door. She was wearing a cotton dress that was almost entirely covered by a large floral apron.

"We are here to look at the room for rent," I said.

"Come on in," she replied, opening the door wide and stepping aside as we entered. "The room is upstairs and it's a double. Follow me."

Up we went to view a large twin bedroom with two beds, a desk, and a closet, light and airy and immaculately clean.

"I'm Doris Zimmerman," she said," and I live here with my husband and my two little boys. They're out with their Dad right now." She fixed the window shade, which was rattling, as she continued: "We only have two rooms for rent a double and a single, and the single, which would have been $5.00, is already taken by a local working girl. She's lived with us for several years. The double room will cost $7.00. But you can surely find a nice roommate and only pay $3.50 each." Her face lit up. "Now isn't that ever a bargain?"

My mother immediately replied, "Oh that won't be necessary. I am sure we can easily afford $7.00 a week." I wondered about how

I would find a roommate and started to speak, but my mom cut me off.

"Esther will be better off living here by herself. But what about the cleaning and the laundry?"

"Well, I'll be cleaning the room once a week and, on that day you can leave your towels and sheets and any small laundry items you have."

"That sounds just fine," my mother said.

"Why not?" Mrs. Z continued. "I am doing the family laundry anyway."

That clinched it. We signed an agreement and my mom smiled with satisfaction.

I left New York for Madison in September 1944. My dad bought me a ticket on the overnight train from New York to Chicago, the Pacemaker, which left from Grand Central. He made sure that I had a seat assignment in the all-women's car. A seasoned traveler, he believed that I would be more comfortable stretching out in the company of women on an overnight coach ride. I, however, was upset that he was preventing me from striking up conversations with nice young men whom I believed I might meet on the train. After changing trains in Chicago the following morning, I finally arrived late in the afternoon, excited by the prospect of a new chapter in my life.

'Mad-i-son,' the conductor called out. I grabbed my bag and made my way to the cab station and then on to 935 N. Johnson Street to be greeted by the Zimmermans: Doris, her husband Earl (an inter-city bus driver I later learned), and their two small sons, Darryl, a five-year old, and Dana, who was about 3.

"Hello there!"

I greeted the children, stooping down with my hands extended, waiting for a hug. But they immediately ran to hide in their mother's apron, grabbing on to her skirt, and not looking at me at all. Doris gave me my key and I was on my own, in a new school, a new city and a new home.

Doris was less than ten years older than I, but I never thought of her as a contemporary. She was reaching the end of her girlhood bloom and rapidly showing premature beginnings of middle age. Raised in the small city of Eau Claire, Wisconsin, she had dropped out of high school and had married her childhood sweetheart. She cared for the house, the children, the cleaning and cooking and spent most of her nights alone while Earl, an inter-city bus driver, was away in some far-off town. She spoke with a Wisconsin accent, and added phrases like "You betcha!" or "Is it ever!" when she agreed with what you said. Earl was taciturn and barely said a word to me. But Doris was bubbly, and seemed to like to talk; she had no one to talk to except the children and later, she talked to me when she got the chance. When Earl had a day off from his bus-driving job, he changed out of his blue serge uniform into comfortable trousers and a woolen shirt to do chores around the house. The kids would follow him around, glad to see him. But he also slept a lot because of his night shift and they had to keep quiet, so as not to wake him. He had his beer delivered once a week, something I neglected to tell my mother. The family belonged to the Lutheran Church in town and went to services on Sunday mornings. They had few friends and no relatives in Madison, so their social life was almost non-existent.

Six weeks after I moved in, the house across the street was put up for sale. Doris and Earl seized the opportunity to sell the small one they lived in and buy the larger one. They also decided to convert it into a boarding house for women university students. It was an old spacious wooden house, which sat squarely on a small hillock, with a driveway on one side and a path to the backyard on the other. Painted dark brown, it was twice as large as the little white cottage we lived in. The ground floor with its living room, dining room, kitchen and two bedrooms was perfect for the Zimmermans. Up one flight of stairs were two large bedrooms and a small single room with just enough space for a bed and a desk and chest of drawers. There was also a suite, with its own alcove, which could be used as a living room-study and small bedroom for two. The top floor was an apartment with its own kitchen, bath, entrance and stairway.

The sale was completed in no time. The working girl was asked to leave because she was not a student, and I was offered the single, which I was happy to accept. Doris listed the house with the University as a residence for women students.

"Esther, do you know anyone who needs a room?" Doris asked. "I called the housing office, and they told me they have no girls looking for rooms now that the term has begun." I already knew of five possible tenants. "Sure, Doris," I replied. "I know a few people who would be interested if their landlords will let them go."

The house filled up quickly. A few weeks before, I had bumped into two girls I had met the previous summer in New York. They had been looking for housing closer to the campus than their temporary quarters and left me their telephone number in case something turned up.

I called. "Are you still looking?" I asked Carol, who answered the phone. "My landlady is looking to fill two doubles."

"What's the address? We'll come this afternoon," Carol responded with an excited voice. They signed a lease right away and moved in a few days later. Mary and Carol had worked together as copygirls for *The Daily Worker*. Although they prided themselves on befriending the working class, they had little to say to Doris once they moved in. She was happy to have them but had few interactions with them. And they were happy to keep to themselves.

I found another tenant for Doris, another Doris. Doris Jacobson was my friend Dick's younger sister. She was entering the University as a freshman from New York and needed a room. She had flaming red hair, wore sweater sets, plaid skirts, and penny loafers, and she would have loved dorm life had she had a chance to get it. But she had to settle for our off-campus place. I paired her up with Zelda, a biology major from Brooklyn with a genius level IQ. The two became enemies almost from the first day, but the housing shortage kept them together. Zelda was poor. Unlike her new roommate, she had almost no money to spend on herself.

Finally, a month or so later, I brought in Sorelle, a transfer student from Newark, New Jersey, whom I had met in one of my classes. By then the only room left was the suite with the alcove.

"Wow," said Sorelle. "This is a beauty. I would love to have it but I can't afford it."

She looked at me with her pretty round face and deep brown eyes: "Esther, Esther, why don't we take this one together?"

I struggled with this new idea. I had just gotten my single and was enjoying the privacy. But my room was tiny and the only comfortable seat was the bed itself. "We can have a real living room with a couch and chairs," Sorelle pleaded, "and sleep in the alcove. Or one of us can have a bed in the living room and the other in the alcove. You'll have more space than in your single, Esther. Let's move in together." And that is what we did.

Later, Sorelle warned me that if she were to get a boyfriend she would expect me to leave for the night, but that never happened. (The war was still on and the soldiers had all left the campus to go overseas.) Having Sorelle as a roommate opened up new doors for me. I met and became friends with Trotskyists for the first time. And through her brother, who worked as an economist in Washington, she had close ties with a group of older students in the Sociology Department, all devoted followers of Hans Gerth, the world renowned Professor of Sociology, who was teaching at Wisconsin in those years.

One day, Zelda, the IQ genius who had scored so high on the Stanford-Binet in fifth grade that she was taken to the Board of Education Brooklyn Headquarters in an ambulance, arrived at my room announcing: "Esther, I just heard that the Nutrition Department is looking for volunteers. They are doing an experiment to determine whether yeast, which is an inexpensive source of protein, could be used as a dietary supplement to feed thousands of refugees. It's sponsored by UNRRA—a UN agency." Entering the doorway, she added, "They need people to follow a strict diet. You get all your meals—breakfast, lunch, and supper. C'mon Esther, let's do it together."

"What's the hitch?" I asked as I moved over on the couch to make room for her to sit down. "Well," she replied, "you're not allowed to eat anything but their food. They measure it." She had an impish grin on her face, and then she added, "You have to save all your urine and your feces, so they can measure that too. Oh Esther, do it with me." She grabbed my arm as she said, "We can both use two weeks worth of free food."

I knew that she was going to do it with or without me and couldn't wait for me to mull it over, so I agreed. It sounded like fun and a way to save money. The next morning we climbed up a huge hill to the Ag School, found the designated room, which was actually set up as a café, signed an agreement to abide by the rules, and were given a hearty breakfast: juice, home made bread, home made butter and jam, homemade hot cereal, a hard-boiled egg, a container of milk, and coffee. As we left, we were each given a large dark green bag made of cotton with an oil cloth lining and a drawstring closing. It contained two large bottles, one for feces and one for urine and some collecting paraphernalia to ease the process. The worst thing about the adventure was how boring the food got to be. There was no meat, no fresh fish, no dessert. We ate the same thing day after day. "Oh God, not again!" Zelda cried out as another hard-boiled egg was given to us as our dinner protein. We yearned for our old favorites, like the "Hot-Fudge Mary Jane," a brownie, covered with vanilla ice cream and smothered in hot fudge sauce that had become a treat we loved to order at the counter of the local Rennebohm's drug store. The best thing about the diet was the ease with which we handled the excrement. Zelda and I marched out each morning with our waste collection, joking about the jars, and threatening our housemates that we would bop them with our swinging bags. One day, as we were swinging our bags, we bumped into Doris Zimmerman on our way out the door. "Whatcha got there?" she asked. "And what's so funny?"

"Oh just some lab specimens," Zelda replied with a smile.

Doris shook her head the same way she did when one of her little boys had just done something silly.

At the end of the two weeks both of us had had enough. Zelda planned to return, but not for at least a week of real food. On the day after the diet ended, we ran together to the Rennebohm's that was just a block away from our house. It was 8:30 AM. We took seats at the counter:

"We'll have two Hot-Fudge Mary Janes," I called out to the waitress before she even had time to remove the pencil from behind her ear.

"Oh I'm so sorry," said the waitress. The brownies haven't arrived. I can give you two hot-fudge sundaes."

Zelda and I looked at each other. We both had made the same slightly disgusted face.

"Hot-fudge sundaes! For breakfast?" Zelda asked, her voice rising. "No thank you." And we proceeded to order toast and coffee and fried eggs.

As students in an off-campus residence, we each had our own keys and came and went as we pleased. Because there was no common living room for us, the house was considered to be a private dwelling, rather than a mini-dorm with strict rules for women students. It was great for us tenants. No one was monitoring us. But it also meant that we interacted less with each other and certainly less with the family downstairs. Doris managed to clean our rooms when we were in class. I only saw her on chance meetings if we were both coming in or going out at the same time. Even when she did my laundry, she took it and returned it when I was away. Occasionally, however, she would knock on my door to ask my advice about something that troubled her.

One day I heard the sound of the front door closing, someone running up the steps, and a knock on my door. I opened it to see Doris. "Esther, I just showed the apartment to a couple who answered the rental ad." She was out of breath and sat down on my bed. "You know what?" she said. "They call themselves Mennonites and they come from Indiana. They're in Madison because the man is working here. You know, they look nice and they are clean and they say they are married, but I looked at her hand and she had no wedding ring. Now what do you think of that?" "Oh Doris, Mennonites are not allowed to wear jewelry. It's against their religion." Her eyes widened and her face blushed. "Is that really true?" she asked. "Well then, if you're right, I guess I should let them move in."

Never had she had a better set of tenants. They were so quiet that one would hardly know they were there. They dressed simply in cotton or woolen clothing. The wife wore long skirts, dark colors, and no jewelry. The husband was always dressed in black trousers and a black jacket. Their religion forbade them from taking part in the military and the husband was assigned to work in a program for Conscientious Objectors. The apartment they rented actually had a separate staircase, so we hardly saw them except to get a glimpse of the woman in her long woolen coat and flat shoes, coming and going with her groceries. We would exchange hellos. Unfortunately, they were transferred out of Madison before I had a chance to really talk to them about their beliefs. I would have liked to know more about them.

As I was returning from class one wintry day, I bumped into Doris on her way home from the small neighborhood shop where she had gone for a few last minute groceries.

"It's so expensive there," she complained, "and I tried to Jew him down but no such luck."

Until then I had never heard the expression "Jew down the price." I was astonished to hear such a thing from Doris's mouth. Should I tell her that what she was saying was blatant anti-Semitism? Didn't she know that I was Jewish, which made it especially hurtful? I decided to ignore it and said nothing. She was not worldly but she was truly goodhearted. Later I learned that it was common lingo in the Middle West at that time.

One day, towards the end of my stay in Madison, Doris Jacobson and Zelda decided they had had enough of each other and each found another place to live, leaving an empty double room in the house. A few weeks later, Doris Zimmerman knocked on my door to tell me that the University Housing office had called her that morning. "They wanted to know if I had a room for two Negro women students who are having a hard time finding a place to live?"

"So, what did you tell them?" I asked

"I told them I would think about it" she said, "but I really don't want to get involved. What do you think, Esther?"

"Oh Doris, it would be such a good thing to do. I would be happy to have them as house-mates, and I'm sure that all the others in the house would feel the same way."

"I don't know," she replied. "I don't think I want them, although no one else has even asked about the room and it's been three weeks now."

As soon as she left I went to search for Mary and Carol.

"We've got to do something to get her to change her mind."

Carol remembered that the pastor of the Lutheran Church in town was on the Board of the local NAACP. I ran down and knocked on Doris's door.

"Why don't you discuss it with your pastor? I'm sure he will help you decide." "Hmm," she said, " I hadn't thought about that. It's a good idea. I'll call him."

A week later the two black women moved in. They were so self-contained that none of us saw much of them, but they were excellent tenants and Doris was happy to have them.

As graduation approached, Mary decided to marry a classmate who had grown up in Wisconsin. They planned to remain in Madison, a city that most of us New Yorkers, and many national magazines, had decided was the ideal place to live in the United States. The wedding would be held later, some time after we all left. But Carol decided to buy Mary's gift in advance. On the day the gift arrived, Doris came running up the stairs, knocking on my door and bursting with news.

"What is it?" I asked.

"Esther, do you know what Carol bought Mary as a wedding gift?"

"No."

"She bought her a huge set of books!" And as she said "books" she broke into a half- smile, half-smirk, placed her hands on her hips and snorted "What kind of present is that?"

"What books did she buy?" I asked.

"Come on, Esther, help me carry the package upstairs and you'll see what it says on the label."

I ran down to help her and saw: *The Complete Works of V.I. Lenin*.

As I was dragging my end of the heavy package up the stairs, I laughed to myself. "Oh Carol, you are so true to form! Oh Doris, you must think we New Yorkers are crazy!"

I left Madison in the fall of 1946 with enough academic credits to get my degree as soon as I finished an independent study paper that could be done in New York.

"Good-bye Doris." I said as I hugged her. "I loved living here and I'll come back to visit. It has been a great two years." "You bet," she replied, brushing back a bit of straggly hair.

She walked me to my waiting cab, telling her boys to stay on the porch.

"And have a safe trip." She closed my cab door and we both waved until the cab turned into University Avenue. "I'm comin'," I heard her yelling to Darryl and Dana.

I enrolled in graduate school in New York and never saw her again.

Doris and Earl Zimmerman, Madison 1946

# AN UNLUCKY STRIKE

One evening in the fall of 1946, our reunited family was sitting in the living room. Jack had returned from the army, safe and sound. I was back in New York, taking classes at Columbia. My father was sitting in his special chair, with cushions piled behind him to ease his back pain. And my mother was busy puffing up his pillows. The telephone rang. My mother rushed into the bedroom to answer it. "Mrs. Edelman," the doctor said, "I have bad news. Your husband has an inoperable lung cancer for which there is no cure. His life could be prolonged, but not saved, by x-ray treatments." He then described this new procedure, which was in its primitive stages and involved burning of the skin each time a treatment was administered, causing increasingly severe discomfort as the treatments progressed. "You can call my secretary in the morning and arrange with her for your husband to start the radiotherapy." My mother hung up, rose from the bed on which she was sitting and slowly walked back to the living room. She looked dazed. My father asked who had called. "It was the doctor's office," she said. "They want us to call in the morning to arrange a set of appointments to treat your back pain." My mother later told my brother and me what the doctor had said and made us promise not to talk about it where my father could hear us. The truth was that my father knew how ill he was. The extent of his pain, the doctor's look when he examined him, had made it clear that the original diagnosis of "bursitis" was wrong and something much more serious was going on. But my father never talked about it to my brother and me.

My father died just seven months later, at home, in his own bed, surrounded by my mother, my aunt, my brother, and me. His visitors, a best friend, Milton, and my cousin, Lou, who came to see him every other evening once he had been confined to bed, had just left. My father had lapsed into a coma earlier that day, just after he had trouble speaking, a symptom that implied that the tumor had spread to his brain. I was in the room at the time, watching his face turn white and his body stiffen. He struggled to get out his last words: "Vault in bank." He knew he was dying and he never forgot that he was leaving behind a family. He then lapsed into a coma. At about 10 o'clock that night we who had been sitting next to his bed heard a loud gurgle. So this was the legendary death rattle! Jack grabbed a hand mirror to put near his mouth, a trick he learned from the movies to determine whether a dying person was still breathing. The mirror was clear. I picked up the phone from the night table next to Daddy's bed and called our family doctor who lived in the next building. "I'll be right there," he said, and he arrived about ten minutes later. After a brief examination, Dr. Guggenbuhl signed the death certificate, citing the cause of death as cardiac arrest, which technically was what had happened.

But the real cause of death was lung cancer from smoking Lucky Strikes for forty years, ever since he was sixteen. Smoking cigarettes was the normal thing for men to do in those days. And "Luckies" was a household word. *The Lucky Strike Hit Parade* was one of the radio shows my brother Jack listened to every Saturday night. It featured the most popular songs of that week and ended in a contest. The prize went to the listeners who correctly identified the top ten songs in correct order. The prize? A box of fifty Lucky Strike cigarettes was sent to the winner with no questions asked about the recipient's age. Jackie won once, when he was fifteen, and we were as excited as if we had won a lottery. The package arrived. It contained a reusable dark green tin box with a red circle in which "Lucky Strike" was printed in black letters and it held fifty cigarettes. Jack proudly presented it to our dad.

A few months before his death my father had read an article in *Reader's Scope*, a muckraking magazine that used the *Reader's Digest* format, which linked lung cancer to cigarette smoking, some twenty years before the monumental *Surgeon General's Report on Smoking and Related Diseases*. "Don't light that cigarette," he commanded, as I pulled one from the pack in my hand. "I just told you about the article."

"There's no proof that cigarettes cause cancer," I shot back. I lit my cigarette. He shrugged his shoulders and then turned on his heels and walked away.

I had become addicted to cigarettes two years before, in Madison, when we non-smokers helped the smokers by buying a pack of cigarettes every time we saw them in the drug store. It was wartime and most cigarettes were reserved for the soldiers. The civilian supply was limited. So the packs were only put out once a day and you could buy only one pack at a time. I did this for a friend, a graduate student in the English Department, who would come to my house once a week to pick up his haul. In the meantime I tried some of his cigarettes and forced myself to like them. Soon, I couldn't do without them. Besides, in my Psychology I class, which I had taken at City College, Professor Kenneth Clark (the Kenneth Clark of *Brown v Board of Education* fame), a chain smoker who smoked in class, suggested, between puffs, that the correlation between smoking and early death could be attributable to factors other than cigarettes. Armed with this bit of self-serving "information," plus my own addiction, I argued with my father, but I knew deep down, that he and the author of the article in *Reader's Scope* were most likely right. *What I had not realized, but should have, was that lighting a cigarette so close to a person with lung cancer was selfish and inconsiderate.*

My father died in May of 1947, at the age of 56, shortly after my 21st birthday. He had been sick for a year and a half. His symptoms started with a terrible case of flu he had developed during a flight home to New York from Seattle. Later he developed back pain, severe enough for him to cancel the trip to Madison, Wisconsin to attend my graduation in June of 1946. When I returned home shortly thereafter, my father had been erroneously diagnosed with bursitis by an elderly incompetent GP who was a wartime substitute for our own family doctor. "Just apply heat, the doctor had said." But my father was getting worse each day. We watched him suffer, dragging himself to work in the morning and returning home in great pain each evening. Finally a friend of the family referred my parents to a doctor at Mt. Sinai who agreed to see my Dad a few weeks later. After examining my father and analyzing the results of a tissue biopsy, Dr. John Garlock, the chest surgeon, called on the telephone to tell my mother what they had discovered.

In the fall of 1946, at the time of the diagnosis, I was taking classes at Columbia and living at home because I wanted to be near this man whose face lit up every time I came into his view. My father was still working and only stayed at home for the day of his X-ray treatment, to which I accompanied him as the designated driver. On one of those days, we were asked by my mother to stop in the grocery store on the way home. My dad was standing near the cashier and I was across the room choosing something from the shelves when I heard him call me: "Ketzela," he cried out, "Don't forget the bread." I was so embarrassed I wanted us both to disappear. I ran back to where he was standing and rumbled between my clenched teeth: "Will you stop calling me that! I'm almost 21 years old." I was furious. "Oh," he said, with a fallen face that quickly turned into an impish grin, "I'm so sorry. From now on I shall call you Miss Ketzela." After that, we went back to the car and, still mad at him, I drove him home to rest after his horrible, painful burn treatment.

I came to realize how hard it was for my father, the source of strength in the family, to become confined to his home and then become a bed-ridden patient. One day, our family doctor, now safely returned from the war, was taking blood from me to give to my father in a later transfusion. As my, now skinny, pajama-clad father went past the room where this was taking place, I saw his look of anguish and heard him groan with sorrow. Dr. Guggenbuhl came to our home once a week towards the end of my father's illness, to check his condition and later to prescribe the morphine injections as the end was nearing. With one freckled hand on the syringe and the other on my father's buttock, he taught my brother how to administer the needle so that my father could remain comfortable.

In the funeral parlor, my father lay in an open casket, dressed in a dark suit wearing a tallis and a yarmulke, items that the undertaker provided and had placed on him without asking us if we wanted him to be dressed that way. He seemed shrunken, having lost as much as 40 pounds. My Aunt Becky, my father's brother Sam's wife, looked into the casket and announced, "Oh he looks just like a Bar-Mitzvah boy!" It irked me to be left with such an inappropriate image of such a man. My father was a completely non-religious person and he would have been astonished to see himself with a yarmulke and a tallis, two garments he almost never wore in real life. Oh well, if there is a heaven, he is surely there, playing cards and swapping jokes with all the other secular humanists, and forgiving us for our little stupidities.

# MT. HOLYOKE

A few months before I left Wisconsin, I read a posted notice advertising a graduate fellowship in Political Science at Mt. Holyoke College. At that point I was prepared to go to Columbia for my graduate work and to live at home. But a full tuition scholarship and funds for living expenses sounded even better. I applied, was accepted, and planned to attend as soon as I received my undergraduate degree. In the meantime, however, my father had become terribly ill, so I decided to go to Columbia after all.

One year later, I was traveling in Europe on a summer tour. There was a double ring on the phone in my hotel room in Prague.

"We have a transatlantic call waiting for Esther Edelman," said the operator. "That's me," I replied.

"Please come to the lobby telephone booth to receive it."

I raced down the stairs. My mother was on the line.

"Esther," she said, "I just got a call from Victoria Schuck. She's the Chairman of the Political Science Department at Mt. Holyoke. She wants to know if you would be interested in a job as Instructor in the department starting in September. An opening has suddenly developed."

"Oh my Gosh! Are you sure she wants me to be on the faculty and not just come as a graduate student?" I asked.

"I am very sure," my mother replied. "She said that she knew that you had teaching experience and a year of graduate work at Columbia and she wants to talk to you."

My heart was beating fast at the thought of a possible job waiting for me. "Be sure to tell her I am interested," I instructed my mom. "Tell her that we are due back in New York in just two weeks. I'll call her as soon as I can."

I returned from Europe as scheduled and Jack, my mother, and I drove to South Hadley where I met Victoria Schuck in her office. She was a short, compact woman in her fifties whose unmanageable short, dark hair lay askew around her head. She kept tugging at her tortoise-shell glasses, putting them on and taking them off as she rapidly spoke to me, and to the secretary at the other end of the buzzer, and to the person on the phone who had interrupted our conversation. I liked her right away. She had my old application for the master's program on her desk and we talked about my work at Columbia and my teaching job at City College. The man who had been hired for the Holyoke position had pulled out just a few weeks before and Ms. Schuck was desperate. We agreed that I would teach the same course I had taught at City College. I gave her the telephone numbers for Sam Hendel, my Government professor at City College, and Franz Neumann, my advisor at Columbia; she could contact them as references. I signed the contract a week later.

"I'll miss you, Ketzel," said my mother, as she helped me pack a suitcase filled with clothes and books. She sighed as she looked at me. "But you'll be coming home on weekends, so it won't be so bad," she said, knowing that I had already signed up for a Saturday morning class at Columbia. I helped her close the bag and gave her a kiss.

Arriving in South Hadley, I was impressed by the reds and yellows of the changing maples, by the charm of this tiny New England town, with its commons, its main street that was commercial for only two blocks before it turned into the street upon which the school bordered. The campus buildings were a mixture of old, newer, and new. Many were made of stone; others, in colonial style, were of red brick. Everything looked substantial, and classy, and well kept. The dormitories were scattered among the classroom buildings. Each had a name and a housemother and a big lock on the front door. I discovered later that at precisely 10:00 PM on weekdays, and a bit later on weekends, the doors were bolted shut. Coming in after hours was a serious offense and merited disciplinary action. Men were, of course, not admitted beyond the downstairs parlor, where they were allowed to greet their dates and whisk them off campus, to be returned before curfew. For me, this was in sharp contrast to my own experience in Madison where we undergraduates had keys to come-and-go as we liked.

I met my first class on opening day and we decided that I should call my students by their first names, as was the campus custom. The strange thing was that, although the class list consisted of two dozen Christian names: Anne, Elizabeth, Margaret, Katherine and an occasional Jill or Joanne, the names my students were actually called were Betsy, Ibby, Nan, Pooh, Meg, Kit, and so on. I was struck by how these nicknames sounded so Waspish, so upper class, and so babyish. My own friends from childhood and through my college years were called Ruth, Shirley, Marilyn, Rhoda, Zelda, Doris, or the slightly fancier: Sorelle, Jewel, and Marcella. None of them used diminutives, and there were no Poohs or Ibbys. Another surprise for me was the custom of knitting in class. I made the mistake of not objecting to the knitters on the first day. I wanted to be liked and I wanted to be informal. So even though I thought that knitting trivialized what my students were trying to learn and surely interfered with note-taking, I never forbade it, and a half dozen of them made their sweaters and scarves as we plowed through *Marbury vs. Madison* and *Gitlow vs. The State of New York*. Worse, I found the girls to be too docile and unquestioning. One day we read excerpts from Lenin's *State and Revolution* and I added some arguments from the current newspapers to document Lenin's thesis that the State was indeed the instrument of the ruling class, even in America. After class a few students came to me asking for a refutation of this argument. "Oh Miss Edelman" one of them begged, "Tell us that it isn't really like that!"

A few weeks into the semester, the President of the College, Roswell Hamm, a forbidding looking man in his sixties, with a long, thin nose, steel rimmed glasses, and a strong baritone voice, held a reception for new faculty. As I entered the room, Miss Schuck, who was standing next to the President, told him my name. "Ah Miss Edelman, he boomed, I am so glad...," I beamed as he said this and rushed over to him only to hear him finish the sentence: "that your signature on the petition to restore Ralph Grundlach's tenure was one of only five from Mt. Holyoke." (He was referring to the decision by the University of Washington to fire three tenured faculty members, including Dr. Grundlach, who was an eminent psychologist. The "crime" was their refusal to answer the question about membership in the Communist Party before a legislative committee in the State of Washington.) My face must have been bright red as the faculty members who were already sipping their wine turned to look at me. Only five had actually signed the petition that I had been handed a few days earlier and that I had signed immediately. I thought then, "I've got to get out of here as soon as I can."

The Holyoke culture was far more conservative than that of New York City or Madison, Wisconsin. 1948 was an election year with three major candidates running for President. Truman won in the real world, but at Mt. Holyoke, in the straw vote held on campus, it was Dewey, the Republican, who won by a landslide. Out of the thousand votes cast, Henry Wallace got 12, one of which was mine. But this was in keeping with his national percentage.

At Holyoke, afternoon tea, served once a week in each dorm, was a fairly well attended ritual. The first time my students invited me I was shocked to see them wearing dresses, stockings and heels for the occasion. At each such tea, one student poured the tea, and one poured the water from silver-plated vessels. They were learning how to be hostesses, supervised carefully by the housemother. There was also a weekly sit-down dinner in each dorm, with table linens and good silver to which the students invited special guests, like me. Here too, the object was to encourage dressing up, proper table manners, and pleasant conversation. I coveted the invitations, but I also found those evenings to be part of the same ritual and tradition that I would have rebelled against had I been one of those students. Years later on a visit to Oxford, I was reminded of the Holyoke dinners when the tour guide led us into the dining hall at King's College, and described what it was like during the school year with full table service and waiters and all of the formalities that were part of the ritual there. It was the training ground for what was to come and, for all but the scholarship students, what they experienced at home during school vacations. It was all so upper class and so alien from my own experience as a girl from a Jewish immigrant family. One of my students, Missy (Melissa) Gamble, finding out where my family lived, rushed up to me one day to tell me that she too was from the

Bronx. Her family, the Proctor and Gamble soap manufacturers, lived in Riverdale in a mansion on the Hudson River. Technically it was the Bronx, but hardly my Grand Concourse Bronx.

To escape from what I considered a stifling atmosphere, dominated by unmarried women, I was glad, especially at first, to run home to New York every weekend. I was 22 years old, closer in age to the students than to my fellow faculty members. I could not help comparing what I considered a stodgy atmosphere in South Hadley Massachusetts with the vibrant life I had had in Madison, where there were lots of men, lots of graduate students, and a huge Student Union where so many of us hung out, exchanging ideas as we broke for coffee in the Rathskellar, a basement café that was open until midnight. The one thing I failed to note was the paucity of women professors at Wisconsin, compared to the large number at Mt. Holyoke.

In December, I received an offer to be a Congressional Intern with Representative Jacob Javits, to start in January 1949. I told Miss Schuck that I was hoping to leave Mount Holyoke if she would allow me to do so. She did not hesitate to reply, "Just think how it would look on your resume to have left an academic position after one semester." I turned down the job in Washington and I agreed to stay at Holyoke for the spring term, but I never even thought about spending another year in that cloistered atmosphere; I just wanted out.

For many of the students, however, the unmarried women on the faculty, especially our department chair, Victoria Schuck, were inspirational. Vicky believed that women could, and should do everything that men did in public affairs. She used her telephone and her position as Chair of the Political Science Department at a Seven Sisters College to persuade important women in public life to spend a few days on the Holyoke campus as Visiting Lecturers. During their time on the campus, the visitor joined the students at breakfast, lunch, and dinner, and was able to chat with the young women in a casual setting. One of my Political Science majors, Joanne Hammerman, had been asked by Miss Schuck to escort a visiting lecturer, Eleanor Roosevelt, to the room she was to stay in on the campus.

As Joanne deposited the suitcase she was carrying, Mrs. Roosevelt asked her to stay and talk with her. "I want to know all about you, Joanne," said Mrs. Roosevelt, who was then serving as the United States Ambassador to the United Nations. They talked about the role of women in public office, a conversation that led Joanne, many years later, to run for Lieutenant Governor of Illinois. She did not win that election but it paved the way for her entry into Chicago city government.

I left Mt. Holyoke at the end of the spring semester, sad to part with some of my favorite students, but glad to return to bustling New York and to resume my studies at Columbia.

# IT CAN HAPPEN HERE: PEEKSKILL, 1949

"From border unto border, from ocean unto ocean, arise triumphant, the brave Russian folk…" The deep baritone voice boomed into the night from the City College campus on 138th Street in Harlem. The year was 1946. The song was one of Paul Robeson's favorite encores: one that he had popularized during the war when the Americans and the Russians were on the same side.

Paul Robeson

"From Border Unto Border"
http://www.youtube.com/watch?v=Vyd2PMj_qoM

A great advantage of summertime living in New York in the forties was going to Lewisohn Stadium at the uptown branch of City College, and attending the outdoor concerts. And there was no concert quite like the ones Paul Robeson gave there. Every seat was filled.

Minnie Guggenheimer, a wealthy philanthropist who provided the money for the stadium concerts, introduced Paul. (She called him Paul and we all called him Paul, as if we were personal friends. He was a man of the people and we-concert-goers were his people.) Minnie Guggenheimer was a tiny woman, about seventy years old. She spoke in a high-pitched, a bit breathless voice, pronouncing her words more like the British do than typical New Yorkers. But there was no limit to her enthusiasm for the giant who stood next to her on the platform. And the audience went wild. There was Paul, singing under the stars in his rich baritone, loaded with feeling for the subjects about which he sang. They were all about peace, about brotherhood, about justice. He loved to sing in Spanish, (Viva La Quince Brigada), in Chinese (Chee Lai), in Russian (Polyushko Polye), in Yiddish (Kolybel'naia). His enunciation in these languages and his accent were flawless, his passion unbounded. The only bad part was that it had to end. The audience tried not to let him go. With thunderous applause at the end of each encore, he did another and another until finally he knew he had to leave. And then the foot stomping started and often that would lead to still another encore and maybe even another. And when we left, there was a sadness, not just because the concert was over, but also because we knew how embattled he was and how the days of hope for a better world had come to an end. The cold war had begun.

For young leftists like me, Paul Robeson in the early forties was our "All American Hero" as well as a designated All American football star. For us, he was much more than an athlete. He had been a brilliant student, an amazing actor, an opera singer, and most of all a black man who understood how racism permeated America; and he fought to combat it. For that reason he chose to live in Europe where racism would not cripple his life, making his home in England first, and then in the Soviet Union in the thirties. My first introduction to Paul Robeson was hearing him sing the *Ballad for Americans*, buying the record and listening to it so many times that I knew all the words. "In Seventy-six the sky was red, and thunder rumbled overhead, and bad King George was asleep in his bed, and on that stormy morn, old Uncle Sam was born...Some birthday!"

"Ballad for Americans"
http://www.youtube.com/watch?v=rnXyGr668wg&list=RDn8Kxq9uFDes

I attended as many of his performances as I could, at concerts for progressive causes, and also at concerts like those at Lewisohn Stadium. In 1945, I was at the University of Wisconsin when he and Uta Hagen arrived as Othello and Desdemona, performing to a sold out Student Union theater. His popularity at that time was at its peak.

In 1949, Paul Robeson scheduled a concert near Peekskill, New York, but there were so many threats on his life from the local people that the concert was cancelled for a later date when more security could be provided. An increasingly strong anti-Communist frenzy was rumbling in the United States, a harbinger of the spectacular rise of Senator Joseph McCarthy the following year.

The concert was rescheduled to take place in a more secure place in Peekskill, despite the ugly, anti-negro and anti-Semitic protests of the white, mostly working class residents. The new concert was going to be held in a large open field, which was enclosed by hills. The idea was to place an "honor guard" of brawny union men on those hills to be on the watch for, and stave off, any violent attacks. Calls went out to every New Yorker who had supported Henry Wallace in the recent campaign, to show up at the concert and by mere numbers to overcome the opposition.

The Saturday before Labor Day my phone rang: "Esther, it's Jon Naar. Eric is driving up to Peekskill for the concert tomorrow. He has room for us. We're meeting at 116th Street and Broadway at 9AM—in front of Chock Full O'Nuts. Want to go?"

"I'd love to go if I can make it," I said, "I'll call you back."

It was the last weekend of the summer, and my mother, brother, and I were still in Belle Harbor in the Rockaways, where we had rented a beach house. I had to figure out a way of getting to the city on time and a story for my mother who, I knew, would put up a fight before she let me go to the already highly publicized demonstration. I told my mother that some friends from Wisconsin had arrived in the city and I wanted to see them, so I would go early Sunday morning and spend the day with them. "OK," she said, as she busied herself putting cereal boxes and canned goods into a carton. "Have a good time. But be home in time to start packing. We are leaving by noon on Monday." I called Jon back and told him I could make it. I asked my brother Jack to drive me to the train the next morning and to be sure not to tell Mom where I was going. He agreed. "Just be careful," he warned, as the car pulled up to the station.

Eric Josephson, a graduate student in the Sociology Department at Columbia (and the son of Matthew Josephson, who wrote *The Robber Barons: The Great American Capitalists, 1861-1901*) had just bought a vintage car and there was room for five of us: Jon and me, Eric, and an older couple whom Eric knew through his parents. The man's name was Oscar and he came with his wife, an artist. Oscar was an African American who had fought in Spain in the Lincoln Brigade.

The weather was beautiful. It was a sunny but not too hot day in early September. We met Eric in front of the restaurant on Broadway where he had parked and was waiting for us in his newly acquired automobile, a 1932 Chevrolet cabriolet with a tan body and an off-white canvas roof that could be lowered at will. I sat in the front seat next to Eric, and Jon got into the back. "Wow, Eric," Jon said. "Where'd you get such an amazing car?" Eric beamed. "It's a long story. Tell you later." Because it was so sunny we decided to keep the top up and proudly drove along, enjoying the admiring or quizzical looks from the passengers of the cars that drove beside us. We were especially visible to all who cared to see us because the car had only a windshield in the front. There were no side windows. As we got close to our destination, the Peekskill campground, we found ourselves squeezed into a two-lane highway with huge crowds of people on our side of the road, screaming and jeering and cursing us as we drove in a single line at a speed of about ten miles an hour, the fastest we could go because of the traffic. The protesters were carrying big signs "Commies! Go Back to Russia!" Their faces were red with anger as they shouted at us. "Nigger lovers!" Fortunately we arrived inside the heavily protected concert site without incident and rolled out our blankets and picnic, waiting for the music to begin. Robeson sang as he had at Lewisohn Stadium: songs of freedom, of workers struggles, of unity of all peoples, of peace and justice, of a world without racial hatred.

"Joe Hill"
www.youtube.com/watch?v=n8Kxq9uFDes

When the concert was over, a voice came through the loudspeaker: "Those of you who came by car rather than by bus, stay in line, close together! Keep your windows shut! And, above all, keep moving." What windows? Eric, Jon and I had a moment of anguish until Oscar told us about a trick he had learned in Spain. We took our picnic blankets and held them taut from the front seat to the back. It was hard on Eric who had to hold his end of the blanket with one hand and drive with the other, but he managed. What we faced as we left the grounds was now a one-lane road with crowds on both sides, and this time they were throwing rocks at each passing car. The cops were doing nothing to stop the riot. The sound of broken glass was everywhere, except in our car, which had no glass but the windshield. We felt the rocks hitting the blankets and hoped that they were ricocheting back into the crowd. This part of the drive lasted for what felt like an hour of driving at walking speed. When we finally reached the highway and could drop our blankets, I found it hard to believe what we had just experienced. It was like a scene out of a Fascist country: the sight of broken glass all over the roads, the distant sirens of ambulances, the faces of those screaming people and the passivity of the cops. We knew that rocks had hit all the cars ahead of us. "So now we know," said Eric, "that it can happen here."

Pete Seeger on The Peekskill Riots
http://www.youtube.com/watch?v=wuO7XpFelNw

*The story of Paul Robeson after that is a sad one. In the fifties the U.S. Government confiscated his passport and he no longer was permitted to travel to England, to the Soviet Union, to Africa, all places where he had been greeted with adoration and his celebrity acknowledged. For eight years, 1950-1958, he was confined to the United States. The government pressured impresarios not to book his concerts and even black churches were asked to avoid him. He was harassed and bullied by the press and the government who wished they could silence him once and for all. His "crime" had been his belief that racism was tied to capitalism. He had decided to use every means at his disposal to talk and to sing in opposition to the Cold War and the direction in which the American government was heading. The decline of his influence was overwhelming and he gradually succumbed into a deep depression, became demented, and died of a stroke in 1976.*

# ALL MIXED UP

As a graduate student at Columbia University in the early 50s, working for a PhD in the Department of Public Law and Government with one of the world's greatest social scientists, Franz Neumann, my deepest wish was to get married. I wanted to be married, to have children, to live near my relatives and friends and have a career, in that order. Columbia was a great place for me. I lived at home and was thus near my Dad in his last year of life. I would go to class at Columbia in the mornings, and three days a week in the late afternoons, I went down to City College on 23rd Street, where I had a job teaching the introductory course in the Government Department. At Columbia, I took the required courses, had lots of interesting friends, long lunches, long mid-afternoon breaks, and even a small office of my own in the library stacks, once I started on the dissertation phase of my degree.

In 1950 I was dating Gilbert, a tall freckle-faced dentist, who lived with his parents in the Bronx, and had an office in Manhattan. What I liked about him most was that he read *PM,* the left-leaning daily newspaper that took no advertising. We *PM* readers were practically a cult, sharing a pro-labor and "one-world" view in a period when the cold war had begun. Other than that, I searched for a reason to admire him and came up with a flimsy: "I like you because you know what you are good at. You are not a rejected doctor, you like being a dentist." I knew deep down that I did not want to marry him, so I applied for a Fulbright in London, mostly to get away from him. When he took me to meet his parents with whom he lived in a modest four-room apartment in the west Bronx, not far from my own home, his mother, a short, square-faced woman said to me. "Gilbert's father and I are happy that he finally wants to settle down, and with a smart girl like you from the Concourse. But," and she looked at me quizzically, "why then are you applying to go to England for a year? Why don't you stay at Columbia, and plan your wedding, and not be so far away from my son?" It was a good question. My answer could have been. "Because I don't want to be trapped in the Bronx with Gilbert and with you." But I said nothing more than, "I am just applying. It's a long shot. We'll see what happens."

I had my doubts about a life with Gilbert, whose interests were narrowly focused on enlarging his private dental practice, not much more than that.

Fulbright application photo

With Professor Neumann's help in defining a project and a strong recommendation from him, I wrote the Fulbright application and I attached a picture of myself, hoping to win their hearts by looking serious as well as light-hearted, and sent off the document. If I were awarded the Fulbright, I would be working with the great Professor Harold Laski, who had also been Neumann's mentor at the London School of Economics. I would be starting in the fall of 1950. I would have to find a place to live in London, and with Laski's blessing, work on my project: "The influence of the Fabians on British Politics and Political Thought." Beatrice and Sydney Webb, the leaders of the great English socialist movement, the Fabians, were still alive, and living in London. The plan was to interview them as part of my dissertation. On a cold day, near the end of March, I was on the way to teach my class at City College, turning the pages of *PM* on the D train, when I read "Harold Laski Dies in a London Hospital." His death was sudden, from influenza, and hard to believe. It suddenly occurred to me that I might not want to go to England after all. Now that Laski was dead, who would be my sponsor? On June 21st I stopped to get the mail in our apartment house lobby. There it was, a letter from the U.S. Department of State. I tore open the envelope and read: "My dear Miss Edelman, The Department is pleased to award you a United States Government grant… authorized under…the Fulbright Act." I was thrilled. I could hardly wait for my Mom and Jack to come home from work. "Look, look," I showed them the letter before they even got inside the door. My mother hugged me and my brother asked, "How much are they giving you?" A few days later, a subsequent letter detailed the terms of the award: £ 400 for the academic year, which was half of that awarded to those in my cohort. The reason for that was that I had mentioned that I had $5000 in my bank account, a legacy from my father, who had died a few years before. I wondered whether they gave me the fellowship because I cost them so little. But I accepted the award and the terms.

In the following weeks, the London School of Economics wrote to assign me a new sponsor, a man I had never heard of, and housing with an elderly widow whom I would help with chores. Did I want to do that? Much of the thrill was gone. I was still having doubts about the year in London and Neumann had already gone to Switzerland for the summer. I could not decide whether to go or not. I talked about it with my friend Billy Asch, as we drank coffee in the basement café at John Jay Hall. "Esther," he said, banging his cup as he hastily put it down on the saucer, "You are hopelessly mixed up. You need a good psychotherapist. I've always thought you needed that kind of help, but now I'm sure." A few days later, I had an appointment to see Dr. Anthony Totero, a short, plump, balding man, in his sixties, at his office on 5th Avenue and 67th Street. My cousin Lou knew him and recommended him. Dr. Totero and I sat on opposite sides of his desk and I talked about my dilemma. "Yes," he said, "I think you would be making a wise decision to stay here and sort out your life, instead of running off to England. Let's start next week."

I made an appointment with the director of the Fulbright program in New York, a man in his fifties, dressed in a Brooks Brothers style navy blue blazer, who led me into his office as he was barking orders to his secretary.

"What can I do for you?" he asked, as he stacked papers on his desk into neat little piles. I told him that I was there to give up my Fulbright. He stopped stacking and stared at me. I told him about my visit with the psychiatrist and my decision to remain in the United States to sort things out. Slamming his pencil onto his desk, "I am truly sorry to hear that," he said. "I think that relying on a psychiatrist to help make one's decisions is popular these days, but dangerous. It ruins people's creativity. Our society will be stuck with a bunch of namby-pambys, instead of leaders who are willing to take risks." I looked at him, dumbfounded at his lack of sympathy. And then he added: "I wish you had come sooner so that we could have given the fellowship to someone who really wanted it."

I decided that I hated this guy.

Instead of going to England, I said goodbye to Gilbert and spent the following two years sorting things out with the help of Dr. Totero. My mom and brother and I moved to Manhattan to a great apartment that was near everything I wanted to be near. I found a new topic for my dissertation, one that I started working on in the Special Collections at the Columbia library.

# DESTINY?

Childhood memory: It was a hot July day in the summer of 1937, and we campers of Bunk 10 had just returned from lunch to stretch out on our cots for an hour of reading, napping, or talking softly to each other. Sonia was at one end of the row of cots and I at the other. In between were Jeannie, Gerry, and Rita. We were all eleven-year-olds, good friends, who had returned to Blue Ridge year after year. Sonia was the newest to the group. She was a short, wiry, redhead with a face full of freckles. The fact that her Dad owned Sally Togs a popular children's dress company, and that the family was loaded with money, did not make her snobby. She was, in fact, a comic figure, and she loved that role. She never sat still and was always up to some act of clowning, like opening a fixed-cap Coke bottle with her teeth, a feat for which she was famous throughout the camp.

At lunch we had started to talk about our favorite topic, boys, and when we got back to the bunk the conversation continued. We were exploring the idea of how and when we were going to meet our future husbands. Sonia came up with the idea that when we were born God paired each baby girl with a boy who was going to become her husband. As she said this she was lying on her back on her cot, and tossing a ball into the air. All of a sudden she stopped throwing, sat up straight and said: "But what if my boy dies before he meets me?" Rita and Gerry weren't listening any more; Jeannie was reading a book. "Oh come on Sonia," I shouted from the other end of the room, "Do you think God has nothing better to do than matching up every baby in the whole world?" "Would you please stop shouting," said Jeannie, "I'm trying to read." "Sorry, Jeannie," I replied. "But Sonia is being ridiculous. I'd like to believe her but it's impossible." And as I reached for my postcards to write my daily note to my parents, I wondered how I would recognize the boy that was just right for me.

Ten years later I was in graduate school at Columbia. The war was over. Young veterans were taking advantage of the GI Bill to complete or enlarge their educations. It was the perfect place to find a husband while preparing for a career. I knew I wanted both. I wanted to be a married career woman and also a mother. There were loads of eligible men around in 1947; many were already married, but many more were still single. According to the sociologists, the ideal places for mates to meet were schools, churches, community groups, or summer-camps. I was heading for a PhD but I knew that I would put my career on hold to become a wife and a mother, once the right guy came into view.

As I turned 22, 23, 24, I was still in graduate school but with no husband in sight. My best friends at Columbia were married men, women, or single men who were friends but not potential lovers. I was living at home in the Bronx with my mother and brother, going out on a lot of dates, but being very selective about who was a candidate for marriage. My ideal person had to be as politically engaged as I was, had to be well educated, had to be tall and handsome, and had to have a good way to earn a living.

As I was approaching 25, my brother Jack and my mom were getting tired of the long subway ride to the fur district where they both worked in my father's business, and I welcomed the possibility of living nearer to Columbia. Was there any reason for us to remain in the Bronx? As I thought more about it, I realized that such a move would be exciting. Jack and Mom agreed. I began to read the classified real estate ads in the *Times* for a two-bedroom rental in Manhattan and one day found two apartments that looked interesting and were affordable. Knowing that you had to get there as early as possible, I raced out of the house and showed up in the lobby of a red brick, Georgian style, small apartment building on 88th Street between 5th and Madison Avenues.

"I am here in response to the ad for a rental in this building," I announced to the doorman.

"Ah, yes," he replied. "You are the first to arrive. Please take a seat. The agent will be here in a few minutes."

Soon a well-dressed woman showed up, carrying a briefcase and a huge set of keys. We took the elevator to the fourth floor where she showed me a two-bedroom apartment that also had a maid's room. What a bonus that would be; each of us could have a room for ourselves. The place was perfect. I was dazzled by the location. Imagine living that close to Fifth Avenue and to all the museums, and great bus routes to Columbia and all over the city. I told the agent that I was very interested; that my family members would be available to come right away to confirm my enthusiasm.

"Hold on," she said. You must fill out an application. We need bank statements and two references."

"Great," I replied. She had application forms in her case and I gave her the name of our bank and the names and addresses of two fur coat manufacturers who were also close friends. Things were looking good. I took a subway down to the other listing, which turned out to be in an Art Deco building on Second Avenue between 22nd St and 23rd St. This too was a beauty, but lacking the third bedroom and the fancy address. Once again I was one of the first lookers. I filled out an application—this time in a rental office that was right in the building. I told Jack and my mom about the two places and they too were excited by my descriptions. "The one on 88th would be better," I reasoned. "It's got three bedrooms." "I'm not so sure, Esther," my mother replied. "The one downtown is closer to the office."

As it turned out, our decision had been already made for us. That evening I got a call from the real estate agent on the Upper East Side. "Don't you have any references that are not Jews?" she asked. I was astonished and I quickly added the name of our banker, Mr. Maher. "Come on, Esther," my brother said, when I told him what the phone call was about. "She's telling you that we did not get the apartment."

Two months later we moved into to the Art Deco building where I shared a room with my mom. It turned out to be a great apartment and a great location for all three of us. It was the move, plus Murray, that opened up a new world for me.

I met Murray when I was teaching at Mt. Holyoke College and he at the University of Massachusetts in Amherst. My cousin Teddy, who had known Murray well when she was a student at Sarah Lawrence, had given him my South Hadley phone number. We finally got together a few months before we both returned to Columbia to work on our PhDs in the Public

Law and Government Department. Murray had grown up in Brookline, Massachusetts, had been an undergraduate at Harvard, and was a great tennis player. He was top-heavy, tall and rotund, with a big body, skinny legs, and a small balding head. Armed with his racket, a blue Chevy sedan, and the names of friends of his family, mostly the rich and beautiful young women at Sarah Lawrence College, he conquered New York in no time. He invited me to meet his New York friends, people whom I do not think I would have met otherwise. There was no romantic involvement between Murray and me; he was more like a brother. He was happy to treat me as his companion with no strings attached. It was a perfect arrangement. Through Murray, I met Leo Huberman and Paul Sweezey, who were about to launch the Marxist magazine, *Monthly Review*. Leo and Paul introduced me to still others such as Yip and Eddi Harburg. Yip was the brilliant lyricist who wrote the songs for *The Wizard of Oz, Finian's Rainbow, Bloomer Girl,* and probably his best-known single, "Brother Can you Spare a Dime?" Eddi, was his extroverted wife who loved entertaining young people and who threw parties in their large Central Park West apartment. They had a huge living room facing the park on a high floor in a building right on the corner of 86th Street. The dominant piece of furniture in the room was the grand Steinway piano.

"The Eagle and Me" from *Bloomer Girl*

www.youtube.com/watch?v=i0Zad8aC4Bg

On a typical evening, a young visitor would be playing a song from *Finian's* or *Bloomer Girl* and a smiling Yip would be singing the lyrics in his scratchy voice. "If I'm not near the girl I love, I love the girl I'm near." At these gatherings, Eddi spent time with each of us, and knew our names and our histories. She prided herself as a matchmaker and she gave my name to Jack, an ENT surgeon, who was seeking a wife or mistress with leftish politics and good looks. (Unbeknownst to me, Eddi also knew Bud Rowland, whom she matched with a young jazz singer, Anita Ellis, who was just starting her career, and who was too busy to return his phone calls.)

Jack invited me out for dinner one night at the beginning of June 1952 and spent most of the evening telling me how great he was. "I'm a surgeon," he said, "but at heart I am really a classical musician. I practice the piano every day even if I don't get home until midnight. I love art too," he added, drawing some lines with his butter knife across his empty bread plate. "I spent last summer in Juan les Pins and met Picasso. I met him on the beach and we talked—in his bad English and my bad French. And you know what? He invited me to his studio. We took a picture together." Jack chuckled. "And he made me sit down because I am so much taller than he that he looked like a dwarf." Jack removed a picture from his wallet to show me a smiling seated Jack and a standing, serious Picasso.

At the end of the meal, as he waved to the waitress for the check, Jack invited me to a big party the following week. It was a fund-raiser for his organization, the Physician's Forum, a group of politically progressive doctors who supported a single-payer system of national health-care. Even though I was not enthusiastic about Jack, I agreed to go. A party of doctors who believed in universal health care had definite appeal. When the night of June 6th arrived, I wore my new Claire McCardell dress, a navy and white polka-dot silk, with a band collar, a plunging neckline, and a sweeping long skirt. It was a beautiful dress, perfect for the occasion.

The party was held in the home of Dr. Buddy Meyers, a psychiatrist who lived in a posh brownstone between Park and Lexington Avenues, in the East Sixties in Manhattan. As we entered, Jack said, "Look, Esther, I'm an officer in the Forum; I've got some business to work out with the others. So make yourself at home and I'll be back in about an hour." And with that declaration he took off down a long hallway turning his head back toward me as he said, "I'll see you later." There I was, at the bottom of a grand staircase, feeling abandoned, looking around for someone to talk to, and reaffirming my earlier impression of Jack as an inconsiderate egotist. At that moment a young couple was descending the stairs. She was wearing a smashing yellow linen suit, sporting a deep tan that enhanced the radiance of her blond hair. The guy was tall, with dark hair and horn-rimmed glasses, wearing a tan twill suit, a button down white shirt and a bow tie. I stared at them, as one does at beautiful people, and staring hard, I realized that I had met the girl before, at the home of the Harburgs. As she reached the bottom step, I said, "Oh Shirley, you look so great, I didn't recognize you." Looking at me quizzically, she replied instantly and smoothly: "Oh, have we met before?"

The handsome man, seeing the embarrassed expression on my face, broke into a laugh, "Come on girls, I'll buy you each a drink while you sort it out." We walked to the cash bar, and as he paid for and then handed me my glass of wine, he introduced himself as Bud Rowland and the girl was indeed Shirley. I was really impressed that he offered to treat me, a total stranger, but gladly accepted his gracious invitation while making small talk with Shirley. With drinks in hand, we three moved away from the bar and began to circulate in the crowd that had now become sizable. Suddenly one of my good friends popped into view. It was Aleine who was there with her husband, Abe. She knew Shirley well and she also seemed to know Bud and greeted them both warmly. A few minutes later she pulled me aside and said: "Esther, do you remember me telling you that I had met I the perfect guy for you?" she said, pointing to Bud. "Well there he is."

# THE "PERFECT MATCH"

The evening was getting better all the time. So this guy was that "perfect match" Aleine had talked about. So far he did look pretty perfect, especially if he and Shirley were not a fixed couple. Aleine would have known if they were, and, if so, she would not be matching me with Bud. To top it off, Bud was a doctor, (a Jewish girl's dream), and a progressive doctor (an Esther Edelman's dream), who believed in National Health Insurance.

'Esther, I'm back." It was Jack. He also knew Bud and Shirley and said hello. He knew Abe and Aleine and they chatted for a moment. And then he turned to me:

"It's getting late," he said to me. "Why don't we go back to my apartment where we can relax and I'll play the piano for you?"

"Sounds like a great idea," said Bud. "C'mon Shirley, let's all go to Jack's place." And that is what the four of us did.

I spent the weekend with friends at Shelter Island and returned on Sunday. As I entered the door of our apartment, my mother greeted me, with a hug and a huge smile. She couldn't get the words out fast enough.

Mama in the 1950s

"Oh Ketzie," she said, " a fellow named Bud called you. We talked on the phone for a long time and he told me all about himself. Finally you found a real mensch. He thinks you are beautiful and smart and wonderful and that I must be too, since I'm your mother. He's going to call again tomorrow evening."

And sure enough, the next night the phone rang and I rushed to answer.

" I'm Bud Rowland. Remember we met at the Forum party?

"Yes, I remember and I am so glad to hear from you. But how did you get my number?"

"I called Columbia Department of Public Law and Government. I spoke to Miss Black and she gave me your telephone number right away. I told her I was a resident at the medical center and I had met you at a party. Are you free to have dinner with me next Sunday evening?"

"I'd love to. What time?"

"Oh around six, I guess. I have a date with my Dad for Father's Day. We're going to a Dodgers game in the afternoon and I'll call you as soon as it's over."

Sunday came and as the hours passed I was feeling abandoned, no call, perhaps no date. And then at 6:30 the phone rang. "The game turned out to be a double- header. I'm so sorry. I'll pick you up at 8, if that's still OK." At 8 o'clock he came and took me in his Plymouth to Luchow's, a German restaurant on 14th Street, not far from where I lived. I loved everything about him: his beige Haspel cotton suit, his button-down blue shirt, his bow tie. His eyes were deep brown and you could see them behind long, very straight lashes. I only hated the way he drove. If there were a red light at the end of a street we entered, he put the car in second gear, slowed down to a snail's pace, and thus did not have to come to a full stop when he got to the corner and the light had changed to green. The fact that all the cars behind him also had to creep along did not seem to bother him.

At dinner he told me about his neurology residency at Columbia. When I asked him where he went to college and to medical school his reply was, "New Haven."

"Do you mean Yale?" I asked.

"Yes," he replied. But it was clear (then and now) that instead of boasting about his privileged education, even mentioning it made him uncomfortable. I loved him right away.

The next day he told his Mom and Dad that he had met the girl he was going to marry. They invited us to dinner a week or so later. Bud picked me up in his car and we drove to Eastern Parkway, to the spacious apartment the family had lived in for the past twenty years. It was furnished in traditional taste but everything looked perfectly matched and in great condition. Bud's father sold fancy upholstery to professional decorators.

His mother, Cele, a fairly large woman with a face like the then popular movie star, Myrna Loy, honey colored hair, and the same brown eyes as her son, greeted us at the door. "Well, hello," she said in a low husky voice. And his dad, chimed in an even lower and huskier voice, "Welcome to Brooklyn." She wore a greenish-blue silk dress, cut low and fitted tight. He wore a bright red silk tie, a starched white shirt with gold cuff links.

Cele put her arm around me to usher me into their living room. She made me feel welcome. They offered us cigarettes and whiskey before we sat down to dinner and I couldn't help comparing them to my own parents. Bud had described his mom to me in the car on the way to their house. She was ten years younger than my mom, she bleached her hair; she smoked heavily; she loved to cook, to dance, to vacation in Florida, to play cards, and to spend a lot of time with her friends, women of her age who also ran households in Brooklyn. She was also the youngest of the children in her family, but she took care of her siblings as if she were the eldest. That bit of information helped me get to appreciate her. Henry was American born, unlike my father, but they were both businessmen who liked to play cards and to smoke. I think my dad would have liked Henry had they ever had a chance to meet, but I was not sure that Cele and my mom would have much in common.

Bud and I saw each other as often as his hospital residency schedule allowed, once or twice a week. Sometimes we just had dinner by ourselves. Once we went to Atlantic Beach where Bud's parents had a cabana and we swam and met their friends. Once we dined with my cousins Arthur and Teddy when Arthur told Bud, "I think I know you. I've seen you before." And as he stared at Buddy, he suddenly smiled in recognition. "I got it!" he said. "I saw you in my shaving mirror this morning."

One evening in early July, we were driving past the *SS United States*, a newly built, huge American ocean liner, which was docked in a pier along the West Side Highway. Many-decked and freshly painted in white and red, I gaped and said, "Wouldn't it be fun to take a trip to Europe on that ship?" "What a great idea!" he replied. And from that moment on we started to plan our wedding. "How about on my birthday, August 3rd?" he suggested. We mentioned it to his parents and his dad said: "Gimme a chance to breathe. Esther hasn't even met my sister Rose." So we postponed the wedding to August 31st, the Sunday of Labor Day weekend. Union Temple, a reform congregation where Bud's family attended services, had just completed renovating its catering facilities and we were able to reserve the space on short notice. We had nearly 300 lunch guests that included our close friends, our families, almost all of Cele's friends and all the Kahns, a large family of furriers who were my parents' closest friends.

Cele and Henry at Esther and Bud's Wedding

Ours had been a romance that took less than three months from the moment we met until the wedding day. I fell in love with Bud on our first date; it was one of those pitter-pattering of the heart moments. The more we saw each other and the more I learned about him, the more convinced I was that this was a perfect match.

And I believed it even more when one day, after we were married for about ten years, Bud's mother who was cleaning out her closets, brought us some old pictures. One of them was a group picture of the junior campers at Camp Equinunk, the brother camp to Camp Blue Ridge. In the front row of the group portrait of the junior boys sat Bud, age 12, and in the back row was my brother Jack age 14. And I, although not in the picture, was just a stone's throw away, perhaps lying on my cot and talking about how God matches up couples.

August 31, 1952

We had a week to spend on a honeymoon and took Cele's advice to go to Vermont rather than New Hampshire because New Hampshire, she said, was known for its high pollen count in September. Bud had hay fever. We arrived at the Lodge at Smuggler's Notch, a charming country inn, only to discover a huge bush of Golden Rod blossoming in front of the main entrance. We spent our days eating and sleeping and walking the mountain trails, where Bud took pictures between sneezes.

After a week of good food, good sex, and getting to know each other, we returned to New York to settle into our apartment in Riverdale, a nice section of the Bronx that was a short commute for both of us by car, but a long commute by subway. It had not been our first choice. We had wanted something in Manhattan, in Washington Heights near the hospital. And we actually had found a bright, spacious apartment on Riverside Drive, walking distance to Bud's work and a short subway ride for me to Columbia, where I was writing my dissertation. When the apartment house manager interviewed us, he told us that he had another applicant whose financial credentials were less risky than ours. Bud had a fellowship in neurology that paid less than $3000 a year and the other applicant was a professor of sociology at Columbia with a steady income that was twice as much as ours. "So why don't you give him the apartment?" Bud asked.

"Because he is a Negro."

"So?" asked Bud

"If we let him in, others would move out."

"If you don't let him in, don't you think that some other others would move out?"

"Not likely," said the astonished manager and the interview was over and we never heard from him again.

So we settled for Riverdale. We signed a year's lease but made certain that there was a clause that allowed us to leave for military service, something that was looming in the background.

Stowe, Vermont 1952

# CONDITIONS OTHER THAN HONORABLE

Just after Bud and I were married, his dad sent us to comb the sales-rooms in search of furniture for our one bedroom apartment in Riverdale. We spent a Saturday at the high-end Baker showroom, looking at dressers and sofas and chairs, not knowing where to start until Bud spotted a lithograph of Picasso's *White Pigeon* on the wall.

Pablo Picasso: White Pigeon on Black Background (1947)

*The Pigeon* was part of a series of Picasso lithographs that culminated in his portrayal of *The Dove* that soon was to become the symbol of the World Peace Congress in Stockholm Sweden. (Pigeons and doves are from the same bird family, with small differences.) The cold war was getting hotter and the world was divided into the hawks and the doves. Two nuclear powers, the United States and the Soviet Union, were aiming their atomic bombs at each other and the official policy of the United States government was to depict the supporters of peace, and particularly the Stockholm Peace Petition, as disloyal persons, the equivalent of terrorists, who sided with the Soviet Union.

"Wouldn't that be a great wedding present for us to give each other?" Bud asked. "Yes, yes, yes," I agreed. It was clear that that was what we both wanted, more than anything else, and Bud ran to the salesperson to inquire about buying it. "No," was the response; "we just use the pictures as a backdrop for the furniture. It's not for sale." I would have left it there. But for Bud that was just the beginning of the conversation, not the end. Bud talks to everyone. At highway tollbooths every thirty miles or so, he would talk to the toll booth operators, asking each how far to the next toll, and how far to our destination. I was embarrassed by what I considered his unnecessary questions, but he seemed to think that making conversation was not only a duty on his part, but a blessing for the bored guy at the other end. So it was no surprise to me when he heard the picture was not for sale that he asked the furniture store clerk to please find out where they bought it. "Wait here and I'll ask." And sure enough the guy came back with the name and address of a gallery on 57th St., just a few blocks away. "Let's go," said Bud.

The gallery owner produced a folder of Picasso prints and there it was, the white pigeon on a black background, dated February 4th 1947, and numbered 31 of a series of 50, signed by Picasso and for sale for $125. We couldn't believe our luck. It was much cheaper than any of the furniture pieces we looked at and we both wanted it so badly. As soon as it came back from the framer, we hung it on the empty wall of our nearly empty living room, and there it stayed for exactly five months, much admired by our friends. When Bud's parents came from their perfectly decorated apartment, which was loaded with antique furnishings, but lacking in art, to see what we had chosen, his father, circling the room as if he were looking for something that was hidden, said: "Nice picture, but where's the couch?"

One reason we had not paid too much attention to our furnishings was the uncertainty about where we would be living in the early years of our marriage. Not long after we bought *The Pigeon*, Bud received his call to duty. He owed the government military service as a doctor. He was required to enlist as an officer in the medical branch of the military, and to sign a loyalty oath that was mandatory for would-be officers.

Were he to join the Army or return to the Navy, the oath, (a new one) was a multi-page sworn statement that the signer had not been affiliated in any way with a huge list of organizations that were considered subversive. As a medical student at Yale, Bud had been a member of, and later he was elected national president of The Association of Interns and Medical Students (AIMS). The House Un-American Activities Committee had cited AIMS as suspect, either communist or a communist front. Furthermore, a few months before Bud received his notice, a medical school classmate and AIMS member, Charles Nugent, had been called to the Army under the provisions of the doctor draft. He had refused to sign the oath and was drafted into the regular army as a private. (*The New York Daily News* published a picture of Dr. Nugent shoveling coal.) Things did not look good for Bud who knew that he would not sign the new version of the oath, which was not only a potential entrapment, but also a violation of the First Amendment.

But then along came the possibility of working at the National Institutes of Health (NIH) as a member of the United States Public Health Service. This not only would fulfill the duty obligation, legitimately as a physician, but the oath was the old one, one that merely asked that the person swear that he or she did not believe in overthrowing the U.S. government. Bud's boss at Columbia, Dr. Houston Merritt, had been asked to recommend neurologists to staff the new Clinical Center at NIH and Dr. Merritt recommended Bud. Bud had doubts about using the NIH route because he wanted to show support for people like Charlie, who had not had that option. To top it off, we had gone to see Arthur Miller's *The Crucible*, a play about witch-hunts in 17th century Salem, Massachusetts, which Miller portrayed as a metaphor of the McCarthy period in the United States. The day after we saw the show, Bud had to make his decision. He recognized that working for the Public Health Service was indeed the perfect next step in his career and it was useful government service that would fulfill his obligation. "But was it a cop-out?" he asked himself and me. I did not think it was, and I argued that it looked like a perfect solution to the dilemma he faced, but I knew that he had to make his own decision.

NIH in 1953 was a federally funded, medical research establishment, filled with brilliant scientists and physicians, supported by a tremendous budget to cover the important work they were doing. Science had been a high priority during the World War II as well as in the then-existing cold war struggle against the Soviet Union. And there were many physician-scientists who preferred to serve at NIH than in the war in Korea. They were the group that was later fondly called the "yellow berets," a term Bud hated because it implied cowardice rather than a rational choice to do public service and scientific research instead of pure military service.

The papers arrived; the oath was the simple one: "I swear to uphold the Constitution of the United States." Bud signed and was duly accepted. I was relieved.

On March 11, 1953, we moved to Takoma Park, Maryland, a Washington suburb. A few days before, we had packed up the Picasso and lovingly delivered it by hand to my mother's apartment in New York, to keep for us until we returned. When the movers arrived at our Washington area apartment, they unloaded our furniture, our books and records and papers, our dishes and pots and pictures—everything except the Pigeon. Why? Because Washington, D.C. was a scary place in 1953. It was the time of Joe McCarthy, the Senator from Wisconsin who was leading the fast-growing anti-Communist hysteria in the United States. The newspapers had screaming headlines about Red atom spies, about Reds in the State Department. They were filled with articles about people who got into trouble: who lost their jobs, lost their passports, or sometimes went to jail if they refused to cooperate with the inquisitors. Even the ACLU instituted a loyalty oath to its members, weeding out those who had been Communists or who refused to answer the query about Communist affiliations. One story in the *Washington Post* was about a government worker who was under suspicion because an informer had told the investigators that that man owned hundreds of books and classical records. The issue was not even the content of the books, which would have been bad enough, just the quantity. To protect ourselves from the snoopers we were likely to encounter, we left our peace symbol in New York. We even thought of leaving many books and records. A friend of ours, who had a small collection of books published in London by the radical publishers, Lawrence and Wishart, removed them from his shelves once he decided to sell his home and open it to potential buyers in suburban Connecticut. But Bud and I decided to take a chance and bring our books. Besides, no one we knew had extra storage space.

A few months after we arrived in our new flat in Takoma Park, our neighbors, a young couple that lived in the basement apartment in our rented private house, knocked on our door. "We have something important to tell you," the young woman said. "Come in." I opened the door wide. They were newly wedded Seventh Day Adventists, who came to Takoma Park from the American heartlands to be near the headquarters of their church. They sat with us in the living room and the husband spoke. "The FBI was just here and asked us questions about Dr. Rowland. I guess they ask about everyone who works for the government. Don't worry; we only had great things to say about you. We told them about the great music you listened to, and how many books you owned, how intelligent you were, and what nice people you were." Bud and I looked at each other. I shook my head in disbelief. He thanked them for coming and thanked them for their compliments.

When they left, we talked about what they had told us. We were not surprised at all that the FBI would be snooping. After all Bud had been hired to work for a government agency and he had been the President of AIMS, an organization on the list of the House Un-American Activities Committee. We rather expected that. But AIMS was an organization that dealt with health-related issues such as one-class care and national health insurance, so we assumed that being associated with it would not be a reason to be ousted from NIH where Bud was hired as a clinical neurologist. Many people we knew were being called upon by the FBI to testify about someone, or were under investigation, or both.

One day I met an old friend who was married to a serviceman in Washington and I invited her and her husband to dinner. In the middle of dinner we discovered that the husband was working for Naval Intelligence.

Once again, Bud and I looked at each other in dismay, practically choking on our food, and hoping that the evening would not be a long one.

Soon, many of our friends were reporting back to us about FBI inquiries about Bud. One after another told us that their reply had been "Bud Rowland is a great person and a great physician and is not a security risk in any way." One day our friend Walter Freygang told us that when the FBI agents approached him they started the conversation with "We want to know what you know about Lewis (also known as) Bud Rowland. Don't tell us what a wonderful guy he is. Don't tell us what a wonderful doctor he is. We've heard all of that, over and over. We want to know about his political views. He had been the president of the Association of Interns and Medical Students." "So what?" Walter queried, "I was also a member of AIMS." And when the agent asked Walter about his political views, he replied, "Somewhere to the right of Senator Robert Taft." (Senator Taft was a notoriously conservative senator from Ohio, and a leader in the Republican Party.) Walter also became the subject of an FBI investigation a short time later.

When we moved to the Washington area, I was already in my seventh month of pregnancy. Our first child, Andy, was born in May 1953. The apartment in Takoma Park, turned out to be a difficult commute for a family with only one car, a newborn baby at home, and hospital duty for Bud every third night. Thus when the opportunity arose to move into a government-owned apartment house in Bethesda, Maryland, right on the grounds of NIH, we happily made the change, not dreaming that this would become an obstacle for us later.

Not long after our move to Bethesda, in March of 1954, I was expecting Bud to come home for lunch as he usually did, but instead he phoned to tell me that he had been called to the security office at the Department of Health, Education and Welfare and the officers wanted him to answer some questions. At that point, Bud had asked if he could call a lawyer and they said no. Then Bud asked if he could call his wife. They seemed surprised and bemused and said yes. So the phone rang and Bud whispered: "I can't talk much, I'm in the security office and they let me make this one phone call. They want me to answer a bunch of questions. I've decided not to talk to them. I wanted you to know this and I want to know whether you agree." My answer was "Remember Einstein." Just that week we had read that Albert Einstein had been asked, by a young schoolteacher who had been called before a committee investigating subversion in the schools, whether it was alright to refuse to cooperate. Einstein replied that the teacher was correct, that the process of cooperating with these people just gave them a sense of legitimacy, when indeed they, the interrogators, were the real subversives. Bud and I were thrilled with Einstein's reply. It was so refreshing to hear someone proudly advocating saying "no" to the Inquisitors. Bud replied, "I knew you would agree. I better go now. We'll talk more when I get home." He hung up and told the security agents that he would not talk to them without counsel and the meeting was over. Two months later, on May 6th Bud received a letter from the Personnel Chief at NIH suspending him from duty by order of the Secretary of the Department of Health, Education, and Welfare. "The suspension is being effected (sic) in the interest of national security." Bud was to continue on the payroll but not report to work until a decision was made in his case.

At this point it was clear that we needed a lawyer. We hurried to New York, to the office of Kunstler and Kinoy, two civil liberties lawyers we knew of but had never met. Arthur Kinoy was a small energetic man whose mind spun as he gesticulated and talked. "We'll fight back," he declared, banging on his overloaded desk. Then he started to pace up and down the space alongside the window. "We'll carry the case to the Supreme Court if necessary and make headlines in every newspaper." Kinoy's optimism and his fighting spirit stunned us. Was it possible that we could win the case? "Think about it and get back to me if you want to go this way," were his parting words as we rose to leave.

On the ride back to Washington we talked about what Kinoy had said. "We'll make headlines in every newspaper," had made Bud uncomfortable. He immediately thought of his parents who loved him deeply, took pride in his accomplishments, but just did not understand his politics. So he suggested that we get a second opinion. "Let's ask I.F. Stone,"

Bud said. "He should know the right kind of lawyer for us and one who lives in Washington." I.F. Stone was a left-leaning journalist, famous for his independent newsletter, *The I.F. Stone Weekly*, and a good friend of our friends, Leo Huberman and Paul Sweezy, the editors of *Monthly Review*. The following morning Bud called Izzy Stone, told him that we had many mutual friends and that we were in trouble and would like to ask his advice. "I have some time tomorrow," he replied. "Come see me " And he gave Bud the directions to his home in Chevy Chase.

When we arrived, Izzy met us in his garden. With his double-thick eyeglasses and a visible hearing aid that reached from his shirt pocket to his ear, he held his notepad in one hand and his pencil in the other. He thought we were going to give him a story. Bud did not want to get into print at that point. "All we want is the name of a lawyer with an office in the District." Izzy suggested his close friend Gerhard Van Arkel, a labor lawyer who had handled civil liberties cases. Although we had never heard of Gerry Van Arkel, we trusted Izzy to recommend someone who shared our perspective. When we got home we called Gerry, made an appointment and went to see him. He was just the opposite of Arthur Kinoy, and of I.F. Stone. Gerry was a Brahmin, soft spoken and reserved, who reacted to Bud's story without visible emotion. He outlined a thorough, but cautious strategy. When the charges were posted, Bud would decide how to answer them. It would all be done step by step. We liked the idea of having a lawyer in Washington, and his judicious approach sat well with Bud, who was not seeking national publicity. Bud hired Van Arkel right away.

On May17, 1954 Bud received a five-page letter from Nelson Rockefeller, then Undersecretary of the Department of Health, Education, and Welfare (HEW), notifying him of the reasons for his suspension. There were seventeen charges, which were considered to be violations of Executive Order 10450, the governing regulation regarding security in the Department. [This order, when first issued in 1950, had not applied to HEW. But in April 1953, two months after Bud's appointment, it was amended to include HEW, where Bud worked.] The charges covered three categories of offenses: 1) misrepresentation of the facts; 2) association with a person who advocates overthrow of the U.S. Government and 3) membership in or sympathetic association with a subversive group.

The charges were:

• That he was a member of AIMS and elected President in 1948 for one year (1949). AIMS as described by the House Un-American Activities Committee was a Communist front organization. It also was affiliated with the International Union of Students (IUS), a pro-Soviet organization. [*According to Bud's testimony, half of his medical school's class and one third of Yale Medical School at that time were members of AIMS. It was an organization that advocated for the welfare of medical students and interns, for the inclusion of minorities in medicine, for one-class patient care, and for national health insurance, which made it anathema to the powerful American Medical Association. During Bud's presidency AIMS disaffiliated from the IUS*]

> • That he had friends and a close relative who were allegedly Communists. [*Once the anti-Communist crusade had begun, Bud made a point of never asking anyone about political affiliations and he would not disavow a friendship or a family relationship because of someone's political affiliation.*]
>
> • That he supported conferences and groups that were subversive like the Civil Rights Congress [*Bud supported them because he considered them to be causes that advanced human liberties and rights.*]
>
> • That he attended a Marxist discussion group in New Haven in 1946, sometimes in the home of an alleged communist. [*True, he attended, was interested in learning something about Marx, and probably suspected, but never cared, about the affiliations of the host or hosts.*]
>
> • That he supported the American Labor Party in New York City and the Progressive Citizens of America and contributed money to a reception for Henry Wallace. [*True, both were legitimate political parties; Wallace was on the ballot as a candidate for President of the United States.*]

• That he and three "other Communists" organized a rally in New Haven in which Henry Wallace spoke and Paul Robeson sang and that Paul Robeson was a known Communist. *[Bud was an usher at the rally.]*

• That Bud subscribed to *In Fact* *[True. In Fact was an independent newsletter written by George Seldes, a muck- raking journalist who had been thrown out of both the Soviet Union and Italy because of his critical remarks about the dictatorships in both countries.]*

• That he subscribed to the *Daily Worker*. *[Not true.]*

• That he did not cooperate with the security people at HEW on the day they brought him in for questioning. *[He had asked for and was denied a lawyer.]*

• That he did not cooperate with the FBI who had wanted to question him about others. *[True.]*

• That he misrepresented his application to the Public Health Service by not listing AIMS as a professional organization to which he belonged. *[Was AIMS a professional or, as Bud thought, a student organization?]*

• That "various people who knew you during your affiliation with [AIMS], stated you were a Communist sympathizer." *[How does one answer such a charge?]*

The document was filled with hearsay. "Proof" that an organization was "subversive" was because it had been designated "subversive" by such spurious sources as the House Un-American Activities Committee. "Proof" that a person was "subversive" was based on testimonies of unnamed informers.

We were petrified. We knew that we were facing an irrational and hostile force. Bud would not be looked upon as a victim of outrageous charges but rather as another of a long list of left-leaning people who should be dismissed from their jobs because they were risks to "national security." Few people were asking, as Bud asked in his deposition, how could someone with only a physician's medical responsibilities, who was doing medical research, and who had no access to classified material, affect national security? The worst was that the press and the liberals and people in general were so scared that they allowed McCarthyism to happen. This was thought control in the guise of national security.

For the next four weeks, Bud and Gerry Van Arkel worked on the answers to the charges. Bud was absolutely clear about what kind of answers he wanted to give. He told the truth about each charge and whether it was correct, or a lie, or totally out of context. He described the controversy within AIMS, in the year that he was President, about whether the organization should retain its membership in the International Union of Students and thus be official supporters of the Stockholm Peace Petition, and noted that it was in that very year that AIMS decided to disaffiliate from the IUS. He denied that he was present at the Budapest Youth Festival in 1947 and reminded his accusers that he had never been abroad, and had never owned, or even applied for, a passport. As President of AIMS his name had been used to support several conferences whose causes were all valid affirmations of human liberty; Bud did not care if some of the sponsors were or were presumed to be Communists. Every charge was answered factually, with great patience and with little rhetoric. However, in the final summation of his statement Bud wrote, "The obligation of good citizens in a democratic society is to eliminate discrimination and to fight for social justice. This is a demonstration of loyalty, not disloyalty to the United States."

The reply was submitted on June 16, 1954 and the response to it was delivered seven weeks later on August 5th. It was signed by Oveta Culp Hobby, the Secretary of HEW, and stated: "Your continued employment in this Service is not consistent with the interests of national security." The discharge was rendered "under conditions other than honorable."

What we thought would be a more drawn out process, involving a hearing and an appeal just ended suddenly. Bud had a week to gather his belongings at the Institute, and, because we lived in a government apartment, we also had to immediately pack up our household and find a new place to live with our one-year-old Andy. Our lawyer promptly asked for an extension until the end of August but we received only an extension of an extra week. August 20 was moving day.

When the letter from HEW had arrived, Bud and I called our parents: "Hi Mom, bad news," said Bud.

"Oh darling, I'm so sorry. Those people are terrible. But don't worry. Dad says that if you want to start a private practice, he'll put up the money. And, actually, he has always thought you would make a better living in practice."

I told my mom and I added, "and they want us out of here in a week." She instantly replied, "You'll stay with me. You and Bud and Andy can have the bedroom and I'll be comfortable on the couch. The apartment is nice and spacious and I would love having you. When Bud gets another job you'll find a permanent place." I told Bud what she said and we accepted gratefully.

Just before we left we received a phone call from a scientist at NIH, a friend of a friend, someone we had never actually met.

"Do you folks need a place to live?' he asked.

"No, we are moving in with my mother in New York," I replied.

"Well, if you change your mind, my wife and I would be happy to put you up. We heard about your situation, and we are so very sorry that this had to happen."

And a few weeks later, Leonard Berg, a fellow neurologist on the clinical staff at NIH sent us a copy of the letter he wrote to Oveta Culp Hobby. Jeopardizing his own career, Leonard decried the decision to fire Bud whom he described as "a loyal American citizen, a great human being and a great neurologist."

Bud's job at NIH was given to Dr. Gunther Haase, a German neurologist who had married a U.S. Army nurse and settled in the United States after the war ended. He later became a friend, and we found him to be a decent person, even though during the Second World War he had served as an Officer in the Luftwaffe, the Nazi Air Force.

We called moving companies to arrange for the transfer to New York. This time we did our own packing. It all happened so quickly; we had to do so much in such a short time that we barely had time to ruminate about the future. There were no farewell parties, just phone calls or brief visits to say "goodbye" to our friends. Most of them, although they knew Bud had been suspended, only vaguely knew the details of our "case." They were stunned by our sudden departure. None of us knew what would happen next.

# HOLDING FAST

Our little family of three arrived back in New York on a hot August day. My mother's apartment on Twenty-Second Street and Second Avenue was a spacious one-bedroom, with high ceilings and enough fans to keep us comfortable. Bud and I slept on the floor in the living room, where my mom slept on the couch. (Little Andy got the bedroom and remained there by himself for the night, which turned out to be a better solution than trying to persuade him to go back to sleep when Bud and I entered the room to go to bed.) I was pregnant with a second child and each morning I ran to the bathroom to throw up because moving from the floor to a standing position was more than my endocrine system could tolerate.

One week after we arrived, the phone rang. It was Charlie Kennedy, one of Bud's colleagues from the house staff in New Haven, who was working as a pediatric neurologist at the University of Pennsylvania.

"Bud, there's a job opening in our department at Penn. I spoke to Joe Stokes, and he wants you to apply."

"Wow," said Bud. "I would love to work at Penn. What's Stokes' number? I'll call him right away. Wouldn't it be great for us to be working together again?"

Bud and I drove to Philadelphia a few weeks later for Bud's interviews with Dr. Stokes, the Chairman of Pediatrics, and with several staff neurologists and neurosurgeons. All went well and Bud was offered a position, dependent on approval by the trustees of the university. Bud was happy about the move to Philadelphia and awaiting the last step in the process. I was so relieved that he would be working again and, from what I saw of Philadelphia, I thought it would be a great place for us to live. A few days later, Dr. Stokes called. "I am afraid I have bad news, Bud. The trustees did not approve the appointment because of your dismissal from NIH. I argued with them but to no avail. I am truly sorry. And ashamed."

The news hit Bud hard. He looked glum. He buried himself in the work he had carved out for himself and spent even more time in the library reading molecular biology and biochemistry papers. He wondered if his academic career was over.

I spent my days taking Andy to the playground at Peter Cooper Village, a group of apartment houses a few blocks from my mother's. My mom went to work every day and Bud had decided to spend his "free time" going to the medical library at Columbia, doing library research and writing medical articles. We had no friends nearby. At 9:00 AM each day, I would push Andy in his stroller down the streets lined with tall buildings, until we reached the gardens and the playground within the complex so that he could swing and slide and play with other kids' toys. Peter Cooper had an enlightened policy about sharing toys. Each child gave up his or her toy as they entered and was then allowed to choose another from the communal pile. Upon leaving, the child got his or her own stuff back. It was a great system! Nevertheless, for me it was a lonely life.

On weekends, we saw my in-laws in Brooklyn, but we had not yet visited my brother Jack and his wife Dot and Jonny, their little boy who was Andy's age. They were awaiting the completion of a new house in New Rochelle and living for the summer in Croton, in Dot's parents' home, while her mother and father were in Europe. We had been to the Croton house the previous summer. It was a small estate: a big house, a private tennis court, a full-size pool, and lots of grass and trees.

One Sunday the phone rang. It was my brother Jack.

"How would you and Bud and Andy and Mama like to come visit us here in Croton this afternoon? Jonny would love to play with Andy. He's been alone all week. You can come for lunch, and then we can have a swim."

"We would love to come," I replied. "We'll just throw some stuff in a bag and jump into the car. Be there by noon. Thanks!"

I was so happy to be able to get out of the city. I told Mama and Bud and Andy about the call. "Hey, everybody. Let's get going!" I grabbed some bathing suits for Bud and me. I loaded the diaper bag and added a change of clothes for Andy. Just before we left the apartment, the phone rang again. My mother answered. It was Jack. She listened and her smile turned into a frown. She covered the mouthpiece and said, "Jack says that Dot has been thinking it over and she is worried that her father will find out that Buddy and you were there. Jack said that if they were in their own house, of course there would be no problem, but Dot's father would be furious with her for inviting you to Croton. He's got government contracts." I grabbed the phone from my mom. "Jackie, we are coming anyway!" I hung up before he could answer. I was angry. How could anyone in our family treat us as if we were criminals?

Just then, Bud walked into the room.

"Guess what? " I said, "Jack just called to tell us that Dot is worried that she will get into trouble with her Dad if we visit them at his place."

Bud said, "You really can't blame her. Her father is still mad at her for marrying Jack. After all, Jack works for the old man. He's liable to get fired."

"Well, we're going anyway and I told him so," I announced, zipping up the bag I had just packed. "If we give in to her fears, we'll end up destroying the family. I'll never want to visit them. Let's just forget what she said and go."

Bud shrugged his shoulders. "It's tricky, but we'll go if you feel that strongly."

On the drive to Croton I wondered to myself how we would be received. But as we got out of the car, Jack greeted us with smiles, reached for our bag and ushered us onto the patio. Dot was setting paper plates on the picnic table. She kissed us hello, and grabbed Andy with one hand and Jonny with the other, leading them to the seesaw and the toys. There was no mention of her father or of the last phone conversation. The children got busy playing and laughing, and Jack, Bud and I took a dip in the pool. We grilled hot dogs and watched the little boys run and tumble on the grass. The day turned out to be fun for all. Not a word was mentioned about our plight or about Dot's concerns.

A month later, Montefiore Hospital in the Bronx, a Columbia affiliate, posted a job for a neurologist at Bud's level. The administration there had already accepted other political refugees who had been wounded by McCarthyism and the people who knew Bud at Columbia and at NIH recommended him enthusiastically. Two important friends had intervened on Bud's behalf: Dr. Merritt, at Columbia, and the world-renowned Chief of Pathology at Montefiore, Dr. Harry Zimmerman, who happened to be a family friend and who had known Bud for many years. The Director and Trustees of the hospital raised no objection. There were many courageous people who disliked what was going on and quietly condemned it in their own acts of defiance. This seemed to be more true in New York, and in science and medicine than in Hollywood, where people like screenwriters Dalton Trumbo, Ring Lardner, Jr., and Albert Maltz were first put in jail and then denied access to making a living in their chosen professions. Luckily, the newly appointed Chairman of Neurology at Montefiore, Dr. Tiffany Lawyer, was happy to hire Bud as an Assistant Professor. Bud was working again but others, who also had been cited as "subversive," were not. And the country was harmed as dissent was stifled at a time of nuclear buildup by two great powers that were poised for war.

By October of 1954, Bud and Andy and I were settled in a garden apartment in Riverdale, an easy drive to Montefiore. When our furniture was delivered from storage, we set up house, fetched *The Pigeon* from a box in my mother's apartment and hung it prominently on the living room wall. Our new home had a big backyard, and there was a playground across the street. All was back to normal.

# THE SUBLEASE

Riverdale in the Fifties was a New York City neighborhood with a suburban feel. It was the strip of the Bronx that ran from the top of Manhattan to the Westchester border and from the Hudson River east to Broadway. There were high-rises, garden apartments and many private homes, all surrounded by trees and grass. A few main streets were lined with shops and food markets where one could park a car and load up.

The rental apartments like ours attracted a varied group of people including some college professors, some young doctors, and some temporary residents who worked in foreign embassies or at the United Nations. Our apartment was in a two-story building that was one of about a dozen look-alikes in a development called Vinmont, which was named after the developer, Mr. Weinberg.

We had the ground floor apartment with two bedrooms and its own garden. It was the perfect size for Bud and me, and Andy and his new brother, Steve, who was born six months after we moved in. Bud had a good job at Montefiore Hospital as a member of the Department of Neurology, a fifteen-minute ride by car from our home. Things had worked out surprisingly well for us after being tossed out of NIH.

We became friends with the two families who lived in the duplex next door, with whom we shared an entryway. Downstairs were the Bernsteins. Alex Bernstein was a Russian exile with a permanent residence in Paris. He was the son of Osip Bernstein, a Russian chess champion and friend of Marc Chagall. In fact, Chagall had given Alex and his wife a wedding present: a painting of a bride and groom afloat, carrying a huge bunch of flowers. It hung in their living room. At the time we knew him, Alex was serving as a simultaneous translator at the UN, one of those people with huge earphones on his head, translating Russian into French as the delegates were speaking. His wife was a dark-haired, slim Parisian, who spoke little English, and who did all of her housework wearing the briefest shorts and a halter-top, with a large silver bracelet encircling her upper left arm. One winter day, wearing that outfit, she knocked at my door, trembling with cold. "Estair, my door, it locked. I must find ze super with ze key." "You must be freezing!" I opened the door for her and then ran to my closet. "Come in, I'll give you my coat. The super is roaming the grounds. I'm sure you'll find him." I pulled out my worn but warm winter coat, which she could have wrapped around herself twice. She successfully completed her mission ten minutes later, handed me back the coat and ran off shouting, "Merci, merci beacoup."

Above the Bernsteins lived an African-American family, the Harrises: Nat, Mary and their son Donald. Nat and Mary both worked for New York City as professional civil servants. Donald, then 14 years old, was a tall, gangly, quiet teenager, who babysat for us from time to time. He attended Fieldston, a private school in Riverdale that was known for its high quality as well as its high tuition. Nat and Mary and Donald spent their summers in Oak Bluffs on Martha's Vineyard. I shall never forget Nat and Mary's description of how they managed those summer trips. Unlike us, who just got into the car and drove until we needed to stop for food or a restroom, they had to plan the trip carefully, to avoid those places that would not serve them a meal, or not allow them to use the toilets. I knew that the country was filled with racists but I had not known that the North was still so much like the South in 1954. The demand for equal rights was still an urgent cause. The Harrisses' stories further inspired us to move from a passive "Isn't it a shame" stance to active participation in the civil rights movement as the demand for justice became a major movement in the United States as the sixties approached.

In our building, the apartment upstairs was occupied by a family of four. Lee, the wife/mother was an outgoing, aggressive woman, who loved to garden but had no garden of her own. Without any invitation from me, she became the self-appointed caretaker of my backyard. She would pop in unexpectedly with some new soil or new plants and with a hoe or rake and a big smile. "I just bought this for us," she would say. "I'll run out to plant it." And then she would stride through our living room to the glass patio door (the only entrance to the garden) and stake her claim to our yard. The next day she would be back to water the new plant. I couldn't bring myself to restrain her, but my neighbor, Alex, had no such compunctions. "Get your hands off my tree!" I heard Alex screaming. I ran out my back door to see Lee with shears in her hand running away from him. "I did not ask you to trim it. Hors d'ici! Get out of here!"

Bud had just passed his Neurology Boards in the fall of 1955, and he and his boss decided it would be a good time for him to learn new lab techniques by taking a six-month sabbatical in London. As soon as Bud was accepted to work at the Medical Research Labs in Hampstead Heath, we started to make our arrangements to go. The last task was to find a tenant for our apartment; we were leaving in less than a month. My father-in law's bank manager, who was arranging a letter of credit for us in England, advised us to charge twice as much as we were paying and demand the entire rent in advance. (Bud and I, however, knew that asking for a large amount of rent in advance would probably ruin our chances.) "Otherwise," the banker said, "how can you protect yourself from strangers walking off with all your possessions?" I laughed to myself. Little did he know that our meager possessions would not be worth stealing. We decided to advertise in the *Riverdale Press*, citing the price of $150, the rent we were paying each month, plus one-month security. We were prepared to settle for even less, feeling desperate at that point, and knowing that if we were unable to get our monthly rent paid in New York, we would be hard pressed to rent another apartment in London.

The ad produced one potential customer, a nicely dressed slim man wearing a camel's hair coat that matched his light brown hair. He appeared at our door and in a deep southern accent said, 'Good Morning, Ma'am, mah name is John Tompkins and ah'm here about the ad. This place may be just what ah'm lookin' for.' He was an engineer, in New York for six months, and his family was back in Georgia. As we walked through the apartment his enthusiasm grew, and when I showed him our washer and dryer, which had not been mentioned in the ad, he was really happy. "How 'bout the school" he said.

"The neighborhood school is just a block away."

'That's good. I hope there are no Negroes in the school."

I froze. "Look here, Mr. Tomkins," I replied. "I'm sure there are a few." My face must have turned bright red as I continued in a firm voice: "And I think that if you are living in New York for a short period of time, you might just want your family to enjoy and to learn from that New York experience. Live like we do, that's the reward of travel."

He looked embarrassed and murmured a soft "I guess you may be right." And we left the laundry room and started back up the stairs. "But at least there are no Negroes livin' in these apartments. Right?" he added.

"Oh" I responded, "It so happens that the family just across the courtyard is Negro, but you don't have to worry that your children will be in school with their son. He goes to the best private school in Riverdale!"

We stood in the hallway, facing each other. After a brief silence he said, "I don't mind that they live there, but I hope you all will understand that we will not be friends with them." And I replied in a loud and firm voice: "That's fine with me as long as you are polite and do not ruin *our* friendship with them. And the rent is $165 a month including the use of the washing machine, one month payable in advance plus one month's security, also payable in advance." Once again there was a brief silence.

"All ri-ight," he said slowly. The deal was cut.

*Our Southern tenants were exceptionally neat and clean and left the place in better shape than ever. They did not befriend the Harrises, but there was never an incident between the two families.*

*Seven years later, after we had moved from Riverdale, we read about a civil rights activist in Americus, Georgia, named Donald Harris. A picture accompanied the article. We recognized Donald, then a college student, who was working, along with several others, for voting rights. Donald and his friends were arrested for "inciting insurrection in the State of Georgia," an act that was defined by state law as treason and punishable by death. Donald remained in jail from August until November 1963, when a judge ruled the insurrection law unconstitutional. Shortly after his release, Bud took our two* *sons to a rally on Donald's behalf, which was held in the Neighborhood House in Riverdale, just across the street from the apartments in which we and the Harrises had lived. It was a great victory rally. Bud introduced himself to Donald and our boys met their old babysitter with hugs and congratulations. We always wondered if our Southern tenants were back in Georgia at that time, reading the headlines, and if they recognized their former neighbor. A few years after his acquittal, Donald Harris married Kate Clark, the daughter of Kenneth Clark, the psychologist who was instrumental in convincing the Supreme Court, in its decision in <u>Brown v. the Board of Education of Topeka, Kansas,</u> that separate education could never be equal education because of the deleterious effect such separation had on black children and on white children. Dr. Clark, who had been my instructor in Psychology 1 at City College in 1944, died at the age of ninety in May 2005, with an obituary in "The New York Times" that began on the front page, a highly significant news item. Bud and I went to the wake and there met Donald and Kate. "What a small world we live in," I said to Bud, as we sat together at the service. "My psych professor became this legendary figure in the civil rights movement. His daughter Kate married Donald, our former neighbor. And our tenant, who did not want to have anything to do with the Harris family, had the opportunity of knowing significant actors in American history, but chose to ignore them because of their race."*

# LONDON, 1956, ARRIVING

When we boarded the Pan Am flight from Idlewild Airport (now JFK), we were escorted to the three bulkhead seats, reserved for families like ours. A bassinet was hanging from the front partition that separated our coach from business class. The flight attendant helped Andy, who was two and a half, into the window seat and then offered to help us place nine-month old Stevie into the basket, without realizing that he was twice its size. So we were resigned to having a baby on one lap or another for the next seven hours. Fortunately, the kids mostly slept through the flight.

It was Bud's first trip to Europe. He was looking forward to a new experience and to finding out for himself why those of us who had been to Europe before were so anxious to go back. I had told him about the summer trip I had taken in 1948 as part of a World Study Tour to examine social change in the immediate post-war period. Our group was mostly college students from the Northeast, but there were three boys from Texas, who were total misfits. "'We want bacon n' eggs!'" I tried to imitate their demanding voices. "They would call this out to the waiter as they were asked for their breakfast order. Can you believe that? It was still the time of rationing. And, even *without* a food shortage, those places wouldn't have served bacon and eggs." I laughed as I recalled, "They were total misfits in our group. The Texas boys were looking for a fun trip to Europe where they could get bargains for their valuable American dollars, and have a good time eating, boozing, and sightseeing."

"So why did they join your group?" Bud asked.

"There was a pileup of people who wanted to go to Europe, but there weren't enough ships. The best choice was a tour. Little did they know that our tour was a serious one--to study the impact of the war on the European social order. It was so embarrassing to be with them."

The February day we arrived in London was crisp and clear. After we gathered our luggage and walked outside to get a cab, we passed a news-stand. The headlines on the tabloids announced that day as the "Coldest

Day of the Century." It was 29F. Wearing winter clothes, we seemed comfortable, so we were mystified to hear that 29 degrees was low enough to make the headlines in England. We hailed one of those roomy London cabs to take us to our hotel, which was located in a residential section, quite far from downtown. As we rode through the streets, I saw that the London I had known in 1948 had been completely rebuilt in the past eight years. There were no more bombed-out buildings. Everything had been cleaned up.

When we arrived at our hotel I took off my coat to get busy tending to the needs of two small children, and no sooner was the coat off, I put it back on. The room was freezing! While Bud was calling the front desk to ask about the heat, I went to the bathroom to run hot water in the sink to warm up the children's bottles. But there was no running hot water. The pipes, which the British placed outside the buildings, were frozen. Only the gas fireplaces, for which one needed shilling coins to activate the system, heated the room. Bud went down to the front desk and asked to exchange pound notes for shillings. "I am terribly sorry, sir, but there is a shortage of shilling coins throughout the country. There are none to be had."

Just when we realized that the temperature in the hotel room required us to remain fully dressed in our coats, we discovered that Andy had lost his gloves. In the meantime, Stevie developed diarrhea, so Bud set out, with Andy on his shoulders, to find a shop for gloves and a pharmacy. Our hotel, the Brent Bridge, was in Golders Green, a section near where we wanted to find an apartment. By the time Bud got to the stores, they were all closed. It was Thursday afternoon; 2:00 PM was closing time for all the shops in that neighborhood.

There was only one dining room in this lovely old hotel, and all the places were set banquet style: three heavy silver forks on the left of the Crown and Darby porcelain dinner plates, three silver knives on the right, three spoons of all sizes at the top; crystal water glasses and wine glasses to the right; snowy white table cloths and napkins. As soon as we sat down Andy started banging the knives against the crystal and Stevie began wailing for his food. The people sitting near us were clearly shocked, staring at us with disapproving looks and murmuring, "Oh my Gawd's" to each other. We ordered our meal but decided to leave before it arrived, arranging to have it delivered to our icy-cold room where we ate all meals for the next two days, dressed in our outer clothes.

The first task was to provide Kaopectate for Stevie and mittens for Andy. The second was to get us out of the hotel as soon as possible by helping us find a place to live. We spent one day looking, deciding, and completing that mission. American friends back home, who had just spent a sabbatical year in England with their two small boys, had told us to avoid rentals with kerosene heaters, which, although popular, had proven to be dangerous fire hazards for small children. We actually found our flat the first hour of the search. It was a newly renovated house that had been partly destroyed in the blitz, and it had central heating, a requirement that we had been advised to insist upon.

The rent was forty guineas a month, which we thought acceptable, assuming that a guinea and a pound were the same. But we later discovered that a guinea was worth $5, not $3 and we were therefore paying more than we were getting for our apartment in New York. However, at least we were finished with the hotel. The next morning, we moved to 16 Canfield Gardens, centrally heated at a fixed 65F. For extra warmth there was a large coal-fed fireplace in the living room, but it turned out to be unusable because a national coal shortage that year restricted coal delivery to the existing customers. The bathroom had an open window, tiny to be sure, but mandated to remain open because of some safety requirement. We dressed in layers in the house and slept under electric blankets that we ordered from home. (The Brits preferred hot-water bottles.) We engaged a "nappy" service for our endless number of diapers (there were no disposables in 1956—even in America), and we hung all the infant clothes on the backs of chairs to dry, after being told at the Laundromat that they did not have dryers because, "Dearie, it is so much better to hang the wash to dry in the sun!" We never knew what sun the Laundromat lady knew about; we didn't see it for another three months.

No matter how much I had resolved to understand and not to complain, I found myself sharing these stories with my American friend Judy Ruben. She and I would snicker at how the Brits, stuck in their ways, insisted on placing their water pipes on the outside of their buildings and how they tore out central heating if they moved into a new home where it had been installed because: "a steady flow of dry heat obviously causes colds." In Bud's lab, they broke for tea at ten in the morning, lunch at one, and no sooner was an experiment underway, they broke for tea again at four in the afternoon. They were so quaint, clinging to old habits and justifying it all as the better way to do things. The British themselves were experts at not adapting to, or appreciating other cultures, especially as colonizers. And now we, the Americans who had escaped the domestic hardships of war, who tore down old buildings in the blink of an eye, who had unlimited access to oil and gas, who never thought about natural resources as finite, were the ones passing judgment.

But Bud and I never failed to praise the socialist benefits of the free National Health Service, (which included our family even though we were just visitors). We were assigned to a local practitioner, Dr. Levi, who saw the children in his "surgery" a few blocks away from where we lived. He turned out to be just the kind of practitioner we wanted: a practical and sensible man who used caution when dispensing medication. He also dispensed sensible advice. When Andy contracted rubella and was miserable, I suggested: "Maybe it was a mistake to have brought the children to London at such an early age." Dr. Levi's immediate response was, "Children are adaptable to everything except being left behind by their parents." There was also a subsidized milk service, delivered in bottles to our door every day, and a subsidized National Theater, where we saw Shakespeare, Shaw and Ibsen, the best plays of our lives, for one £ apiece.

Ron Fox worked with Bud at the Medical Research Council Labs. He lived in the suburbs and had to commute by rail from a station close to our house in Canfield Gardens. So on my nightly mission to pick up Bud in our rented Morris Minor, Ron would almost always hitch a ride with us to the station. As he entered the car I would say "Hello" and he answered with one word "Right." I would then comment on the weather: how rainy it was, or how pleasant it was, or whatever. He would again answer with one word: "Quite." Finally, as we pulled into the station, he made his final comment, "Goodnight!" Five months later, he invited Bud and me to his home for dinner, which we readily accepted. It was a real breakthrough. We had a lovely meal, interrupted only by Mrs. Fox excusing herself to place their six-month old child on the potty. We joined her to keep her company, but also because I couldn't believe that anyone would wake up a baby of that age to toilet train her. Andy, our three-year-old, had just been trained in the past month.

On the other hand, Bud and I were spending more time with, and growing very close to, Judy and Al Ruben, the American friends whom we had known only casually in New York. The Rubens lived in London because Al, a scriptwriter, worked with Hanna Weinstein, the producer of a new series of TV programs about Robin Hood. Weinstein chose London as her site, not because Robin Hood required a British set, but because she was free to hire screenwriters who had been blacklisted in the United States. Al was the script coordinator, receiving stories from Ring Lardner Jr. and others, whose names were not made public so the series could be repeated in the United States. It was a huge success in both countries. The Rubens had been in London for two years by the time we got there and Judy was tuned in to British ways. I called on her for advice about all the little day-to-day things that were proving more difficult than I had expected, such as finding a nanny for the kids so that I could spend time at the British Museum to do research on my dissertation. With two small children, both still in diapers, and no family to help, I was desperate. I had called a Nanny Employment Service. "I would like to hire a nanny for two little boys. One is almost three years old and the other is almost one. We are living in London and will be here for six months."

"I am sorry madam, but, as you must know, there is a terrible shortage of nannies. We only deal with people who have used our service before. There are many English families that are already on our waiting list. And the idea of hiring a nanny for less than a year is out of the question. I am afraid I cannot help you." I hung up feeling more than ever like an outsider.

Then I called Judy. "Don't pay attention to them," she said. "Do as I did. Put an ad in the *Evening Standard*. Say you are an American family looking for an au pair, for six months, the time you'll be spending in London. You know, British families treat au pairs as apprentices and pay them a pound a week and give them bread and butter to eat. So be sure to mention that you are Americans." She was right. As soon as the ad appeared my phone started ringing. Our biggest problem was who to choose from the several eager applicants I interviewed. Within a few days I hired Dominique, a twenty-year-old, dark haired, green eyed Corsican, who spoke English with a French accent. She was stylishly dressed in a tight, short skirt and a long, loose pullover, looking very Parisian. She impressed me right away by her self-assurance and her cheerfulness. I was holding Stevie in my arms when she walked in the door, and as soon as she took off her coat, she asked if she could hold him. "What a wonderful bébé," she exclaimed, "he's so beeg and healthy." And she put her face down next to his, "J't'aime, my leetle boy."

I was liberated to go to the library every afternoon, have lunch with Judy once a week, and do my daily shopping, all without the kids.

# LONDON 1956: FITTING IN

At first, I was so unaccustomed to having a live-in baby sitter that, when Dominique asked each morning if we intended to go out that evening, I almost always said she was free to go, since we rarely had a date. Then I realized that I could reasonably ask her just to take a few nights off, leaving us free the rest of the week to take a walk or a ride or to make our way down to the West End theaters.

Having Dominique live with us also made it easy for us to have guests for dinner. I loved living in London, where people we knew rather casually in the United States, stopped by because they were lonely and had some free time. My friend Colstan Warne, Professor of Economics at Amherst College and the President of Consumers Union, was in London for a conference about a proposed British edition of the magazine. He stopped in to say hello, something he would not have done in New York.

Our neighbor in Riverdale, Alex Bernstein, the Russian-to-French translator at the United Nations, was in town on UN business. He called to say hello and I invited him to dinner the following evening. When the bell rang, Dominique ran to open the door.

"Good evening," she said.

"Is this where the Rowlands live?" Alex asked, a bit surprised to see this green-eyed beauty instead of me.

"Mais oui," she replied, recognizing his French accent. "Je suis Dominique, l'au pair."

"Ooh la lah!" was his response, savoring every syllable.

When he left us to go back to his hotel, he pulled me aside and whispered, "Estair, are you not worried about having your husband and Dominique living in the same house?" Somehow, that concern had never entered my mind.

One day in June, we read in the *Manchester Guardian* that Reverend K.H. Ting, had delivered a sermon at a church called St. Martins in the

Fields. K.H. was one of the people my brother Jack had befriended in China when he was stationed there during the Second World War, and whom I had also known in New York when he arrived for a year in 1947. I called the church.

"I read in today's paper that the Reverend K.H. Ting was in town. I am an old friend. Can you tell me how to reach him?"

"Just a moment please, and I will connect you to the Rector." I repeated my question to the man who came onto the phone next.

"Ah, yes," he said. "Reverend Ting is staying at the Lambeth Palace."

"Oh," said I, "Do you have the number of the Lambeth Palace Hotel?" thinking that it must be a branch of the Royal Palace Hotel in Piccadilly.

"My dear lady," he replied, "The Lambeth Palace is the residence of the Archbishop of Canterbury!"

He gave me that number and I called and K.H. agreed to come to our flat for dinner. Bud and Andy went off to the Palace to pick him up in the Morris Minor, our tiny rented car, a sight that must have amused the guards at the gate who were accustomed to dealing with Rolls Royces and chauffeurs. A week later Bud and I received an invitation to attend a reception at the Chinese Consulate in London. When we arrived at the door, we gave them our name. Thereupon, a fully garbed English Beadle, shouted out for all to hear: "Doctor and Mrs. Llewis Rrrowland." It was our first entry into the fabled world of British high society, all thanks to the Communist government of China.

At about the same time as K.H. appeared in London, so did Bud's favorite boss from his NIH days, Seymour Kety, the Scientific Director of the National Institute of Mental Health and a world class research scientist. Seymour was in London just at the time we had three tickets to the Glyndebourne Festival, tickets we had ordered five months in advance when we thought my mother would be visiting us. Glyndebourne was, and perhaps still is one of England's most peculiar and most popular institutions--a summer opera festival, at that time mostly Mozart, the dress code for which was "Black Tie for Men and Formal Attire for Women." The concerts were held in a small auditorium on the grounds of an estate in Lewes, a village about sixty miles southeast of London. Seymour was free to join us, although he was battling a foot injury that forced him to wear sneakers at a time when sneakers were considered appropriate only on the sports fields. Nevertheless, he and Bud spent the day before the concert renting tuxedos.

The day of the concert, a normal weekday, we three found ourselves dressed in our finery at 2:00 PM in Paddington Station, boarding a commuter train to Lewes where we were to catch the chartered bus to Glyndebourne. Scattered among the usual commuting passengers, there were many others on the train also in formal clothes and they were all carrying huge picnic baskets. We found out that evening that the baskets contained beautifully prepared multi-course dinners, champagne, wine, and all the appropriate china, heavy silver cutlery, crystal glasses, and damask cloths and napkins to go with the feast. (We had chosen to take our dinner in a small café on the grounds, but we soon realized that that was clearly the déclassé way to go.) What a sight it was to walk through the Glyndebourne meadows at the supper-break intermission to see the men in tuxedos and black ties, and the ladies in long gowns and pearls, plopped on the grass, eating smoked Scotch salmon with capers, cold roasted chicken; salads; assortments of cheeses, drinking wine and champagne, as if they were gathered around their own dining room tables. When we returned to London that night, we agreed with Seymour that the juxtaposition of formal and rural, and of reality and make-believe seemed so normal in England. "And," I added, pointing to Seymour's feet, "even though the Brits would probably not agree, wearing sneakers with a tuxedo just fits the bill."

On that trip, Bud and I also discovered that when you are in a foreign country for a few months and you know of people whom you would like to meet, you brazenly call on them. So it was when Bud decided to take a trip to Oxford one day to discuss his work with the neuroscientists there and I decided to call upon the great socialist historian, G.D.H. Cole, whom I had admired for many years. Cole was by then in his eighties. I called for an appointment, which was readily granted and I stopped in to see him in his office filled with books and papers. He was very kind and we had a lively conversation about teaching people who were studying at Oxford, as opposed to teaching those who had to work by day to survive. At one point in the conversation I asked him about a book that had recently been published.

"Have you gotten it yet?"

He looked a bit surprised and replied: "Ma'am, I am at the stage of life when I am trying to get rid of my books, not buying new ones."

I was shocked into the realization that the accumulation of books was not necessarily a lifetime preoccupation. This revelation about mortality had never before occurred to me.

Bud and the boys at the London Zoo, 1956

Most of our sojourns were on weekends when Bud was free from the lab and we wanted to do something as a family. One Sunday we accepted an invitation from a lab friend of Bud's to be his guest at the London Zoo. Our friend had a membership that permitted him to visit the zoo on Sunday mornings before it was open to the public. "Bring the children," he said. "They'll have a grand time playing with the chimps." When we arrived, we were greeted by our friend and a lovely chimpanzee who took a fancy to us. Posing for a photo, the chimp climbed onto Buddy's lap on one side, while an apprehensive Stevie held tight on the other. Andy seemed quite content to look at the camera.

On other weekends, we loaded up the Morris Minor with the two little boys in the back seat, a road map, and a copy of a book called *The Good Food Guide*. Written by socialist historian, Raymond Postgate, the book was an attempt to steer people towards the restaurants that offered the best food in a country that had become known for serving the worst food. Ordinary people, not food critics, provided the evaluations. We stopped for food and snacks at places the book recommended, but despite the guide, the eateries outside of London were places that gave England its reputation for overcooked vegetables and chicken with pinfeathers still in place. One hot day on a visit to Canterbury, we stopped at a pub to get a soda for ourselves and for Andy. Happy to see Coca Cola bottles on display, we asked for a couple to drink there. The lady pulled the bottles off the shelf, opened them and poured them into glasses.

"Don't you have any that are cold?" Bud asked.

"I didn't bile (boil) them, did I?" was the response.

After we were settled in our flat in London, I wrote a note to John Saville, a historian who had just edited a volume of writings by Ernest Jones, the Chartist leader and the subject of my proposed dissertation at Columbia. I asked Saville if I could meet with him and talk about Jones. A few weeks later I received his reply: "I am no longer working on Jones but a good friend, Dorothy Thompson is. I shall be happy to pass on your letter to her."

As it happened, London in 1956 was the setting for an historic crisis in the British Communist Party, and in fact, the entire Communist movement of the West. Nikita Khrushchev had just issued his astounding report on the excesses of Stalin in the Soviet Union, and two major figures in the British Communist Party, John Saville and Edward P. Thompson, had decided to break with the Party and start a new journal, *The New Reasoner*, which was to be published in London. Bud and I had read about this in the London papers. But we never expected to be discussing it in our living room with Thompson himself.

One June day the telephone rang and the voice at the other end said,

"Hello. Is this Esther? Dorothy Thompson here."

"Yes," I said, "I am Esther. John Saville told me that you might call. I am so pleased to hear from you."

"Good," she said. "It turns out that my husband and I are in London today and could pop in if that's convenient for you." We arranged for the visit the very same day, a Saturday. And so Bud and I met Dorothy and E.P. Thompson. He was a handsome, tall, patrician looking figure; she, a short, bustling woman with a warm and open face. Both of them were about our age and also the parents of small children like ours. They had left their kids at home and arrived at nap time so we had time to talk about many things, including Ernest Jones, *The New Reasoner*, and the book that Edward was then working on, *The Making of the English Working Class*, which would turn out to be a pivotal work in British historiography. Not only were they brilliant scholar-activists of world renown, they were also modest, exceptionally warm and friendly, and very helpful to me in the research project that Dorothy and I continued to pursue for the next decade.

By the time we left London Bud and I had made many friends; we were being invited to people's houses. Summer had come and the sun was actually shining. We hated to leave but the sabbatical was over.

# SUBURBAN HOUSEWIVES: RIVERDALE IN THE 1950S

Despite having advanced college degrees, middle class American women of the fifties were mostly housewives, taking care of the kids and the homes. Once the war's disruption of family life had ended, getting back to "normalcy" meant having children, buying houses, living in the suburbs. The husbands went to work while their wives stayed at home to raise the kids and to "keep house."

I met Mona and Sara in Riverdale where we lived in near-by apartments. Our husbands were scientists. Bud worked at Montefiore Hospital. Bill, Sara's husband was a professor of chemistry at Columbia University; and Mona's husband, Paul, was a professor of biology at the uptown branch of NYU. Mona, Sara, and I were the dutiful stay-at-homes with small children and lots of incentive to make our long days as interesting as possible by enjoying each other's company as we went about the usual chores of shopping, homemaking, and child-care.

Mona and I actually lived in the same garden apartment complex and we met when her first child, Wendy, was two-years-old, just a few months older than Andy. Once, we found each other, we became fast friends. We became even closer when our second children were born, my Steve at the end of April 1955, and her daughter Aline the following July. We proudly marched the new babies in their carriages on Mosholu Avenue as the by-passers stopped to look at the infants. Aline got the most compliments as she lay in her full-size baby carriage, looking like a small gem in a large space. "Oh, what a beautiful baby!" the onlookers would say. Steve's carriage was a new-fangled convertible that could be used as a flat bed at first and then changed into a stroller. When he lay flat in it, in his first six months, he took up the entire space. "Oh what a big guy you have!" said the same onlookers as they gaped.

The two sets of children loved to play together in one house or another. But Mona and I also liked to entertain them by weekly excursions in her six-seater car. Mona was an intrepid driver of a 1956 Ford, with its optional "lifeguard safety package" that included seatbelts and a padded dashboard. (A year later, when Bud and I were looking to replace our old Plymouth with a new Ford that had the safety package, we were told that it had been a slow seller and it had been replaced with a car that had big fins and no safety features.)

Sometimes we boarded a car-ferry from Yonkers to the Palisades, across the Hudson River, and drove up to Suffern where we lunched at the Motel in the Mountain, a Japanese-style inn overlooking the Hudson River. Or sometimes we would drive across the George Washington Bridge and down to Edgewater where we watched the shad fishermen tend to their full nets.

When Andy and Wendy turned three, we enrolled them in the Spuyten Duyvil Infantry, the nursery school, just across the street from our homes, which had a reputation for being a good progressive school, run by Lillian Weber, a professor of Early Childhood Education at Teachers College. (Spuyten Duyvil, is the name given to the whirlpool created where the Harlem River meets the Hudson, in the southern section of Riverdale. It is a Dutch name that can be translated as "spouting devil.")

Mona and I were impressed with a large woman who played tennis each day in the courts next to the school playground. Unlike most suburban tennis moms, Sara wore a long, loose housedress and sneakers without socks, instead of the traditional whites. Sara's son, Larry, was in the class for three-year-olds where he befriended Wendy and Andy. One day, Wendy asked her mom and me if Larry could come back to her house to play, along with Andy. We exchanged addresses with Sara and the three-way friendship began.

Spuyten Duyvil Infantry was a cooperative and the parents had work assignments as occasional teachers' helpers. Once a month we were required to attend an evening meeting to discuss policy with Lillian, the Director, who ran the nursery school with an iron hand and had set opinions on the topics we discussed. One such opinion, and the subject of her research, had to do with the separation of the mother from the three-year-old child at the onset of the nursery school experience. According to Lillian, the mom had to stay at the school–in plain sight-for the entire three hours for ten days no matter what.

On the first day of school, as I delivered Andy, and he ran off to play, I pleaded with Lillian to allow me to leave and to skip the ten-day requirement, "But Lillian," I argued, "Andy has been in nursery school in London for the past six months. He is used to being separated from me."

"I don't want to hear about those English schools," Lillian responded with a contemptuous look. "Everyone knows that they are trying to teach the children how to read. Or they have so much staff that they can coddle the children one-on-one. This is different. I can shorten the time slightly but you must stay for at least a week."

I sat down in the "Mother's section." Andy saw me and ran over.

"What are you staying here for?" he asked.

"It's the teacher's rule."

"Oh. Is it OK if I play? Or am I supposed to stay with you?"

"No, go play," I replied and he ran to join two other little boys who were building a wall of large wooden blocks.

During one of my co-op days, weeks later, when I was assigned to be a teacher's helper, I overheard Lillian ask one of Andy's little friends who had had a hard time separating from his mom, "Davey," she asked, "do you miss your Mom?" And Davey started to weep.

Lillian, a left-winger in politics, was an authoritarian at work. She disliked parents who had strong opinions that were different from her own. One could have predicted that there was no room in the same school for Mona the Mother, and Lillian the Director. At one of the evening parents' meetings in March, as we got to "New Business", Mona raised her hand.

"You know, Lillian," she said, "the Spring break is coming next week, but this week most of the children are out with the measles, so why not call this week the vacation week? Otherwise they will be missing two weeks instead of one."

Lillian looked at her in disbelief. "That's impossible!" she declared, and, giving Mona a contemptuous look, she turned her head back to the full group. "Any other new business?"

Mona raised her hand again. "I would like to propose that we change the name of the school to something other than 'Infantry.'"

My hand went up. "And I second the motion."

Lillian glared at us and said in a deliberate tone, pacing the words slowly: "You both are completely out of order. That is not a topic for this group to discuss. Now, are there any relevant questions? If not, the meeting is adjourned."

A week later I received the following letter:

"Dear Mrs. Rowland:

At a recent meeting the Chairmans' (sic) Coordinating Committee recommended and the school Director decided, not to renew your contract for the 1957-58 school year at the Spuyten Duyvil Infantry.

We enjoyed having your child and believe Andy makes a real contribution to any group. We hope the rest of the Spring term will be a productive and enjoyable one for him."

Sincerely yours,

Lois Smiley. Chairman,

Lillian Weber, Director

Mona received he same letter about terminating the contract for Wendy.

I called Lois Smiley the next morning and asked her what provoked this crazy letter. She replied: "It is clear that you and Mona are not happy here so why stay?" I called Liz, another mom, who was a friend from Bethesda days. Her husband, Paul, was a psychiatrist, a friend of Bud's.

When we had greeted each other, the first day of nursery school, her three-year-old son Davey sank his teeth into Andy's arm. "Now Davey," said Liz, "that's not a nice way to say hello to your old friend." Even so, I expected Liz to be outraged when I read her the letter. Instead she said: "But, Esther, it is clear that you don't like the way the school is run, so why not find a more suitable place?"

Mona and Paul and Bud and I decided to appeal Lillian's decision. Surely the Board of Trustees would reverse such an arbitrary ruling. What did our comments at a parents' meeting have to do with Andy and Wendy? So we attended the next Board meeting where we raised the question. There we were told by the person who chaired the meeting, reading from a document that had been prepared by Lillian: "Andy and Wendy are so well adjusted, they will suffer no adverse effects from being asked to leave." The school was absolved from causing harm to the children. The decision was final.

For me, the incident was another disturbance to the normal complacency of middle class life in America. But it blew over when we were joined by Sara. Sara, a trained psychologist, arrived at the school the day after the Board meeting. With racket in hand, she said to Lillian, "What are you doing asking two great normal kids to leave while you are happily enrolling more and more little bullies who don't get along with anyone?" And shaking her racket at Lillian, she continued, "You are behaving outrageously. You can count me out for next year. Larry is not returning."

The three of us found a welcoming, unpretentious school in nearby Yonkers, where our children had a happy play-school experience for that last pre-kindergarten year. It was also considerably cheaper. The friendship among us "outcasts" was cemented for life.

What we three women loved so much about each other was the down to earth roots we shared as daughters of Jewish immigrants. Our lives were less about where we were going, as our husbands climbed the academic ladders, than where we were coming from. That was what gave us our identities and spared us from the loneliness of suburban life. We became a small circle that included husbands, children and our parents.

My mother, Ida, happily became a part of this new extended family. Hearing that Mona, an accomplished pianist, needed a piano, my mother provided her with an interest-free loan of $1000 to buy a much-coveted Steinway Grand, a piano she played for the rest of her life. Mama, as we all called her, was the example of the assimilated Jew, with a Jewish heart. She visited us on weekends and joined our extended family outings.

Sara's mother, Masha, was the woman with a beautiful, strong face and three marriages. She wore a mink coat and her diamond rings when she took her little grandson "Lahree" to the Riverdale playground. She had not always been rich. In fact, her first husband, Sara's father, had been the rebbe in a failing heder in Brooklyn. Anxious to get out of Brooklyn, he moved his family to the Catskills, where he bought a large house, which he filled with boarders as well as his wife and five children. One day, a year or so after the move, he collected rent for six months in advance from each of the tenants, and ran off with the money, leaving Masha and the children to fend for themselves. Masha raised chickens and sold eggs; the kids got part-time jobs as golf caddies or newspaper vendors and the family struggled, but survived. Many years later when the children were grown, Masha sold the house and moved back to Brooklyn where she worked as a practical nurse, married a rich patient, and inherited his money when he died soon thereafter. She found herself an apartment in a nice neighborhood, bought a new wardrobe of clothes, and traveled to Israel where she met Michele, a Jewish man originally from the Soviet Union, who owned and ran a transvestite nightclub in Berlin. They were married, but because of his shady past record as a gambler, a presumed spy, a possible drug trafficker, Michele was denied entry into the United States, so Masha only saw him on her visits to Berlin three or four times a year. When Mona and I first met Masha, she was deeply involved in this travel pattern, returning from each of her trips with armfuls of leather jackets and soccer balls for all of her children and grandchildren. She would boast about how she fooled the customs officials by carrying the loot deep down in her bag of dirty laundry.

One of her best stories was about the time she arrived on an unplanned trip to the apartment she and Michele shared in Berlin, only to be greeted at the door by a gorgeous blonde dressed in a negligee. When she stormed down to the club to confront her husband, she was told that she had been greeted by one of the transvestites who needed a place for the night.

Mona's father, Nick, was perhaps the most colorful of all. He started life in America as an auctioneer. Then he began to buy up inventories from dry goods stores that had gone bankrupt and to sell the merchandise at heavily discounted prices. Thus he made an adequate living through the depression years. He supported a divorced wife (Mona's mother) who raised their little girl in Philadelphia. When Mona was grown and living in New York, her dad made up for lost time. He loved to visit.

When I would enter Mona's house, Grandpa Nick would greet me with a bottle of Schnapps in hand, a piece of herring, a chunk of rye bread and an onion which he called "hun-yun." "Esther, mein schvester," he would say, "eat this and you'll live forever."

Once, when Nick came to visit me, he asked me the name of our new poodle. "Manfred," I replied. (My children had named the dog after Mighty Manfred The Wonder Dog, a popular cartoon character on TV.)

"Vot's the name?" he asked.

"Manfred," I replied a second time.

"Vot?" he asked again.

"Manfred," I answered a third time, raising my voice a few decibels.

"Vot kind of name is dat?"

"It's Friedman said backwards!" I shouted. His scowl disappeared; his face broke into a huge smile.

"Aah, Friedmahn!" he said. "Now dats a name."

# THE RABBI'S WIFE

When our boys were five and three and getting too big for the tiny room they shared, Bud and I decided to search for a house of our own. It would be hard to leave Riverdale, which was so convenient, but it was prohibitively expensive to buy a home there. Our friend, Sara had already moved to Leonia in nearby Bergen County, New Jersey, just over the George Washington Bridge. Her husband who worked at Columbia found the daily commute to be relatively simple. Houses in Leonia, Tenafly and Englewood were plentiful and the thought of having three or four bedrooms was appealing. One of the wealthy neurologists who had a large private practice at Columbia lived in a small mansion in the fancy section of Englewood. Hearing that we were interested in buying a home in Bergen County, he offered us the name of his real estate agent.

I met Mr. Charles Baker, the agent, a tall, muscular man in his fifties, at the office of Birtwhistle and Livingston on Palisade Avenue in Englewood. He was dressed in Ivy League clothes: a button down oxford shirt, grey flannel pants and a navy blue blazer. On the phone, a few days before, I had told him we were looking for something in this part of Bergen County, very close to the George Washington Bridge, and had given him our price range. As he shook my hand he said: "Dr. Vicale told me about you. I sold him his house a few years ago. What a great guy he is." And then opening the door, and waving me out of the building, he continued, "Let's go. I have a number of homes to show you."

As we walked to his car, I asked, "Do you have something in Leonia where my friend Sara has already bought a house? He turned toward me. "No." he said. "But why would you want to live in Leonia?" And he winced as he continued: "It's an old town with lots of old houses. I'm sure you would prefer to live in Tenafly, so let's start there."

He put the car in drive and pulled out of the space in front of the office. As we drove, we chatted. When I told him how much Bud liked Columbia, he told me that *he* was an enthusiastic alumnus of Cornell, for whom he proudly served as an interviewer for their admissions committee.

I immediately thought: I pity the kids applying to Cornell that get stuck with this stuffed shirt. But I just said, "That's interesting. I didn't know that alumni could play such an important role in admissions."

Arriving in Tenafly, the town just north of Englewood, we saw three homes, all too small and not worth the asking price. I was getting impatient. He persisted, "You know, Mrs. Rowland, your neighbors will all be executives and professionals. I'm sure you and your husband will be very comfortable here in Tenafly." I grimaced but did not reply. He showed me one or two more. Once it was obvious that we were getting nowhere in Tenafly, I found my tongue.

"What about Englewood?"

"In your price range your neighbors might be Jewish and there's a large black population—very different from Tenafly."

"But we *are* Jewish and we *would* like to live in an integrated community."

There was an uncomfortable silence, but it just lasted a moment. He rearranged his face into a big smile.

"Well, I happen to have a house for you, that you will love. It's in Englewood, near a good school. It's a charming Dutch Colonial with 3 bedrooms on the second floor, a finished attic, and a playroom and laundry in the basement. And it happens to be just a block away from the home of the rabbi."

I didn't necessarily like the idea of living so close to a rabbi, with an image in my mind of a ritualistic narrow-minded old guy and his subservient, wig-wearing wife, but I agreed to go see the house, which I liked right away. A few weeks later, we bought that house from Mrs. Tiley-the-Third, an uptight Waspy lady who objected loudly when I asked if our painters could take a look at the house before the closing date.

"I can't be bothered waiting for your painter," she snapped. "You can get your painting estimate after you move."

Mr. Tiley had been transferred and he and his wife were relocating to Pennsylvania, but, as we learned shortly after we moved in, Mrs. Tiley's tennis partners in the neighborhood already were searching for grander homes in areas that still kept out Jews and blacks.

We moved into 280 Audubon Road just before Andy was to start kindergarten in the nearby public school. The first day was an exciting moment for those of us who were delivering our oldest children to "real" school. Andy and I walked to Roosevelt School, three blocks from our home and found the kindergarten class to which he was assigned. The teacher greeted each of the children and then, after telling us when to return, she dismissed the mothers. I found myself walking home, in the same direction as a peppy woman of my age, wearing tan shorts, with a rolled up hem, and a faded blue denim shirt.

"I'm Ellie," she said. "I'm Josh's mother. Is your boy Andy?" I nodded. "The kids seemed to like each other," she continued. "Do you live nearby?"

"Yes on Audubon between Meadowbrook and Huguenot."

"Oh!" she said, "and I live on Robin—between Meadowbrook and Huguenot," she said. "Why not stop in for a cup of coffee? I have a zillion things to do today or I'd invite you for lunch, but coffee just takes a second to make. And I have some fantastic strudel from Baumgartens."

"Sure, why not?" I replied.

As I entered her home I was impressed with the lovely oriental rugs she had, one in the front hall and a huge one in the living room, where there was also an antique credenza, comfortable chairs, a couch covered in grey mohair, and paintings on all the walls, paintings that she told me that she herself had done.

"Let me give you a quick tour." She showed me the house including a room, which, she said, "is my husband's study. He's a rabbi and this is where he does his writing."

So this was the rabbi and this, the rabbi's wife.

The more I got to know Ellie the more I enjoyed her company. We saw each other a lot. Our younger children, her three-year-old Daniel and my Stevie became fast friends and went to nursery school together and after school the children played in one house or another. I preferred to do my food shopping in Leonia, where there was a good coop supermarket. But every now and then I accompanied Ellie to the market in Englewood that she preferred. We went to her market early one morning when she was wearing some junky old pants and a man's shirt. Standing on the checkout line with her eyes roaming all the lines to make sure that none of the others were members of the congregation, she seemed to enjoy the challenge of eluding the Temple gossips that would have loved to spot the "First Lady" in her rags. She told me that when her husband had been offered the job as rabbi, he refused to allow the Temple trustees to buy a house for them. It was important for them to live away from the congregation's watchful eye. "Even so," she added, "when we have invited Board members to our home, they would examine the underside of the dishes, and have the nerve to tell me, 'Well, I never expected to see nineteenth century Majolica in a rabbi's house.'"

Ellie grew up in Worcester, Massachusetts where the Jewish presence was large, but it was still looked upon as strange and separate. The Jewish community in those small cities tended to focus around their synagogue. It was a different atmosphere from New York City, where Jews could be observant or as non-observant as their personal tastes dictated, and still keep a Jewish identity. When Irwin, her husband-to-be, proposed that they marry, she thought that the life of a rabbi's wife would be like being the mayor's wife. She relished the respect she would receive, the ex-officio status that would be bestowed upon her. But at the same time she was her own person, an artist. I think she was happy that Bud and I never joined their temple. She could be herself when we were together.

I envied the fact that Irwin spent so much time at home, where he wrote his sermons and even took care of a lot of temple business. I wished that Bud could be at home sometimes during the day, during the week. I imagined that it would be so pleasant to have adult company and to have someone who offered a helping hand with three kids all going in different directions. But Irwin protected his home-office time and did not do family errands during his workday. Bud would have done the same.

Ellie loved to cook and was great at it. She was the person I could depend on for an easy to do, last-minute recipe to wow our dinner guests in those Saturday night dinner parties we suburbanites were forever giving for each other. And as the recipe unfolded from her mouth she would enthuse about the dish, as if she were tasting it, then and there. "It's mahvelous," she would say in her Massachusetts accent, "all you need is a packet of onion soup, some frozen orange juice and you whip it up, spread it on the meat, throw it in the oven for 30 minutes and it'll come out brown and beautiful and every one will think you stahted from scratch and spent all day cooking." But her real specialty was holiday dinners in the traditional style. Bud and I and the children were invited to every one of these great celebrations; Passover, and Chanukah were our favorites. Irwin, who was a natural born teacher, officiated at each celebration by describing what they were commemorating. He was a short man with a fringe of black hair that circled his head and round brown eyes set in a boyish round face. At the Passover Seder he sat at the head of the long dining room table, prayer book in hand, at first chanting in Hebrew, but soon explaining everything in English. We would sing all the songs and feast until we were ready to drop. I never remember having that much fun at my grandfather's Seders, which were all conducted in chanted Hebrew and, for us kids, were totally incomprehensible and boring.

But the side of Ellie that I admired most was her artistic eye and her creativity as a painter and a connoisseur. In those years in Englewood she had little time to produce new canvasses, but the old ones on the walls attested to her talent. They were bold and colorful; some impressionistic, the later ones abstract. And her knowledge of art history was impressive. We were so busy with our families that we could not go to museums often, but occasionally we would sneak off to spend a few hours in New York at the Museum of Modern Art or at the Metropolitan. When we did, I was proud that she knew so much but I was also embarrassed by her enthusiasm. "There's a Diebenkorn," she would say, "He paints just like me." She would get so close to the painting she was pointing out to me that the museum guards would run up to us as if we were about to maul the picture. "Step back!" they would shout. And we did until we reached the next room, where it would happen all over again. It was even more unsettling for me when she pointed to a painting on the other side of the room and said in a loud and excited voice, "Look at that one. That's a Schwitters! He's the greatest! How I love Schwitters!" I had never heard of Kurt Schwitters until that very moment, so I blushed for my ignorance. And I got even redder for her outspoken behavior in what was normally a hushed environment. But later, I realized that it was her perception, her passion, and her extensive knowledge that was on display. That was Ellie.

# PARENTING

Bud and I met on June 6th 1952, and we were married less than three months later on August 31st. At the wedding, during the traditional first dance, Bud's father, who was dressed in his waist-coat and striped pants, said, in his raspy, cigarette smoke-laden voice, "Esther, I really hope that you are going to have children right away. I want to enjoy my grandchildren while I am young enough." I put on my best forced- smile for him as I thought: "Who is he to tell me when to have children?" The music stopped and we walked back to our table. "Thanks for the dance," I said, glad to be away from him and wondering how much more unsolicited advice my new parents were going to offer. But sure enough I did get pregnant immediately, never imagining that a first shot at sex without a diaphragm would lead to a baby. Bud was thrilled with the news and I wavered from being happy about having a child to being fearful about losing my freedom. Things were happening too fast.

We moved to Washington when I was in my seventh month and visited Georgetown University Hospital to see if it was a good place to give birth. As we entered the building, we were faced with a huge statue of the Virgin Mary occupying a major part of the main hall. It brought back memories of a film I saw as a child in which the pregnant mother is offered the choice of saving herself or saving her baby, and she makes her decision in favor of the child after checking it out with the Virgin. So I said to Bud, "Let's get out of here. I want to have the baby at George Washington." And we fled.

Andy was born on May 20, 1953 to two novices. We were educated in school, but we had no training in baby matters and neither of our mothers lived nearby. In fact, when I was about to leave GWU Hospital, the nurse asked Bud to bring the baby a blanket so we could wrap Andy in it to take him home. And much to the amusement of the two discharge nurses, he brought a full size adult blanket. "And he's a doctor!" one of them said as soon as Bud walked out of earshot. And they both laughed.

Andy and Bud, July,1953

Once home, we did the best we could with a new baby who was either eating or sleeping or crying, with a lot more of the latter than I had expected.

"Don't babies just lie there and gurgle?" I asked my pediatrician, a rather stern guy whom one of Bud's colleagues had recommended.

"Newborns eat and sleep, and in between they cry. That's all they know how to do. It's normal." He said it so matter-of-factly that I believed him for the moment.

He then went on to encourage me to buy a Foley's food mill. "When the time comes for the baby to eat solid food, you'll use it to chop up your leftovers and save money!"

I decided then and there that this doctor was not going to be my type. We never had leftovers. I did not want to spend an extra minute in the kitchen. Why was everyone else using Gerber's jars of baby food?

It took a while to get used to Andy's baby-cries and to figure out what he needed. Bud tried to be as helpful as possible but he could not neglect his work. He was working in a research lab with a team of neuroscientists. When he came home, after the experiments were over, he would light his pipe, take out his book, and push the bassinet-on-wheels with his foot, back and forth to quiet a restless newborn. A few months later, when the Clinical Center at NIH opened, Bud became a resident all over again. He had to stay at the hospital overnight every third night, leaving Andy and me alone in the house. I did not mind the middle-of-the night feedings. It was easy to grab Andy and nurse him. But when it came to changing his diaper, I had to do it in the bathroom, where, the minute I turned on the light, the enormous black water bugs that emerged at night, would freeze in place and then scamper back into their hideouts. Feeling alone and unable to get rid of them, I wanted to cry. I complained to the landlord who told me I was lucky—my neighbors in the basement apartment had a lot more.

Thus when the opportunity came for us to move to the grounds of NIH, we grabbed it even though it was just a one-bedroom apartment. Bud and I slept on the sofa bed in the living room and Andy got the bedroom. Bud only had to walk across the street to get to the hospital, which meant that he could remain at home at night, even when he was on call. That was so much better!

Later, after we returned to New York, we moved to a garden apartment in Riverdale. Bud had a job as clinical neurologist at Montefiore Hospital during the day and was out three evenings a week, studying biochemistry at Columbia. I was again left alone with Andy, a toddler who had a hard time going to sleep for the night. He loved the swings in the playground across the street and begged me to take him there night after night, before he would finally settle down in bed. So there we were, dressed in our outdoor clothes with me pushing Andy on the swing, in a dark empty park.

The next big challenge was weaning Andy from the bottle. I had tried breast-feeding and it lasted for three months. My nipples were inverted and therefore difficult for Andy to grasp. I supplemented my hungry baby's diet with bottles of Similac, which he got so used to that the breast-milk dried up. So we moved from the breast to the bottle, which Andy loved. There were no pacifiers in those days. When Andy was two-and a half, my friend Mona, whose two-and-a half year old, Wendy, had been weaned a whole year before, persuaded me to toss out Andy's bottles, much to Bud's dismay. Bud argued, "Have you ever seen a person walking down the aisle sucking a bottle. Leave him alone. He'll know when he's finished." And I was sure that once again, the absentee father was abdicating his role as parent and choosing the easy way, non-intervention, which was his style. But Mona's solution, which I tried, was a harsh one: "Tell Andy that the bottle is lost or destroyed and there is no substitute other than the cup." It was the cold turkey approach and it did not work. Poor Andy was beside himself, hunting for the "lost bottles," crying bitterly, his nose dripping, "Where's my baba?" I couldn't stand it. "Look, darling, I found your baba!" I finally said. He grabbed it, sucked it and held it tight.

And then there was toilet training. We arrived in London when Andy was about three months short of his third birthday. I knew that the nursery schools in Riverdale would not accept children who were not toilet trained and I assumed that in England, where children were potty-trained early, the same rule would hold true. So I tried frantically to train Andy and the more frantic I was, the more anxious he became. Once, I even slapped his behind after he pooped in his training pants.

And Bud's "I never saw a guy walking down the aisle in diapers" was no help at all. Finally, after all my idle speculation, I decided to check with the local nursery school, The House on the Hill, which was just two blocks away and had a great reputation. Did they have room for Andy who was not yet three? Did they require a toilet trained and a fully weaned toddler? They assured me that they had room for Andy; they had a staff of many young Swiss women apprentices, who were living at the school, learning

English and child-care. There was plenty of help to change diapers and to fill bottles, and to take full care of the toddlers' needs.

*we arrive at the House on the Hill fr. Andy's first day  3/5/56*

Andy had a place. On his first day of school, Andy, looking very American in long corduroy pants, a plaid shirt, and a ski jacket, his hair in a crew cut, walked with me the few blocks to a 19th century Victorian house, just off the busy Finchley Road shopping street. When we arrived, two scrubbed looking Swiss girls, wearing striped cotton dresses and long white aprons greeted us. One said hello to me as the other stooped down to talk to Andy with a big smile and a warm hug, and within minutes she took his hand and led him off to play with the other children and the toys. "Come back at 3 o'clock," I was told, "or call us if you would like to fetch him at a later time." When I arrived back at 3, Andy was happy to see me but also hugging the Swiss girl who delivered him to me. He had had a good time. One afternoon I picked him up and off we went downtown to do some clothing shopping at Selfridges. At the store he needed the bathroom so I found a WC with an adult toilet seat upon which he lifted himself and pooped right into the bowl. I hugged him as I helped him button up. He was so proud and so was I. It was a memorable occasion. Six months later, when we had to leave London, he was wearing short pants, a white shirt with a collar, and his brown wavy hair was cut long. There were no more diapers and no more bottles. The example of the other kids did the trick; no force was necessary.

We parents learned-by-doing on our first child. The younger kids benefited from our growing expertise. Stevie was born two years after Andy, a spacing that turned out to be a bit too close when the boys were little--both in diapers and both on bottles. But that only lasted a year. The good side was that Steve had Andy as a model. By then we were completely relaxed about weaning and toilet training and just let things happen as they were bound to do.

Steve was big and strapping and so well coordinated that he could broad jump at 20 months, and win a fight with Andy a few years later. Thus he challenged Andy's self-perceived entitlement to be the boss. When Steve was four, a little sister came along to alter his position as the baby of the family.

Judy arrived to two well-experienced parents. What a celebration we had. My women friends, Mona, Ellie, and Sara telephoned each other with the news. And when we were discharged from the hospital, they greeted our arrival back home in Englewood with a bottle of champagne as they congratulated me for producing a daughter.

As a third child, Judy was by far the easiest. She was musical, artistic, and good in school. Once she was old enough for music lessons, she almost never missed an opportunity to practice. After school, racing into the house with a "Hi Mommy!" she would pass into the dining room, coat still on, arrive at the piano and, either standing or seated, play at least one piece that she had been studying. When she was in second grade at the neighborhood public school, she had an inventive teacher, Mrs. Watson, who placed prints of the great artists, (Klee and Chagall that year) on all of the classroom walls. Then, and ever since, Judy could spot a Chagall or a Klee wherever they were on display.

Judy age 7, 1966

Bud and I had assumed that the hardest part of parenting was the age when the children could not be spoken to because they were too young to understand. Or the reverse; they could not talk and thus tell us what was troubling them. We could not wait until they were old enough to express themselves. But I remember that a friend once warned me: "Little children little problems and big children big problems." I could not believe that that was possible, until the children grew and child-parent relationships took on a new and hostile dimension.

For example, one evening in Englewood, when Stevie, was about 11, the kids and I were sitting down to dinner, without waiting for Bud who was going to be later than usual that night. Steve was acting up. He pushed his chair away from the table and threw down his napkin. I cannot remember what the fight was about but I remember yelling at him.

"Shut up, Stevie! And just pass the chicken."

"Here's the chicken, I'm passing it!"

He then threw the platter on the floor, scattering the food and the broken crockery all over the kitchen.

"You horrible brat," I screamed. "Look at what you've done! You've ruined it for all of us. How dare you?" He ran; I ran after him, still screaming,

"Come back here this minute and clean this up."

He ran out the front door, slamming it behind him. He picked up a small rock and tossed it through the dining room window, cracking the pane. Hysterical, I called Bud to tell him what had happened. And Bud called Steve at his best friend, Daniel's house, where he correctly assumed he had gone, and told him that he was going to pick him up for a ride to the airport, where Bud had a tissue sample to fetch. They would talk and Bud would be able to make peace. Bud called me back:

"I just told Stevie that he could ride with me to the airport this evening and get him off your hands until the two of you make up," he said proudly. "Yes, I want to find out what the problem was between the two of you."

I slammed the phone down. So Stevie and I were to be regarded much like two little kids having a fight and Bud was the mediator.

When Bud and Steve came home that night, I had already gone to bed. I did not want to see either of them. The next morning I was still smoldering and I told Bud, "What happened yesterday was a nightmare. We've got to do something to change the way Stevie treats me."

Bud shrugged and turned back to the mirror as he continued to tie his bow tie.

"Let's call Ian, to see if he could help us," I suggested. Ian was a neighbor and a psychiatrist. "And ask him to recommend someone for Stevie."

Bud sighed. "I'll do whatever you really want us to do, but you know I hate to involve strangers in a family dispute." He had never gone to a psychiatrist himself. I made the call and Ian suggested we come right over for a quick chat before he and Bud had to start the working day. As we entered Ian's home on Maple Street, Bud greeted him with a collegial arm around his shoulder. "Esther is having a hard time with Steve, perhaps you can help her." I looked at him in disbelief as he did that. "Two smart docs feeling sorry for the helpless lady," I thought to myself.

Ian invited both of us to sit down in his office. Bud held out a chair for me but I walked past him and sat in the other one. As Ian settled into his own chair behind his desk, I told him the story of the chicken and the rock.

"Can you recommend someone to treat Stevie?" I pleaded.

Ian stood up and replied: "Why don't you and Bud figure out what you both are doing that's making him behave that way." Ian looked at us, from one to the other and then stood and opened the door for us. "Think about it. And come back to me when you are ready."

That is a discussion Bud and I never had and we never returned to Ian. Whatever was bothering Stevie at that moment seemed to pass, and nothing quite like that happened again.

Steve at age 11 with our poodle, Pipsqueak, 1966

A few months later, seven-year-old Judy was taking a bath and calling for a fresh piece of soap. Bud walked by, grabbed soap from the linen closet and entered the bathroom.

"When did you get those marks?" he asked, pointing to two large black and blue marks on her torso.

"I dunno," she replied as he sat down on the edge of the tub to examine her more carefully.

"Uh-oh," he said in a serious voice. "Turn around. I think there are more on your back."

He discovered a half dozen blotches spread across her body, and called me to show what he had found.

"Did you fall, Judy?" I asked.

"No," she replied. "They just came."

"Tomorrow, first thing I'll call Dr. Wolff," said Bud, referring to our pediatrician at Columbia, who was also a hematologist.

"I hate going to the doctor, and I don't like Dr. Wolff!" Judy shouted as she splashed the new piece of soap into the water.

"Up you go," I said to Judy as I brought her towel and helped her out of the tub. "We just have to make sure that these bruises will go away and that you are fine. It's important to see Dr. Wolff."

Bud, who had been mostly a "Take-an-aspirin-and-we'll-see-how-you-feel-in-the- morning" kind of doctor for the family, really looked worried this time. He knew that Judy needed to be examined and tested as soon as possible and confided in me that leukemia could be the diagnosis—but there were other, less serious possibilities as well. I became morose when he mentioned leukemia. Was it possible that one of our seemingly healthy children could have such a terrible disease? I couldn't get it out of my mind. We had a date for dinner at the home of friends and I could barely get through the evening. The following day, we took Judy for the exam and for the blood tests. Her platelets were practically all gone. Her condition was serious and we would not know her diagnosis until she had a painful blood marrow exam that was scheduled for a week later. We told no one in the family, to spare them from the agony of thinking that Judy had a fatal illness until we knew for sure. But that did not help either Bud or me from thinking the worst, as much as he tried to reassure me, and himself, that it was too early to come to any conclusion.

Two weeks of agony led to a final diagnosis of idiopathic thrombocytopenic purpura (ITP), a disease that affects children and tends to cure itself. There was no medicine to give Judy. She had to have weekly blood drawings, which were painful. She screamed as she saw the needle pointing in her direction and I held her tight. She hated those sessions but the test results showed that gradually and steadily her platelet count was building back to normal. The disease just faded away.

And so did many of the parenting problems that baffled us at the time.

# CIVIL RIGHTS IN ENGLEWOOD
# IN THE 1960S

It was a morning in mid-September 1962. The boys were walking to Roosevelt School, a few blocks away from our house, and I had dropped Judy at her nursery school at the Jewish Community Center. From there I found my way to an address I had scribbled on a pad, the result of a phone call I had made the day before to the Lincoln School Boycott Coordinating Committee, asking if they could use me as a volunteer. "I've never taught small children," I apologized, "but I have three kids of my own, and I have taught in colleges."

"Don't worry," the woman reassured me. "We have some trained teachers who can help you, if needed. Right now we need volunteers to man the classrooms on a daily basis. If you could give us a day or two, that would be great."

The Supreme Court, in 1954, had made it clear that school segregation, based on race, was illegal. But even in 1962 Englewood still had three almost all white elementary schools, one that was almost all black, and one that was 63% black. The civil rights organizers in Englewood decided that something had to be done and called for a boycott of the all-black school. In order to do this without sacrificing the children's schooling, an alternative school was hastily set up in the homes of several families who lived side by side in an integrated neighborhood.

I drove to Liberty Road at the western end of the town to a development of a dozen look-alike houses. They were all ranch style, single-story homes, with backyards, garages, and driveways, just like Pete Seeger's *"Little Boxes"* except these boxes housed people of color side by side with whites. The boycott committee had placed a table on the sidewalk and a group of women was gathered around it. I parked and headed for the group, where I was told how to enter my second grade classroom, and that the Principal would be joining me in a few minutes. One of the women escorted me to my building and I descended the staircase leading to a comfortably furnished "finished basement."

As a college teacher, I was always nervous in the moments before the beginning of the class. Once we started, however, I found myself relaxing and enjoying the discussion. In those days, I had given my students a syllabus, with a specific assignment for that day and all we had to do was launch into the discussion. But second grade was different. And much harder, I soon discovered.

As I entered a large wood-paneled playroom, I was greeted by the clamor of eight seven-year-olds, supposedly seated in bridge chairs that had been neatly arranged into a circle. But the children were mostly on the floor, crawling on the shaggy orange carpet and hitting each other with pencil cases. I stood behind a makeshift desk and shouted above the din: "Hello everybody! I am the new teacher! Please get seated. Just then the door swung open and the newly chosen principal, a black woman with lots of teaching experience, arrived. She rapped a ruler on the back of the bridge table that was to be the teacher's desk. "What is going on here?" She rapped, and she glared, she rapped and she glared, and gradually the room became quiet. She demanded that the children sit in their designated chairs and one by one they sat down. When one little boy turned his head to say something to his neighbor, the principal marched over to him. "Stand up!" as she grabbed his hand and pulled him to his feet. "When I am talking to you, _you_ are listening to _me_! Is that clear? And there will be no fidgeting, no giggling, no sound from you while your teacher is talking. Now you may sit down." Finally, she introduced me and left.

I was on my own. "Good morning, children," I said. "Now that you know my name, I'd like to know yours. So let's go around the room so you can tell me."

"Round the room, round the room," one child repeated, with a mischievous look on his face as he got off his chair and started crawling around the room. I spent the next twenty minutes listening to the children introduce themselves, but one or two were still crawling on the floor. I read them a story; some of us talked about it while others were whispering to each other. They drew pictures and at last it was time for me to deliver them to the recess teacher and for me to go home for my own children's lunch.

I soon learned that to be a successful elementary school teacher you had to have patience. You had to have a lesson plan and stick to it. You had to be able to repeat yourself over and over. You had to make rules and stick to them. You had to be the boss and make it clear that you were the boss. In other words you had to do all the things I was terrible at doing. Fortunately there were enough volunteers to make it possible for me to serve only one morning a week, and to share my class with other volunteer moms. One of them, a great elementary school teacher who was on leave to raise her own small children, kept the class focused on very specific educational goals: arithmetic, spelling, reading. She planned each day's exercises carefully and succeeded in holding the children's interest. Another volunteer, my friend Helen Sprinson who was part-Native-American, kept the children spellbound with her tale of the Trail of Tears, the forced and deadly march of Native Americans, accompanied by African-American slaves, from the southeastern part of the United States to the western Indian reservations in the 1830s. "The children had never heard of this bit of American history," she told me later, "and they were fascinated by the story." I was envious. Why hadn't I thought of telling such a story?

Finally, with pressure from the community, the Governor, and the threat of potential lawsuits, the Board of Education agreed to restructure the entire school system, close the Lincoln school and bus the children to the other three schools and neighborhoods. The boycott ended. The Lincoln School building was converted to the Board of Education head-quarters and the old headquarters, which had been more centrally located, became a single sixth grade school for the whole city. The elementary schools ended after fifth grade. There was one junior high and one high school. The new Superintendent of Schools was committed to a fully inte-grated system and made all the changes that had been promised, but that was still not enough. The resolution was flawed because only the black chil-dren were being bussed.

So we had won a battle, but still had a long way to go. After the rearrangement of the schools was ordered, all of the black children whose homes abutted our ward were bussed from the now closed Lincoln School district to ours. Cornel Satterfield, a tall five-year old, dressed for school in woolen slacks, an ironed shirt, and a tie, was one of them. Because he and Stevie had become best friends in the Roosevelt School, they pleaded with me to give them more time together. Two or three times a week I would fetch Cornel by car at about 10 in the morning, let the two boys play for a couple of hours, feed them lunch, and send them off on foot to their afternoon kindergarten class. They were both big kids, tall and strong, and they had a great time playing in our yard. Cornel taught Stevie how to ride a two-wheeler and how to tie the laces on his sneakers. So imagine our surprise when, at the end of the term, the kindergarten teacher refused to recommend Cornel to be promoted to first grade. I protested to the principal, who had become my friend, describing Cornel's accomplishments in the area of motor skills, as well as his maturity as a guest in our home. What were they looking for, I wondered? But knowing the rigid kindergarten teacher, an elderly white woman who had complained about bussing-in the Lincoln children, I realized that she was the one who had proposed that Cornel be left back. In the end, Cornel did get promoted. He was placed in a different first grade class from Stevie and they saw less of each other from then on.

The next challenge for Englewood was to elect a new Mayor and City Council that would be supportive of civil rights in Englewood. Bud and I who were active Urban Leaguers, (an organization that was dedicated to racial equality), and the Democratic Party stalwarts who also were completely involved in the civil rights struggle, met in each other's homes and devised lists of neighbors to call on and a script of what to say. We attended church gatherings in the black churches, holding hands with those on either side of us, and singing "We Shall Overcome" and passionately believing it.

"We Shall Overcome"
https://www.youtube.com/watch?v=QhnPVP23rzo

I became a member of the Urban League's Education Committee, meeting weekly in Olga Gellhorn's living room on the East Hill, where we monitored the school integration project. The following year, when Andy entered the new Central Sixth Grade School, I was elected President of that school's PTA and met frequently with Leroy McCloud, the school's African-American principal.

Unfortunately, our victory in establishing one integrated school system for all was jeopardized when one white family after another withdrew their children from the public system and, instead, enrolled them in the private schools in the neighborhood or across the river in New York City. Even our friend the rabbi, who had been so active in the civil rights struggle, decided that his oldest son should go to Horace Mann, in Riverdale. Bud and I were angry with him for making that decision.

My last civil rights project before we moved to Philadelphia was more problematic. One day I had read in the local paper that the Englewood branch of the Junior Chamber of Commerce was proudly presenting its second annual "Aunt Jemima Pancake Fest," a Saturday fair in the center of town, to which all were invited to eat free pancakes, supplied by the Quaker Oats Corporation to promote its product. On display was an ad, with a huge picture of Aunt Jemima, all decked out in her long dress and apron, with her brown smiling face, and a handkerchief bandana tied around her head. She appeared to be the essence of black servitude, an image from the antebellum days in the South. The whole thing made me uncomfortable, but I wondered if it would be worthwhile to do more than send a letter to the editor, admonishing the Chamber of Commerce for prolonging the stereotype. I decided to confer with my friend, the principal of Andy's school.

I entered Mr. McCloud's office and placed the newspaper ad on his desk for him to read. "I've come to ask your advice. I can't decide whether this is too trivial an issue to fuss over or whether it is worth a fight."

He read the piece, sighed, and smiled, saying, "It surely does convey the image of black people as happy servants. You know, there's a campaign going on to get rid of Uncle Ben and of Aunt Jemima, but they are such best sellers, it won't happen."

"So, should I forget about it?" I asked.

"No," he replied, "It might be a worthwhile educational campaign. Follow up on it, if you have the time."

So I called the new anti-discrimination office at City Hall and suggested they ask the Chamber of Commerce to back down. "I'm not sure this is the kind of issue we want to get involved with," replied the woman who took my call. "It's not exactly a question of discrimination."

"That's true," I said, " but talk it over with your Committee and see how they respond."

By chance, at that moment, the Committee had nothing immediate on its agenda and they decided to take action and deny the needed permits to the Junior Chamber, who had no idea that their goodwill campaign had a downside. The festival was canceled. But the victory seemed to be a hollow one when many members of the community, black and white, were puzzled by the disappearance of free pancakes, an event that had been extremely popular in the past. The Junior Chamber people did not know what they were doing wrong, and, judging from the angry phone calls they received, neither did the community.

# THE PROCEDURE

In the winter of 1966, I discovered that I was pregnant again. My family was just getting manageable; I had the three children that I wanted to have, and they were a wonderful handful. With children in school full time I was finally free to go to Columbia every day and spend a good five hours in my small library cubicle, writing my dissertation, talking with my friends, and still get home in time to greet the kids as they returned from school and to prepare dinner for the family. It was a time of liberation. Things could only get better from then on. I was hopeful that I would have a life of my own and a career, as well as a husband, two sons and a daughter, all healthy, bright, and reasonably well-adjusted.

And now I had to undo what we had done by accident. I could not go through those painful baby years all over again: the sleepless nights followed by the long days alone with the baby with no one to talk to, diapering, feeding, and trying to find out why the baby was crying. I wanted to finish my degree and get a job. And Bud agreed with me. Fortunately the pregnancy was in its earliest weeks; there was time for an abortion, but how?

Abortion was illegal in the United States, but it was not in some European countries. As it happened, we were already headed for Europe for a neurology meeting in Heidelberg. Irena, our Polish neurologist friend, would be at the meeting; perhaps she could help. Poland was a Communist country; surely they did not oppose abortion. If not Poland, we could try Switzerland. We had a good neurologist friend in Berne. And Switzerland was known as the place where hundreds of French and Italian women were granted safe abortions that were impossible to get in their home countries. I had told my mother about the pregnancy. "Oh my God," she said. "Two children is enough for any family and you already have three." As she said this she laid out her hands, palms up, and said, "What are you doing to yourself?"

So we were off to Heidelberg, and I was looking forward to being in Europe, where, in several countries, abortion had been legalized. I felt confident that something would work out.

Jan van Eyck: The Arnolfini Portrait

When we arrived I found a postcard in a kiosk, a Jan van Eyck painting, The Arnolfini Portrait. I sent it to my old friend Sara who knew of our mission. "Greetings from Europe. Love, Esther and Bud." She appreciated the joke.

It was our first trip to Germany and it was just twenty years after the war had ended, so that one could assume that the people there of our age had been connected with the Nazi movement. Bud was especially aware of the men in their forties who were wearing polished black boots. He said he could just picture them in their Nazi uniforms. On the other hand, Heidelberg was a charming old university town. It was the first place I had ever seen pedestrian streets where automobile traffic was forbidden.

As soon as we arrived we looked for our Polish friend, Irena. Bud found her in the hotel lobby and asked if she had a moment to talk privately.

"Of course. Let's sit over there." She pointed to a sitting area and we followed her. "You both look so serious. What's wrong?"

"Irena, we need your help," said Bud. "Esther is pregnant, just by a few weeks. We need to find a place where she can get an abortion."

Irena frowned. "Oh I am so sorry," she said. "But if you are thinking about coming to Poland for this, I'm afraid that's out of the question. I know you think it would be easy in a Communist country, but Poland is very Catholic. Perhaps a Polish girl could arrange something for herself. But it would be impossible for a foreigner."

So that avenue was out. We had to wait until the end of the meeting and make our way to Berne to see what could be done.

The concierge at the hotel in Heidelberg had arranged for our reservation in a sister hotel in Berne. It was winter and we slept well under the softest and warmest eiderdown quilts in a room facing the mountains. Our friend, Dr. Kurt Richter, met us for lunch at the hotel dining room and Bud told him of our plight.

"Ah," he said, "I am so sorry that you had to come all the way to Switzerland to fix this. It shouldn't have to be this way." He reached into his pocket for a small leather address book, and started turning the pages.

"There's nothing in Berne, but I have the address of a good clinic in Geneva, and an excellent obstetrician. Here write these numbers down," he said as he handed Bud a small business card and a fountain pen.

Time was the most important consideration at that moment so we left the next morning for Geneva and an appointment in a suite of offices in the town center. We were interviewed by a social worker who took a detailed family history-- the date of our marriage, the ages of our children, my age, my reasons for wanting an abortion, the date of my last period. She was accustomed to dealing with unmarried French and Italian women, not with married Americans, so I was a different, and in some respects an interesting case. The fact that we already had three children pleased her. She was clearly of the planned-parenthood persuasion and one of her missions was to curb excessive population growth. I fit.

The next step was to arrange for a physical examination to determine that the pregnancy was indeed in the first trimester. By 10:00 AM, an obstetrician had examined me and had thus confirmed that I was less than three months pregnant. "Good news," he said just after the examination. "We can go ahead with the procedure." Dr. Baum was our age, spoke perfect English, and seemed very sympathetic to my plight. He had exchanged his white coat for a tweed jacket, under which he wore a blue shirt and a red tie. He waved us to chairs at the other side of his desk and gave us our instructions: "You must file the papers and have the counseling session here this morning. An appointment with a psychiatrist will be made for this afternoon or this evening and once the approvals are in, we can schedule the procedure probably tomorrow afternoon."

"And where do we come back to you for the operation?" Bud asked.

"I will do it in the polyclinic. It's a lovely facility in a country setting, with first-rate facilities and an excellent nursing staff." As he said this I couldn't help visualizing the counterpart in the United States: a dirty space, in somebody's basement, and a "doctor" who might even be using unsterilized instruments.

"The social workers out front will fill you in with all the details." Dr. Baum rose from his chair. He seemed to be so confident. Bud and I grasped each other in relief and each of us shook the doctor's hand in a tight grip as we thanked him.

A social worker gave me a lesson in the use of an intra-uterine device, (IUD), which was the preferred contraceptive at that time, and she made an appointment for me to see the psychiatrist that evening. Bud and I had the whole afternoon free with plenty of time to prepare me for the interview. Knowing that in the United States an abortion could only be justified if the patient was likely to do harm to herself, we bought a book about suicidal behavior, a classic that Bud knew about from medical school. We found a medical bookstore, and we found the book, in English. It was a slim volume that both of us could read in an hour or so.

Back in the hotel room, sitting on the bed, we took turns reading the book. Bud decided that he would play the role of the psychiatrist and ask me questions. My job was to answer them as a potential suicidal candidate.

"What thoughts go through your head when you think of this baby?"

"I feel hopeless. I feel useless. I can't cope."

"And how will you deal with this helplessness?"

"I think about killing myself."

And so we went on in our fantasy of him being the psychiatrist and I being the helpless patient, the needy little woman. And suddenly Bud was talking to me as if I was that needy little, helpless woman.

"Do you want to rest now and I'll order dinner in the room?"

I was annoyed. "No! Let's go out like we always do and find a great restaurant near the psychiatrist's office."

The 7:00 PM appointment time was approaching and we walked to the address written on our small strip of paper. It was an apartment house close to the restaurant and not far from the hotel. We found the doctor's name on the board in the vestibule, rang his bell, and were buzzed in. The tiny elevator was nearby and we took it to the designated floor where a tall, slim man in his late fifties awaited us. He wore a brown business suit, had thinning brown hair and a serious look on his face, rather than the smile I had been expecting from a psychiatrist who was greeting a new patient.

"We are the Rowlands." I said. "We have an appointment." I showed him the slip of paper.

"Je suis Dr Martine. Suivez-moi," he said abruptly as he waved Bud to a seat in a waiting room and indicated that I follow him into his office where he pulled a chair for me on one side of a large wooden desk and then he sat down, facing me, holding a pen in his right hand.

"Madame," he said, "Pourquoi êtes-vous ici?" I answered, "Because I am pregnant and need your permission." He interrupted me: "Pourquoi voulez-vous parler en anglais? Américains! Vous nous attendez de parler votre langue et vous donner tout ce que vous voulez!" *"Why do you speak in English? You Americans, you speak in your own language and you expect to get whatever you want!"*

He was livid. I realized that he was thinking that we were rich, privileged Americans who could afford to come to Switzerland for a procedure that the Swiss were offering to poor European girls who lived in Catholic countries where birth control was also illegal. Speaking in English was just another sign of my privilege.

"Pardonnez moi," I replied, conjuring up the best Walton High School French I could remember. "Je suis ici parce-que il n'st pas possible pour me d'avoir un autre enfant." At that point he decided the struggle was not worth it and he broke into perfect English: "Tell me your problem." I told him, in English, and he hardly probed further. He wrote a few notes, dismissed me and said he would pass on his recommendation to the authorities. "Bon soir!" I barely slept that night. Would that hostile psychiatrist recommend me for the abortion?

The next morning we received a phone call that we should report to the polyclinic, where the friendly obstetrician would meet us. The approval had been granted! The procedure was done in an operating room, with every precaution taken, and all did go well as planned. I stayed overnight in the clinic, carefully monitored until the excess bleeding had stopped. When Dr. Baum arrived for the final visit before I left for home, he checked my heart and my blood pressure and while doing so he said: "You know, Mrs. Rowland, I had a hard time freeing the fetus from your womb. It was a strapping boy who clung hard."

I went home, happy that the procedure was behind me. But this "kind" doctor's haunting words made me shudder. I hugged my kids really tight and went on to the next phase of my life.

# WYNNESTAY: OUR HOME

In 1967 Bud left Columbia to become Chairman of Neurology at Penn and our family of five moved to Philadelphia. The arrival of Milton Shy, the new chairman of neurology at Columbia who had the same research interests as Bud, made it a perfect time for Bud to move on.

Selling the house in Englewood was easier than we had expected. Our first customer immediately accepted the full price we had set. She had fallen in love with the color of the kitchen, the color the painter had, with a sneer, referred to as "khaki," when I left him a chip labeled "absinthe." With our closing date fixed, off we went to scout for the new place in Philadelphia.

Our experience in Englewood had taught us that we wanted to live in an integrated neighborhood where blacks and whites lived side by side. With the help of Urban Developers, a new breed of real estate agents who understood what we were talking about, we found our dream house: the oldest residence in Philadelphia, a designated landmark mansion dating back to 1689, that had originally been built as a country house for Thomas Wynne, William Penn's physician, on land deeded to him by Penn himself. The house even had a name: Wynnestay. Our neighborhood was called Wynnefield, named after Thomas Wynne, and it was located on the western edge of the city, just a fifteen-minute car ride from the University of Pennsylvania. The house, listed and pictured in the architectural histories of Colonial Philadelphia, came with a plaque, which read: "Historic House #189. Philadelphia Landmark Commission."

Wynnestay, Philadelphia, PA

Wynnefield was on the city side of the city-line that separated the city from the suburbs. From the 1920s to the 1950s, the area had been referred to as the "gilded ghetto," the place where Jews could buy houses comparable in size to the ones they were forbidden from buying in the Main Line suburbs, which bordered on the other side of City Line Avenue. There were two major synagogues in Wynnefield, which kept the Jewish population relatively stable, even into the sixties when African Americans moved in, in relatively large numbers. By the time we got there both races were still buying in. The prices were more than fair. Our giant "farmhouse" cost $42,000, just $6000 more than the price at which we sold our much smaller house in Englewood.

Wynnestay was an early Georgian country house, made of Wissahickon schist, a crude stone produced from the bedrock that is indigenous to the Philadelphia region. Brownish-gray in color, with shadings of blue, it is flecked with mica. Wissahicken schist was a common material used by the builders of the early twentieth century houses in Wynnefield. But the stones used in these later houses were of one size and evenly cut.

In Wynnestay, however, the stones had been unevenly cut and randomly stacked, making it look almost sculptured, and sparkling, as the sunlight hit the mica.

The gray stone in Wynnestay was offset by brightly painted white wood trim used on the shutters, the cornices, the door hood and the front door. On the outside, it looked like a charming but large farmhouse, with small windowpanes on the ground floor and a Dutch style double-hung door that allowed us to open the top half and keep the bottom half latched.

Inside the house, the three floors above the basement contained six bedrooms and four bathrooms. Best of all, the large living room on the ground floor had a walk-in fireplace, as wide as the room itself, which contained an old cooking pot hanging from an extendable iron arm. There was a second floor parlor with a bow-shaped window, "a bright, sunny sewing room," according to Mrs. Whittier, the previous owner (who, unlike me, knew how to sew); and a ballroom on the third floor. With bathrooms on every floor, a large kitchen, good appliances, and a large pantry; we enjoyed every modern convenience. Below ground was a cool basement, partly paved in concrete and partly dirt, which the previous owners used for storage of vegetables and wine. There was a huge study for Bud on the ground floor with its own door to the garden. There was even room for a full-size ping-pong table and a pool table on the top floor. The house sat back on an acre of ground, surrounded by well-kept hedges, flowers, lilac bushes, and huge plane trees that were hundreds of years old. Furthermore, it was just a short commute to the University of Pennsylvania, where Bud worked.

Just before we moved, I went to the library to get ideas about decorating such a house and to my astonishment I found pictures of the house itself in architectural histories. When Ellie, my Englewood neighbor asked about our new home, I couldn't resist telling her that I had no pictures because I didn't need them.

"See Hugh Morrison, Early American Architecture!" I said.

"C'mon Esther, stop joking."

"Here Ellie I have a copy." I pulled it from the bookshelf and opened it to p.519, plate 437. And there was the picture of the house and a description.

Some of these histories also tell the story of two British soldiers who lie buried in the basement, put there by the lady of the house who shot them when they demanded to be billeted during the Revolutionary War. The family that sold us the house added credibility to this tale by informing us that their dog, no matter how much cajoling, would refuse to walk on the dirt part of the basement, but would just stand on the concrete edge and yowl.

The grounds covered a full acre and included a coach house, which, in an early renovation, had been converted into a garage with bedrooms and a toilet that was supposed to be one of the first flush toilets in America. There was also a springhouse, a small separate building that covered an old spring, now dried up, that had been used to keep food cool. Before and during the Civil War, Wynnestay was said to be a station of the Underground Railroad, with a connection from the main house to the springhouse.

We moved to our new home in July of 1967. After all the twisting and turning of the furniture on its way out of the small house in Englewood, the movers could march into Wynnestay, carrying the pieces straight forward and up the grand staircase with its three foot square landing and the sunlight pouring in from the Palladian window above. "Now this," one of them said, "is a house!"

Our children had their own rooms. "I claim this one," declared Andy as he examined a large square room on the second floor, opposite ours. Steve asked to live on the third floor near the pool table, and a choice of bedrooms up there. Bud and I decided to place Judy, who was 8, in the room nearest to ours. We had of course brought all of her decorations from Englewood: her special dollhouse that had been handed down from an older friend, her Barbie dolls, and her teddy bears, hoping that, despite the size of the new house, she would feel comfortable. There was a shared bathroom between our two rooms, which served as a conduit for her and for us to stay close. We settled in quickly, took on the new schools, new neighborhood, new friends and Bud's new job.

Unfortunately, the enthusiasm that Bud and I had for the house and for the move to Philadelphia didn't spill over to the children who were missing their friends, the smallness of the Englewood house, and Englewood itself. After we moved in, Bud and I thought we had met the requirements for the perfect home-setting in the late 1960s, including a beautiful house with lots of room so the kids could bring their new friends home to play, or even to stay overnight. But the new friends were hard to find, and once found, bringing them home to Wynnestay became an embarrassment. It was too big, and in their minds, too fancy. Although they complained of this at the time, we paid no attention to what we considered to be a passing phase.

I remember an evening at Wynnestay when we were entertaining friends, Mark, who worked with Bud at Penn, and his wife, Rita. They lived in Swarthmore, which was more like a small college town than a typical bedroom suburb. The husband had an hour-long commute each day to the Penn campus, but they were enamored of the life style in what I perceived as a homogeneous, all white, upper middle class community, exactly the kind of place we were trying not to live in, although deep-down, I too liked college towns.

"Oh my God," I thought, "how boring." I asked her, "Don't you think your family would benefit from living in a place that was closer to Penn and that was more like the real world?"

Rita replied, "Even though Mark has a long commute, the children *love* living in Swarthmore. And the children's happiness is our primary concern."

She put down her drink and turned to me.

"Don't you agree, Esther?" she asked.

I said sharply, "The children's happiness *isn't* everything," and she looked at me as if she could not believe what I was saying. I felt my face turning red and quickly changed the subject.

"Dinner is ready. Let's go into the dining room. Bring your drinks with you."

# WYNNESTAY: TRIBULATIONS AND TRIALS

Our life in Englewood had been consumed with the civil rights movement. It was clear to me, and to Bud, that only by integrating neighborhoods, and fighting to keep all the kids in public school, would we win that battle. We thought Philadelphia was on the right track. They had just hired a new Superintendent of Schools, Mark Shedd, who had also come from Englewood, where he had done a good job in the first phase of the school-integration struggle. We knew him and trusted him. But a major change, like overhauling a school system, takes ages, not months or even several years. He was battling Behemoth in a down-sliding economy.

Andy was just starting high school and had been accepted at Philadelphia's prestigious Central High, the showcase public school for smart boys, with a reputation that rivaled that of Boston Latin, or Stuyvesant and Bronx Science High Schools in New York. But there was a downside. In order to get to school Andy had to take two buses to the other side of town, an hour's commute. Once there, he did well academically, but he missed being in a coed environment. More, he considered many of his classmates narrow and obnoxious. They were almost all white and proud to be at what was essentially an all-white place. To enlarge his circle of friends, and after-school activities, Andy answered a newspaper ad that called for high school swimmers to join a community team in North Philadelphia under the leadership of an African-American swimming coach. Malachi, the coach, was devoted to the notion that swimming practice every day was a way to get kids off the streets and a great sport for life. Andy and, a bit later, Steve, signed up, and eventually so did Judy and Steve's friend Sharon. Malachi was happy to have an integrated team and they worked well together with practices and meets. Although the group used the pool, first at Temple University and later at St. Joseph's Prep, in one of the poorest neighborhoods in the city, Andy, Steve, and Judy managed to get there and to get home safely. They loved Malachi and were proud to be on the team.

Andy, our first-born, had many of the characteristics of the typical eldest child, and a child in our family. He was serious and less playful than his younger sibs and he worked hard at his studies. He believed that the burdens of the world were meant to be on his shoulders. Upset by the United States role in Vietnam, and worried about being drafted to fight an unjust war, Andy became an active participant in the peace movement in Philadelphia.

Steve liked to roam the neighborhood. He was outgoing and big for his age. He started junior high school at Beeber, the neighborhood school, where he learned little and, as he told us later but not at the time, he was mugged a few times, by other boys, on his way to school. In 8th grade he transferred to Masterman, which was a magnet school, a public school with a specialized curriculum. This one was a middle school for bright kids, located in downtown Philadelphia. It was not only public and selective, but it included neighborhood children. It was thoroughly integrated, and challenging academically. Steve had a great experience at Masterman, but when he entered Central High, he, like Andy, was appalled at the show of exclusiveness that he found. Although many of the teachers were qualified and excellent, others were rigid. One biology teacher often spent the entire class having the students copy notes. Steve grumbled and whispered to his neighbor: "Why can't he mimeograph the notes and hand them out to us. And then spend the hour doing something interesting?"

"Steve if you have something to say, say it to the whole class, out loud, now!" So Steve repeated his question. The teacher was appalled and called Steve a "prima donna" and ended the "discussion." Steve decided that he would talk to the teacher about it in office hours that afternoon. "You know, Sir, in a biology class this past summer at science school in Woods Hole, we dissected a cat in an anatomy class and it was amazing. I would like a greater challenge in your class. Do you think that if I purchased my own cat specimen from a supply house, I could set it up somewhere and do a series of dissections under your guidance, getting a little help from you?"

"I would never do that," the teacher replied. "When do you expect me to have special time to spend with you? I go home after work."

After two years and many other frustrating experiences, Steve decided to leave Central. He looked at two of the Quaker private schools, but decided that he should stay in the public system and attend Overbrook, the neighborhood high school where he was one of only a handful of white students in a school of 5,000. One of his white classmates was the daughter of Mark Shedd, the Superintendent of Schools. The teachers were predominantly white, and many of them had given up trying to keep the students engaged in the learning process. Some of them seemed to hate the kids they were teaching. In one open-school session, Steve's teacher confided in me: "You know Mrs. Rowland, Steve is a pleasure to have in class. He's so interested in learning. In the old days most of the kids were like that. Now, we are dealing with a bunch of animals." Steve again was academically unchallenged and was able to graduate a year early. Fortunately, he took two classes at Andover in the summer and there got a taste of the joys and the benefits of a rigorous learning environment.

In Philadelphia Judy had a mixed school experience. She attended Samuel Gompers, the neighborhood public elementary school, which was fairly well integrated and just a short walk from the house. There, she had some decent teachers and some who were really bad. The one she complained about the most was Mrs. Jasner, who divided her class into the "live wires," (all white) and the "dead-heads," all black, except for one white boy who lived in a home for orphans.

Actually Judy enjoyed her time at Gompers, but when she moved on to Masterman for junior high school she had a hard time, at first, being accepted by a cliquey group of black classmates. Eventually she found a compatible group of friends and she was happy at school. Still, Philadelphia was quite different from the smaller, friendlier atmosphere of suburban Englewood. Fortunately, my mother spent most of her weekends at our house, first in Riverdale, then in Englewood, and once again, in Philadelphia. The children loved her and she became especially close to Judy.

Living in a home with fifty windows and four entry doors, a huge yard with giant trees, and a suburban mentality that eschewed taking precautions about locking locks and securing windows, we were perfect targets for the neighborhood thieves. We later found out that one of our thieves was Benjie who sat next to Judy in her third grade class. He was the fourth kid in a family whose mom taught her children how to enter homes through small windows and transoms, collect the stuff, and bring it to her fencing operation for resale. We were robbed four times, three of which occurred when we were away for the summer. But the scariest one happened when we were all at home and fast asleep. The robber broke into the house, climbed the stairs and walked into Andy's room. Andy was asleep, his clothes on the chair next to the bed. When he awoke the next morning his wallet had been removed from his pants and was lying on the chair, emptied of whatever money it had contained. Bud and I were at breakfast when Andy, noticing the empty wallet, shouted the news. We scouted the house and sure enough small appliances and a bike were gone from the ground floor. Andy was shaken. Years later Steve met a guy who, when he found out where Steve had lived, confessed to being the owner of Steve's bike that he had stolen in that robbery.

In the winter of 1969 I was at home watching the snow falling hard and fast. Just as I was wishing that someone would ring my doorbell, offering to clean our walk, that scenario was happening at a doorway on Drexel Road, just around the corner from our house. When that neighbor answered the door she was confronted by a man, carrying a shovel, who forced his way into her home, tied her up, raped her, and killed her elderly father who was in a bedroom upstairs. I found out about it from ten-year old Judy who was walking home on Drexel Road from the neighborhood public school, wondering why the street she was on was filled with police cars and yellow "Crime Scene" tapes. The following weekend Bud, Andy, Steve, Daniel (Steve's friend who was living with us for a few months) and I watched a performance of *Little Murders,* a play by Jules Feiffer that was previewing in Philadelphia. A dark comedy set in crime-ridden New York City, with shoot-outs in the streets and triple locks on the apartment doors, it was both real and absurd. I was laughing and crying at the same time, denying that this could be the new urban life-style, but agreeing that Feiffer was describing a phenomenon that was on its way, if not already here.

In the fall of 1972, *The Philadelphia Inquirer* ran a story about a middle-aged white woman who was stabbed to death, as she was about to enter her home about five blocks away from our house. In the next few weeks several other middle aged white women in our neighborhood were attacked, none killed, but all badly frightened and a few severely wounded, slashed by a knife. One of these women, the elderly baby-sitter who worked for our neighbors, the Prockops, was attacked and slashed on the sidewalk next to our driveway. We had heard the story the night it happened. The woman was in good condition but had immediately told her employers that she would never return to them. And that evening, when Bud and I went to see if they were okay, the family had already decided to sell their house and move to the suburbs.

"Don't you think you should move out of here too?" Leon asked.

"No," I replied, feeling that I had to defend my principles, and smarting at what I considered their impetuous decision. "All of these stabbings are obviously the work of one crazy person. It could happen anywhere." Bud and I both refused to consider the option. We preferred at that time to stand firm and stay with the Amsterdams, the Hendlers, the Hurtigs, and the Stones, all friends who had also chosen Wynnefield because it was an integrated community. We preferred to work with the Residents' Association to tighten up security and not to give up our affordable, landmark house in a neighborhood that was within the city limits.

The Sunday after the driveway stabbing, a man emerged from a patrol car and walked to our property, checking the spot where the woman was attacked. We were sitting in our backyard as he approached.

"I'm Detective Williams," he said as he pulled his wallet from his pocket and opened it to show his badge and handed us his card. "Can I talk to you?"

"Of course," said Bud. "Come sit down." And he called Steve and Judy to join us.

"I want you to be very careful," he said, pointing his finger as he spoke. "There's a potential killer in this neighborhood. So far all of his victims are elderly white women." As he said this, the cop looked straight at me. I was in my forties, but I guess I could qualify. "I want you to pay attention to who you see walking in the street and call me immediately if you see someone who fits this description: 'light brown skin, modified Afro hair, anywhere from 16 to 25 years old, medium height, blue sneakers, chinos, and a green wind breaker.' If you see someone like that, call the number on my card. Be careful. He's dangerous."

When he left, we all looked a bit shaken. I was glad that the potential killer was not attacking children. And the women who were his victims had so far been a good twenty years older than me. Steve and Judy went back to their homework, not saying a word.

The next day Stevie was playing in the backyard. I had the door open and from the kitchen and I saw a figure running through the yard. His hair was a modified Afro, he was wearing blue sneakers, chinos and a green jacket.

"Steve," I shouted, "Did you see that guy?"

And he replied impatiently, "Oh Mom, that was Freddy Bowers, the kid who lives two houses down."

I was nervous. Was it really Freddy, Steve's classmate from junior high, or were Steve and I witnessing the stabber. I thought about it for a while and then, to ease my anxiety, I decided to call Freddy to see if it really had been he and I did so.

"Is this Freddy Bowers?" I asked the voice on the other end of the phone,

"Yeah," he said.

"Freddy, this is Mrs. Rowland, Steve's Mom. Did you run through our backyard about an hour ago?"

"No-oh," he replied, which told me yes.

"Freddy," I said, "I don't mind if you use our yard as a shortcut, but you know we are all so jittery these days about the stabbings. I would like it if you would just yell out to me, 'it's only me, Freddy, Mrs. Rowland' when you do that. OK?"

"I guess so," he answered.

The next morning Freddy was arrested; someone else had spotted him. He was jailed, but soon freed on bail. Freddy Bowers was the son of a popular minister who reigned over a huge Baptist parish in West Philadelphia. The congregants raised the $25,000 to get him out. After several more incidents, which happened while he was out on bail, Freddy was tried in a Philadelphia court. His lawyer, the most expensive defense attorney in the city argued that, among other things, Freddy Bowers was born under Capricorn, the same sign as Martin Luther King, Jr. An almost all-black jury acquitted him. The Bowers family fled to Willingboro, New Jersey just as soon as Freddy was freed. Ironically, at least two of the Wynnefield families who had felt threatened by Freddy had already escaped to that part of New Jersey. A few years later Freddy was tried in New Jersey for new crimes, this time sexual assaults on middle-aged white women, and he was convicted and sent to prison for 54-72 years.

*The trials and ultimate conviction of Freddy Bowers was reported in Philadelphia Magazine, February 1980. The investigator for the Prosecutor's Office in Burlington County, New Jersey searched for the motive behind Freddy's attacks on middle-aged white women with graying hair. After talking with a psychiatrist, she concluded that the assailant might be "paying the women back for some unnamed, distant wrong, real or imagined, that the assailant had suffered at the hands of an older grey-haired woman. Reading this I wondered if perhaps Freddy was one of the children who was classified as a "dead-head" by a middle-aged white teacher in Gompers elementary School—his neighborhood school.*

# HOW ONE SUMMER ENDED

The last days of August in Woods Hole were especially precious, despite the jellyfish that arrive only when the sea has warmed up, despite the earlier sunsets, and even despite the end of science school and the absence of a schedule for the kids. We had spent the entire summer there and we should have been ready to get back to real life in the city, but this never happened. Instead we swam, we barbecued, we played tennis; we visited our friends with the same enthusiasm as we had shown in the beginning of July. We clung to the last days.

So, when the telephone rang on the Wednesday before Labor Day in 1968, and it was Bud calling, I was about to ask him if we could leave for our trip home the following Sunday, an hour later than planned, so that I could have my morning swim at Nobska Beach. One last swim would be so nice.

"Esther," he said, in a serious voice, "I am calling to tell you that the Trojaborgs have arrived in Philadelphia, from Copenhagen, all six of them, and they are staying with us. I am calling to ask you to come home tomorrow."

"But tomorrow is Thursday. Do you mean that you are not coming up this weekend? You are not going to help us pack and load the car?"

"Look, Doll," Bud replied. " I never ask you for big favors. But if you were here, it would be so much nicer for them and for me. You could help them find a place to live. You could help with the school arrangements, with the food shopping, with showing Ruth where the markets are."

"But what about the packing?" I asked.

"Let me talk to Stevie. He's old enough to help. And I'll speak to Andy this evening when he finishes work."

"Well, I guess you really mean it. I'll get Stevie. Andy can help pack but lucky Andy is committed to working at the drug store until Sunday.

He'll have to get a train ticket." I shouted to Steve to come to the phone and went to find Judy to break the bad news.

All the kids helped with the packing and I found myself throwing Bud's stuff into a duffle bag. We managed to fit everything into the Dodge station wagon, leaving just enough room for Stevie and me in the front seats and Judy and the dog in the back. Off we went early the next morning. It was a hot sunny day, even more reason to resent the shortening of our time up there, but once packed, there was no alternative. We had already made plans to drive as far as New Rochelle, where my brother and his family lived and where we would spend the night, to break up the long trek to Philadelphia. My mother would be there and the children were looking forward to seeing her and seeing their cousins. We stopped for gas after about three hours of riding and I vaguely remember a moment when the tires of our car scraped a curb, but nothing seemed to be amiss and we continued the trip.

As we passed the sign for Mamaroneck, a suburb just north of New Rochelle, riding in the center lane, I turned my wheel slightly to keep the car adjusted to the road. To my shock nothing seemed connected. The car wheels did not respond to the steering wheel. I braked as hard as I could and the car took off on its own course, veering to the left in an almost right angle, hitting the guard rail, bumping off the guard rail, turning itself around completely and coming to a full stop back in the center lane facing in the opposite direction. As soon as I realized that I was no longer driving this vehicle I moaned "Oh God" over and over and ducked my head. I later learned that Stevie, and Judy in the back seat, on the other hand, kept their eyes wide open in horror as we veered left and then bounced and then did the full circle. Steve couldn't believe that I took my hands off the wheel and ducked. He was stunned. It was lucky that we hit no other car. They were well spaced and apparently driving slowly enough to escape the path of my out-of-control wagon. Those behind me had been able to stop. The driver of the car directly behind me got out to see if we were okay and took the opportunity to compliment me on my expert driving. He was serious. He thought I had guided us the whole way, and got us back to the center lane so that others could pass left and right. That I was facing in the wrong direction did not count.

Within minutes, the police arrived. They stopped all traffic so we could get to safety. I told Judy to put the leash on the dog, and get out immediately despite her whining that she had been tossed about. She wasn't bleeding and I refused to hear any complaints. We were to abandon the car, march across the highway to the shoulder where the police car awaited us. I was in full control and, at that moment, in full denial that anything unusual had happened. The police had called the tow truck; the car would be taken to a repair shop where we were to meet it. At the shop I called my brother and told him what happened. He said, "I'll be right there." And within minutes he arrived in his car. We packed our belongings into Jack's car and he delivered us, and all of our stuff, to his home in New Rochelle where my mother rushed to greet us. "Are you sure you're all, all right?" she asked. She hugged Judy and examined her arm and her shoulder for possible bruises. My sister-in-law, as sympathetic as she tried to be, was preoccupied with her own troubles, her thirteen year old son Danny was to have surgery the next day for Crohn's disease, a development that no one had told us about until we got there. I telephoned Bud immediately and assured him that we were not hurt and promised to call again later when we knew the fate of the car. Within the hour the phone rang. It was the mechanic telling us that the car was not fixable and I called Bud:

"Well the car is gone. The garage guys just called to say that fixing it would cost more than it was worth, so I told them to junk it." It was an old car that was ready for a trade-in.

"That sounds right," Bud replied. "But how are you going to get home? If I came to get you, we couldn't fit into the Fiat. So, I'd have to rent a car. I have service rounds in the morning and a patient at noon, so I wouldn't be able to get to you until late tomorrow afternoon."

"I guess we should look into the rental from here," I answered.

"Are you sure you are up to it?" Bud asked

"Well I guess I'll be rested by the morning," I said in an uncertain voice. "And I'll ask Jack for the name of a local service. He's taking Danny to the hospital, so he's not going to work tomorrow. And he will help me load up. All our things are here in his house."

"Great!" said Bud, "I'll try to get home early enough to help you unload."

So there I was, playing the game that nothing bad had happened because nothing bad had happened. Nothing except the possibility that we all could have been killed or badly hurt or one of us could have been killed and the others badly hurt. My husband was relieved to find that we were unhurt; the car was of no importance. And we were all busy on the phone with the rental company and the mechanics, figuring out how to get home and not interfere with Danny's trip to the hospital in New York. Only my mother was able to grasp the horror of the accident. She patted me and kept asking if I was okay.

We made it back to Philadelphia the following afternoon. The Trojaborgs greeted us with many hugs. I learned that they had volunteered to come fetch us, but Bud had refused the offer. He always hated to ask "outsiders" to help. He believed me that I was going to be rested and ready for the last hundred or so miles. And, recalling the old wives tale about getting right back on the horse after the fall, I got behind the wheel of the rental. But when we arrived and I heard about their offer, I wished that Bud had let them come for us. Or, even better, that he had come himself.

Two weeks after the accident, I received a bill in the mail from the State of New York, Department of Highways, charging me for the damage to the guardrail. I paid the bill and believed that I had gotten away cheap. I never learned for sure what caused the accident. When the car was in the repair shop, I was told that all the tires were flat. The heat and the heavy load could have been the cause. Or perhaps it was damage I had done to the tires by jumping the curb in the gas station. But a few years after it happened, I read that the Chrysler Company was looking into complaints that, in some of their cars, the steering mechanism had inexplicably separated from the wheels.

# ON BEING A DOCTOR'S WIFE

Philadelphia was, in the early seventies, an "eat–in" city, which is to say that people gathered for dinner in each other's houses, and social life was primarily home centered. The University of Pennsylvania School of Medicine faculty members and their wives were constantly giving dinner parties, and Bud and I were often invited.

One Saturday evening we were guests of the Chairman of the Obstetrics and Gynecology Department and his wife, Elaine. I was chatting with her and with Jane, the wife of the Chairman of Biochemistry, when Elaine turned to Jane and said, "Let's ask Esther to join us on the Mrs. Club panel."

"What a great idea," replied Jane, as she reached for the peanuts in the small silver bowl. "Esther, Elaine and I, and one other faculty wife, have been asked to talk to the wives of the medical students. Can you join us?"

"What are you going to talk about and when and where?" I asked.

"The subject is: 'What Is It Like To Be a Doctor's Wife?' They call themselves 'The Mrs. Club' and they meet on the campus. The panel will take place early next month." And as she offered me the peanut bowl, she added, "They'll be *thrilled* to have the new Neurology Chairman's wife join us. Will you come?"

"Sounds good," I replied. Even though I shook my head in disbelief when I heard the name of the sponsor and the title of the talk, I was flattered by the invitation. "I'd love to."

Jane replied, "I'll be sure they send you an invitation with the exact time and room number."

I received the invitation a few days later, replied that I was flattered by the invitation to join the panel, and I noted the time and date on my calendar. As the time for the event approached, I decided to think about what I should say. All I could think of was what was I doing on the panel? What kind of subject was this?

The meeting was held in the late afternoon in a small auditorium in the medical school. We helped ourselves to tea and cookies and at 2:00 PM the moderator, a young blond woman, wearing a cashmere sweater and a matching pleated skirt, stockings and heels, and a touch of cherry lipstick on her mouth, called the group to order and introduced each of us, as we sat in a row at the oblong table in the front of the room. The first speaker was Elaine, M.D. PhD, a woman in her mid-forties, with straight black hair and dark eyes, wearing a well-tailored suit. She adjusted the mike, cleared her throat, and said, "I am Elaine, the wife of the Chairman of Obstetrics. It is a pleasure to be here." Then, using the Heloise model (Heloise was the famous columnist of the time who specialized in gimmicks for housewives to use to make things work), Elaine immediately won over her audience with tales of cooking second dinners for the doctor who comes home way too late to sit down to eat with the kids. "The solution?" she asked. "It's simple; just buy a stove that comes with a hot plate that can be used to keep the doctor's food warm." Ingenious Elaine was spared from cooking twice, and Dr. Luigi, her husband, could come home, whenever he got there, to a nice warm meal. "Best of all," she continued, "before he comes home, you can get all your pots washed, put the kids plates in the dishwasher, get the kitchen squeaky clean, and have the choice of eating with the children, or the warm-ups with the Doc--- or both." Everyone laughed. The eager audience of soon-to-be doctors' wives wrote little memos to themselves about this miraculous stove that one day, not too far away, they too would be able to afford. Encouraged by the success of her first tip, Elaine went on to describe the second problem endemic to doctor's families: the kids answering the phone! Racing for the phone, answering it with a slurred "Hullo" and then screaming; "Mom, it's for Dad," had happened once too often in Elaine and Luigi's house. No more of this would be tolerated. The children were taught that they could never answer the phone without saying, "This is Doctor M's residence. May I help you?"

The second speaker was Jane, M.D. still laughing at what Elaine had to say. Jane, who was taller and slimmer than Elaine, had reddish hair and spoke in a high-pitched voice. She sounded scattered and tired. She described her life of packing and moving, something she had done

216

four times already and was certain to do even again. Howard, her husband, could never decide which medical specialty was right for him. He first chose research and they moved to New York; he later chose surgery and they moved to Wisconsin; then biochemistry and they moved to Philadelphia. By now there were four children, each of whom had to be accommodated in the move--new housing, new friends, new schools, new pediatricians, new piano teachers, new Little Leagues, and on and on. Jane didn't say much about herself and her own needs in all of this, she just was the real estate agent, scout, packer, mover, facilitator, and glue that held the family together. The audience took turns gasping in disbelief, and laughing at the droll way in which Jane unfolded her story.

Next came me. Unlike Elaine and Jane, my talk was not going to be modeled after a sit-com that depicted the idealized suburban family, but it was clear that the sit-com mood had permeated the atmosphere. Given the informality of the occasion, I tucked away my prepared speech.

I started by asking the question: "What kind of subject is this? Who among us wants to be known as a doctor's wife rather than the person she is? I have an 'all but the dissertation' degree at Columbia. I have taught Political Science at City College, at Mt. Holyoke College, and at Drexel. When I married and had my three children, I assumed that to fulfill my obligation to my husband's career and my children's well-being, I had to postpone my own career and stay at home."

I paused for a moment, hoping my audience was catching on. But there was no head-nodding yet.

I continued: "But one day I attended a lecture by Anne Eaton, a woman economist, who described the economic exigencies of the post-war world. She said, 'the first obligation was to provide jobs for all the returned soldiers and sailors. The next was to convert war industry into peacetime manufacturing. To do these two things, it was necessary to keep women out of the work force, and to convince them that it was their job to care for the home, and children, and to buy the stuff.' I was shocked. Was it true that women had to stay at home for these reasons? Don't we have a say in the matter? Can't we be wives and mothers and also have careers of our own? I am asking you to think about yourselves as women of great potential at the same time as you think about being a doctor's wife."

There was polite applause as I sat down, not nearly as much as there had been for Jane and Elaine. But at that moment I did not care. I was anxious to get to the question period.

The final speaker was Mrs. Sylvan, the wife of a much beloved and highly acclaimed medical practitioner who had a huge private practice. Mrs. Sylvan, who was ten years older than Elaine, Jane and me, was wearing a beige suit and gold jewelry that matched her teased hair. She described her charity work, her volunteer work, and how she helped with the billing in her husband's office. She was pleased with how she had arranged her life to be fulfilling to herself and, at the same time, to be the best possible helpmeet to Dr. Sylvan.

When the question period came, there were none for me. The first question had to do with ordering stationery; the members of the Mrs. Club were caught in the early seventies dilemma of husbands and wives names and needed to be reassured that one always uses Dr. and Mrs. His first name, His middle initial, His last name. Mrs. Sylvan answered that one and the rest of us had nothing to add. There was the inevitable question to Elaine about her stove and where it could be purchased. Finally, the blond president closed the meeting by announcing, "Remember to bring your recipes for the Mrs. Club cookbook, which is almost ready to go to press."

I returned home that night feeling angry, humiliated, and surprised that I was speaking a different language to an audience that I had thought would have embraced my ideas. These were young women in their twenties. It was 1971. How could they not see that the time was arriving for women to be major players, not just shadows of their husbands?

A few weeks later, the phone rang:

"Mrs. Rowland?" "Yes," I answered.

"Mrs. Rowland this is Guil Dudley, I am Dean of Students at Penn. I am calling to ask you if you would be interested in taking a shared job as one of two pre-med advisors in the undergraduate school."

"Well," I replied, "I'm really flattered that you ask. But you must know that I don't know anything about pre-med advising." As soon as the words came out I realized that I was still apologizing for myself. So I hastened to add, "But I have worked with undergraduates and I know many people on the faculty of many medical schools."

"Don't worry about that," Dean Dudley went on. "You can learn what you need to know very quickly. Can you come to my office tomorrow and we'll talk about it. Libby Rose thinks you might be perfect for the job."

Dr. Libby Rose, the faculty advisor of the Mrs. Club was a close friend of Dean Dudley. She had been in the audience at the Doctor's Wife panel and heard my talk, which luckily also included my resumé. My new career was about to begin.

# JULIA

I arrived for work on a January day in 1972. The Dean's office was bustling with students, most of whom were just a bit older than my oldest son Andy. Like him, they wore their hair long; their clothes were rumpled Army-Navy-store bell-bottoms and shirts. Most of the girls had long straight hair and were dressed like the boys.

As I entered the office, the Dean, Guilford Dudley the Third, a sandy-haired, tall and slim man in his early fifties whom everyone called Gil, greeted me with a friendly, welcoming smile. He had already assured me that I would learn all about medical school admissions fast enough from the pre-med secretary who had been there for years and knew everything. This turned out to be true. Reba Aronoff, a white-haired woman in her sixties, was very willing to help me learn the ropes. She loved mothering the students by making small talk, reminding them about deadlines, and telling them to get enough sleep. She knew a lot about medical school admissions. She typed and mailed their recommendation letters, listened to the stories about their interviews, cheered when they got in, and groaned when they were not accepted.

On the day I met Reba, she introduced me to Julia Chase with whom I was sharing the new job. Together we were to oversee the students who were interested in becoming health professionals: doctors mostly, but some vets and dentists, and an occasional optometrist or podiatrist. Julia had arrived on the scene a day or two before me. Together, we were replacing the former health professions advisor, an elderly professor of clinical psychology. Unfortunately, he believed that all good doctors should be white men. But the culture of the seventies didn't allow for that. So he was persuaded to resign and Gil, a dean who knew which way the wind was blowing, decided to split the job, and to hire two women.

Julia had come to Penn as a post-doc in Biology, but with limited funding. The Biology Department had asked the Dean's office to take her on halftime until a full faculty position opened up. To fill the other half of Julia's job in the dean's office, Gil hired me.

Julia was 30 at that time, sixteen years my junior. She had long black hair, sparkling brown eyes, and a low-pitched, sonorous voice. "I've never done this before" she said, "but it should be great fun, don't you think?" She chuckled as she shook my hand hello. I was worried stiff that I would not be able to handle a job I knew nothing about, and she was laughing.

Julia had grown up in Groton, Connecticut, a girl with five brothers in a large Catholic family of formerly landed gentry. She was a passionate long-distance runner who, as a college student, had trained for the Olympics. Her education, at Smith, and then graduate school at Indiana, was supported by scholarships and part-time jobs. The day I met her at Penn she was dressed like the students, in pants and sneakers, ready for a biology field trip, or to hop on her bike, her chosen means of transport.

I liked her right away. And I think she liked me but I knew she had her doubts. After all, I was dressed in a silk blouse, a wool suit, nylon stockings, and leather shoes, all signs of the "establishment." In addition, I was a forty-five-year-old woman with a husband who was the Chairman of Neurology in the medical school, in a culture that did not trust anyone who was older than thirty and had its doubts about the hierarchical nature of academic departments.

So there we were, Julia and I, on that first day. Neither of us knew anything about pre-med advising. Reba showed us our office, explained the system, and what we were supposed to do on a day-to-day basis: seeing students by appointment, helping them with their programs, and later with their applications. Julia and I talked about our schedules and how we could share the responsibilities. Reba suggested that we call Dr. John Hadley, the internist in the medical school that Gil had hired to be our consultant. I was relieved when I heard that we were to have an expert to rely on. Reba dialed, using her pencil to touch the raised keys of the telephone. "Dr. Hadley? This is Reba Aronoff. I am calling from the pre-med office in the undergraduate school. We have the two new advisors here that Dean Dudley spoke to you about, Mrs. Esther Rowland and Dr. Julia Chase."

Turning to us, Reba smiled and said, "He said, 'Send them over, if they can come right now. I know all about Mrs. Rowland's husband and I will be happy to meet her.'"

John Hadley Jr., wearing his long white coat, had thinning red hair and a face splotched with fading freckles. As Julia and I entered his carpeted office, he rose from his desk chair and greeted us with a handshake across the table. "I'm so sorry that my regular nurse-assistant is out today." He then dialed to call the floor nurse to bring coffee for us, something she finally did ten minutes later, with a look of disdain on her face as she banged the tray onto his desk. As soon as she left, he shook his head from side to side and said: "I apologize for the nursing staff. They no longer take pride in their work."

Our interview with Hadley, Jr. was mercifully short and we accomplished little but an exchange of general schedules and phone numbers. I told him that we would call him if and when problems arose, and he seemed pleased with that. As he escorted us to the elevator, he pointed to Julia's sneakers and with a contemptuous look said: "Young lady, the next time you come I hope you will be wearing shoes. You are a professional and you must dress more suitably." As soon as the elevator door closed, Julia looking humiliated, angrily grumbled, "On my take-home pay, I can't afford a pair of fancy shoes." I interrupted her saying, "You know, he's the kind of guy my kids would call an MCP (Male Chauvinist Pig)." Hearing this coming from me, Julia, laughed out loud, vigorously nodding her head. I could see that she had decided right then to trust me.

The idea of sharing a job was beginning to take hold in the seventies. We improvised as we worked, sharing the large number of advisees (half to Julia and half to me) and learning together. Because we were in the office on different days, we communicated by notebook in which we recorded what each of us had learned that day and what each of us had done.

The notebook started out in a formal way. Julia would write: "What are the chances for out-of-state residents to get into our medical school?" I would answer: "It's not a state school but they may give preferences to state residents. I will call Tommy Thompson, a neurologist friend who is also Dean of Students at the medical school. I'll let you know as soon as I get the answer."

But soon we were swapping stories.

I wrote, "Can you believe that John Morris, the kid I told you about who got the D in Organic Chem at Northwestern summer school, refuses to apply to Chicago Med because he's sure his Dad's influence in Chicago will get him into a better school?"

And Julia would write: "Amy Adams, the pre-vet from Kansas, just got a summer job scooping poop at a race track. I really like the pre-vets more than the pre-meds. They are laid-back, even though it's harder to get into Vet School than Med School."

When Julia was not in our office as a pre-med advisor, she was either doing her four-mile runs or pursuing her research as a social-biologist. As a college student at Smith she had joined the track team in her freshman year and tried to break into an all-male road race in Manchester, Connecticut. Turned away in 1960, she tried again in 1961, after running in a seven-mile race in Massachusetts that had generated a huge write-up in the Boston papers. Manchester, thanks to Julia, made history in 1961 by opening the competition to women as well as men.

Julia in Manchester, CT Road Race, 1961

Julia was also a volunteer researcher at the Philadelphia Zoo. Knowing that she would be there, one lunch hour I drove to Fairmount Park, just ten minutes from our office, to the Monkey House. There was Julia, seated outside a large cage. She was observing the gorillas as they played with each other, watching and recording in her note pad every gesture and grimace. On alternate days she would go to a nursery school and do exactly the same thing with the three-year olds.

What a team we were. She was the one whom the students could relate to at first sight, and I was the one with the medical school connections. After a year in the pre-med office, Julia was able to return to the Biology Department as a fully funded researcher. I became the Chief pre-med advisor, working four days a week. To replace Julia I hired another woman, Dr. Jane Rasmussen, who had been a co-panelist at the Mrs. Club, the one who had an MD degree but was spending all of her time settling and resettling her family as her husband searched for his career. Jane loved being back at work. Things were going well for me, but less so for my children.

# THE CLASH OF CULTURES—
# PHILADELPHIA IN THE 1970S

I remember, as a graduate student in the fifties, reading about the huge numbers of radical students in France, in Italy, in South America, who were self-proclaimed Marxists and who were protected in their radicalism by a well established protocol in those countries that the civil government was separate from the university and had no business there. The students were militant, organized, and seemed to know and care more about politics than their counterparts in our country. I wished that North American students were more like the ones in Europe and in Latin America. Why were ours so conservative? At the time there seemed to be no answer, but a decade later the campuses in the United States were rumbling. We were at the beginning of a student rebellion that changed, or at least at the time appeared to change, so much in our country. The movement towards change started with civil rights and added the struggle for peace, for women's rights, and the right to acknowledge one's sexual orientation. It resulted in changes in the dress code and hairstyles, in attitudes about work, the environment, child rearing, and marriage. It questioned the values of the previous generation. I was thrilled to be a part of this, even though, by that time, I was already out of school, in my forties, and considered to be a member of the older generation. It was a genuine cultural revolution, the kind that Antonio Gramsci, the Italian Marxist-humanist, might have dreamed of as he sought the way to bring about revolutionary change by consensus.

Studying to be a doctor or a lawyer was a painful choice for some of the most militant college students, and could only be justified if it could be used to help the poor. And even that might be regarded as "elitist." My son, Andy, decided that were he to go into medicine, he should become a nurse. Bud thought that was a crazy idea. But he also knew that Andy was not alone; one of the most promising medical students at Penn that year had already quit medical school for the same reason. Many students chose to live in communes, sharing all the household chores and expenses. We knew Josh and Eva, a married couple in Philadelphia, who decided to live in two separate communes so that each of them could experience collective life in much the same way as the singles were experiencing it, rather than being a small family unit within a large one.

Even the University accommodated the students of the new culture. At Penn there was a section of the career service office that was devoted solely to non-conventional jobs, such as teaching in alternative schools, or working as community organizers, overseas in the Peace Corps or at home in Vista, the domestic Peace Corps. Penn offered new curricula opportunities such as the one Andy chose that combined his studies with practical experience in the community. The faculty and administrators were listening to the groundswell and responding sympathetically.

So it was with some surprise that I found my second son, Steve, arriving home from Overbrook High School in the winter of 1971, announcing that he had been suspended for wearing his hat, an Irish herringbone Jeff cap, inside the school building. He had put it on at his locker at the end of the day and was about to exit, when he was stopped and sent to the disciplinarian. The only way for him to be allowed back in class was to have a parent come to the school and speak to the vice-principal. I could not believe that Steve had told me the whole story, although I trusted him implicitly. He was an honest and straightforward kid. But suspension for wearing a hat between the hall and the front door was beyond my comprehension.

The next day I went to see the vice-principal, an African-American man in his fifties, who confirmed the reason for Steve's suspension. "Yes, he wore his hat inside the building and that is against the rules." My eyes widened as he continued, "Wearing hats indoors is a sign of disrespect. If we allow our children to be disrespectful, to have no manners, to break the rules, we all will be in deep trouble."

I replied: "Don't you see what is going on in the society? Don't you realize that, due to the influence of the Muslims like Malcolm X, who have become powerful role models in the black community, African-American children are wearing caps all day, indoors and out. It gives those kids a sense of self-respect!"

"Yes" he responded, "Most of the students do wear hats, and I spend most of my day suspending them."

I stared at him to make sure he wasn't pulling my leg.

"Where I work, at Penn, the dress code was dropped by the administration, in response to the students who considered that the way they dress is a personal choice."

His immediate response to that statement was a shrug of despair.

"You people in the universities ought to know better. We are trying to raise children to respect their parents, to respect their Church, and to show that respect by dressing properly."

I asked to speak to the principal. Judging from his name, I thought that he was Jewish and therefore maybe a liberal. He would surely understand what I was talking about. The vice-principal made a telephone call to accommodate my request. Hanging up the phone, he walked to the door that separated his office from the principal's. "You can go in now. And Steve can come back to school if he does not wear his hat indoors."

When I entered the principal's office I saw that the door I had walked through was the only door in the room. The principal was in hiding! Later I found out from Steve that on the day of his suspension, he had gone to his locker, put on his coat and hat, and started walking to the exit door when a strange man appeared and pointed his finger to his head but said nothing. Steve was not aware his hat was on and did not understand why the man was pointing to his head but not speaking. He responded by pointing his own finger to his own head in a mimicking gesture. The strange man then grabbed Steve by the arm and escorted him to the vice-principal's office. And then came the suspension. Unbeknownst to Steve, the man was the principal himself.

After introducing myself and reporting on the conversation with the vice-principal I asked him: "Don't you understand that wearing hats indoors is, for Muslims, as important as it is for Jews?"

"Look," he replied, "we have a system of rules and a commitment to discipline here. I completely support my vice-principal on these matters." And then he began to shuffle papers on his desk and looked at me after a minute and said, "I believe the meeting is over." With that he rose from his chair and waved me to the door. "Goodbye." That was that.

*Much later, after telling this story to African-American friends who taught in the public schools, I realized that in the vice-principal's view, I was a privileged white woman who grew up without understanding the importance of good manners, discipline, and respect. He regarded me as someone who was abetting chaos. I saw him as a rigid person who chose to perpetuate blind obedience to the rules over encouraging the creative empowerment of the new generation. Could we both be mistaken?*

# THE STRUGGLE FOR PEACE:
# PHILADELPHIA, 1967-73

As we stepped into the sunlight that surrounded Union Station, our little family group had no trouble finding the way to the National Mall where the great Moratorium was to be held. We--Bud, Steve, Steve's friend Daniel, Judy, and I-- just followed the thousands of people who were walking, carrying signs that said "Stop The Nixon Murders," "Protest Is Patriotic," "Bring Back Our Troops," and "War Is Not Healthy For Children And Other Living Things." It was a glorious warm day, November 15, 1969. One of the biggest anti-war demonstrations ever held was this one in Washington, D.C. where we gathered alongside of hundreds of thousands of others to hear speeches and to sing songs and to show President Nixon and Congress how many of us there were. As we wound our way to the mall, feeling proud to be part of the massive march, I was stunned to see soldiers on top of each building we passed. There always were cops on horseback in the demonstrations I had been part of for years and years, but soldiers, with rifles that were leaning on stands in short grabbing distance, was a new sight. Were they planning to shoot us?

The rally was in full swing as we found a place for ourselves on the grass. And there was Jay Shulman, the sociologist who used to be a truck driver and still looked like one, with his huge body and enormous hands. He was an old friend from graduate school at Columbia. "Wow, what a stroke of luck to see you after all these years." I said, grabbing his outstretched hand. And with Jay there were other New York friends—a reunion we could never have planned. But it seemed natural, almost inevitable, that we would meet old pals with whom we shared our anti-war sentiments. Half the people in the United States opposed the war in 1969. The speeches were simple and short and all the speakers were saying pretty much the same thing. "Stop the killing; stop the lies; end the war now." Pete Seeger introduced a new song, written by John Lennon and sung in public for the first time. "All We Are Saying Is Give Peace A Chance." And as we left the rally, thousands of people were singing and swaying, hands held high: "All we are saying is give peace a chance."

All We Are Saying is Give Peace a Chance
https://www.youtube.com/watch?v=rhyiqGIJQus

We hugged goodbye to our New York friends and went our separate ways. As Bud, Judy and I walked back to Union Station to meet the boys and to return to Philadelphia, the soldiers were still atop the buildings and the police were on horses, patrolling the streets with Billy clubs clutched in their hands. No one could step off the curb. We were confined to the sidewalk, in rows of about 10 abreast, inching our way, like cattle being herded. We arrived at the station, which was already tightly packed with hundreds of travelers, and awaited the train, which was delayed. We walked toward the waiting area when all of a sudden I felt my eyes burning and my throat tightening. A cloud of smoke sent everyone running and screaming in a panic. Bud and I were on either side of ten-year-old Judy, each holding one of her hands, when a swarm of people, trying to escape the tear gas, forced us to let go of each other. "Judy, Judy, Bud. Where are you?" I kept shouting, as I tried to get my bearings. The fog was so dense that people were bumping into one another. I was frantic, shoving through the crowd until I saw them in the distance. I was crying tears of relief that we had found each other, and tears from the gas that was burning my eyes. The boys met us at the track, and we boarded a train, so crowded that we all had to stand for the two-hour ride to Philadelphia. Smarting from tear gas and dying to sit down with Judy on my lap, instead of standing with one hand on the back of a seat and the other holding her hand tight, I yelled at the conductor: "How come you charge the same price for those who have seats and those of us who are standing!"

"It's not a reserved seat train. If it was, you probably would still be standing in Union Station. Count your blessings." I shut up.

Ever since we had moved to Philadelphia in 1967, our day-to-day lives were permeated by momentous events. Watching the news each evening, we became accustomed to, but still never lost our sense of outrage at the persistent reports and pictures of catastrophes: the assassination of Martin Luther King, the assassination of Robert Kennedy two months later, and the chaotic street battles outside of the Democratic Convention in Chicago, where the police were beating up and tear-gassing the anti-war demonstrators. Night after night the TV cameras showed us the bloodied heads of the demonstrators in the United States and the bloodied and blackened children in Vietnam, running from napalm being sprayed on them by our troops, their flesh torn from their bodies and hanging loose. We saw American soldiers torching the grass roofs of houses in the villages, and the peasants, ablaze and screaming, as they tried to escape their homes. The Tet offensive, by the North Vietnamese army in January of 1968, was graphically portrayed on camera. Although the United States ultimately won the battle, the ferocity displayed by the enemy contradicted the optimistic reports of easy victory put forward by General Westmoreland and President Johnson.

The mood of the day was to fight back against our leaders who were dragging our country and our conscripted soldiers into an insane war and lying about its progress. A powerful response was developing. We marched. We sang. We shouted. Some sat still while the police herded them into paddy wagons for not moving on. Many, including our two sons, who were teenagers at the time, went to jail for a night or two for civil disobedience. Small victories encouraged us to continue the struggle. When the trustees at the University of Pennsylvania, a normally conservative group of wealthy donors, decided to ban the Department of Defense from using campus labs to conduct experiments in biological and chemical warfare, Bud and I were proud of our university. Known by its code name: "The Spice Rack," this poison gas research program provoked the wrath of students, professors, and Nobel Laureates. The trustees' action in 1967 enhanced Penn's reputation as one of the campuses that recognized the legitimacy of the student anti-war concerns. Philadelphia was a Quaker city; the Quakers were pacifists. (Nevertheless, in 1971, when a group of Penn students tried to take over the administration building, the leaders of the demonstration were threatened with expulsion.)

The Quakers provided the leadership in a small but energetic group of anti-war activists, called Philadelphia Resistance, who were ever on the alert to organize the community to protest the war. Lisa Schiller and Josh

Markel, two twenty-something year olds, were the paid organizers whom we got to know well during those years. Lisa, a small, slim young woman with dark hair and celestial blue eyes, grew up Catholic and was influenced by the growing movement of peace activists within the Catholic Church. She propelled Resistance into day-to-day action that included handing out leaflets, organizing candlelight vigils, and suing the government in the courts. Resistance engaged in every kind of anti-war activity short of violence. Our older son Andy, who helped found the Peace Club at Central High School, had asked Lisa to talk to his group; they became friends and Andy from then on worked with the Quakers. A bit later, another invited speaker at the Peace Club was David Harris, whose wife, Joan Baez, was one of the most prominent folk singers of that era and one of the celebrity peace activists, along with Bob Dylan, and John Lennon. Harris had served time in jail as a draft resister. His talk inspired Andy's stance on the draft, the moral issues involved, and the practical steps he would take against forcing young men to fight an unjust war.

Andy always had a strong interest in world affairs and a passion for social justice. He read the *New York Times* and he was the one kid at our supper table who eagerly participated in the world-news-of-the-day conversations with Bud and me.

Andy reading *New York Times,* circa 1970

Bud and I had been excited when he was accepted to Central High School in Philadelphia, the school that was renowned for its high standards and celebrity alumni: Albert Barnes, Noam Chomsky, Bill Cosby (for one year), William Glackens, Louis Kahn, among many others. Andy was a serious boy who was looking forward to having a challenging academic experience. He also was searching for friends who shared his social and political views. He found some, who joined him in the Peace Club, but there were many others who were disdainful of the longhaired boys who argued for liberal social change, such as the members of the football team and Andy's classmate, Douglas Feith.

Doug and Andy had an ongoing battle with each other during their four years at Central. Andy, at dinner, would often report some outrageous thing that Doug had said in their history class. Doug wrote a column for a Jewish newsletter in Philadelphia and in one of his columns he defended his stand on social issues by quoting from Rabbi Hillel: "If I am not for myself, who will be for me? If not now, when?" He had left out the important middle line: "If I am only for myself, what am I?" In another column he wrote about "Andy, the anti-Semitic Jew," charging that Andy had criticized Israeli occupation policy after winning the 1967 Arab/ Israeli war. Andy responded with a well-written, thoughtful reply, which his English teacher cut out and commented: "Why can't you write your essays this clearly at school? A-."

At the graduation ceremony in 1971, a few weeks after another massive anti-war demonstration in Washington, Doug, who had the highest academic average in the graduating class, devoted his valedictory address to praising President Nixon and the American flag. I wished that Bud and I could have stood up and walked out, but we sat through it, gritting our teeth.

*In 2001, Feith became Assistant Secretary of Defense for Policy under Donald Rumsfeld, advising the Bush administration to declare war on Iraq, and defending the torture of prisoners. Three years later General Tommy Franks, the general in charge of the Iraqi invasion, made Doug infamous by calling him, in his memoir, 'American Soldier', "the dumbest f—ing guy on the planet."*

Our second son, Steve, was less interested in politics than Andy, but was tuned in completely to the fight against racism and against the war in Vietnam. In the late spring of 1971, I answered a ringing phone. "Yes, this is Mrs. Rowland," I replied to a woman's voice.

"Mrs. Rowland, this is Patricia Robinson, I am a lawyer in Washington, working as a volunteer. Your son, Steve has been arrested for disobeying a police order to move off the sidewalk near the White House." I held the phone tighter as I began to sweat.

"But don't worry," she continued, "He's OK. He'll be in jail overnight. I am sure the group will be freed tomorrow and he will be put on a bus to take him home."

"Is there anything we can do? Shall we come down? Is he safe?" I asked.

"No, stay put. He's fine. I'll let you know if anything changes," she said. And she hung up. I held the phone in my hands for a few more minutes, shocked that the arrest actually had happened but not totally surprised. I was relieved to hear that a lawyer was watching out for Steve, and I believed her when she said that she would call again if he were in danger.

Steve did return the next day, safe but shaken. A sixteen year old high school sophomore, he had joined a group of Quakers to march in Washington to protest the continuation of the war. They had gone to Washington the day before and were farmed out to stay with supportive families in the city. The next morning they met at a nearby church. The instructions to Steve were clear: "If and when we are arrested, if anyone is under 18, do not tell the cops your age. Because if you do," the group leader insisted, "you will be separated from the group and sent to a juvenile detention facility. Our strength is that we are all together." Steve knew about juvenile detention centers from Philadelphia; one of them was located just a few blocks away from his junior high school. It was a place filled with warring gang members and was reputed to be more dangerous than even the city adult jail.

The US Park Police, which has jurisdiction over the White House, arrested the protesters for blocking the driveway. After they were booked, they were turned over to the DC Metropolitan District Police to be placed in jail. And this is what happened, according to Steve.

"At the police station, I waited my turn and was then asked my age. I refused to tell them, and raised some suspicion. I knew I was not obligated to tell them anything except my name and address until I was in front of a judge. They put me in a room alone, and the 'good cop' entered.

'Steve, how are you doing?'

'Good'

'Glad there wasn't any trouble at the White House. You people feel pretty passionately about what you are doing, don't you?' he continued.

'Oh, by the way, do you live in Philadelphia?' .

'Yes, you have my address."

'And what's your date of birth?'

'Listen, I already told you that I'm not telling you my age. Why would I tell you my date of birth?'

'I see, well, that's all I wanted to know.'

The cop left."

Steve sat in the room for quite a while and then the "bad" cop arrived, banging the door shut, and in a hurry. He sat down next to Steve and said:

"I want to know how old you are. You better tell me, or you are going to be really sorry… Listen kid, you are going to the adult jail. You got any idea what that is like? Some of those guys haven't seen a woman in years."

Steve didn't reply.

"They would like nothing better than to see a nice, young, pretty boy like you in their cell. You know what those guys are going do to you? Strip you down, bend you over and you'll be taking a big black stick right up your ass! …. You think I'm playing with you? I want to know how old you are!" He was getting very agitated.

"We are all the same age, anything that happens to me, can happen to anyone." said Steve

"No, you are asking for trouble, kid. These guys are going to be so happy to see you. I'm giving you one more chance. Tell me how old you are, or you are going to really regret it."

"I'm not going to get split from my friends and spend the night at the Youth Detention Center. Either way, I might have to fight. And if that's what I have to do, that's what I'll do."

He was scared, but refused to let the cop know that.

"OK, you are a fool. Suit yourself. But, at least see if you can get the driver to stop on the way over there to get you some Vaseline!" And he left.

Steve was returned to his group. The police took them over to the jail in squad cars, just three or four at a time. The others were taken first and he was left in the car by himself for quite a while, wondering who was going to be his cellmate. Finally they took him in, took away his wallet and keys, put them in an envelope with his name on it and led him down a long corridor of cells. The cells were all full, but none of them had demonstrators. Steve began to panic. They got down toward the end of hall, and opened a cell door and told him to enter. Steve looked around and saw that the cell was empty. He was never so glad to be alone.

At his hearing the next day, Steve told the judge his age and was transferred to a juvenile court where the charges were dropped. Soon thereafter he was released to the custody of a public defender, the woman who had telephoned me the night before. She took him to lunch and they were joined by another public defender who told the story of the case he was working on---a 17 year-old angry black kid who was picked up as a passenger in a stolen car. The young man was arguing with the judge and arguing with the guard. His lawyer feared that his client was going to be beaten and thrown into solitary and he even thought he might spend the rest of his life in jail. Steve was put on a bus back to Philadelphia and could not stop thinking about that other teen-ager who, because he was black, was experiencing life so differently.

Steve at 16

In 1972 Andy, then in his first year of college at Penn, was arrested in conjunction with another massive demonstration, this one to protest the renewed bombing of Hanoi. Offered the option of being freed if he paid $200, Andy and about ten others refused, and stayed in jail for two days. (Others in the group paid up and were released immediately.) Ultimately all charges were dropped against the demonstrators because the police had illegally wiretapped the leaders. While he was in jail, Andy watched the guards brutally beat three black teenagers who were also in their custody. This was done on separate occasions, but in Andy's full view. "It was as if they wanted to demonstrate how brutal they could be. It scared the piss out of me and made me hate jails."

# ROWLAND V. TARR: THE LAWSUIT AGAINST THE DRAFT

In his junior year of high school Andy had a serious, practical issue to worry about: was he going to register for the draft the following year, when he turned 18 on May 20, 1971? Andy read *Win Magazine,* which was written by the pacifists, A.J. Muste and Dave McReynolds of the War Resister's League, and had spent much of the preceding year reading about the history of pacifism and non-violent resistance in the writings of Gandhi, Martin Luther King , and Nelson Mandela. He concluded that he was not a pacifist and therefore would not apply for conscientious objector status. Ultimately he started to think more about becoming a draft resister. Working through this dominated his last two years of high school.

Phil Ochs's "I Ain't Marching Anymore" became Andy's favorite album, played so often that we all knew the words. "It's always the old who lead us into war and always the young who fall."

"I Ain't Marching Anymore"
http://www.youtube.com/watch?v=gv1KEF8Uw2k

The draft also dominated the dinner conversations in our household. Each night when we sat down to eat, either Bud or Andy would say something about the draft, and Judy would groan: "Not again! Do we *always* have to talk about politics?"

"Sorry, Judy," Bud would say, "but this is important." We talked about the options. "Why not sign up for the draft and take the college deferment?"

"Not a chance!" shouted Andy.

"Why not sign up and take a chance on getting a high number? And then…"

"Dad, you must be kidding."

"No. If you get a low number, then you can go to Canada. We have lots of friends there who would help you."

"I'm not copping out and escaping to Canada." Andy pushed his chair back from the table.

"So, what's your plan?"

"I will not sign up and when they come after me, I will go to jail."

"Going to jail is the worst option," Bud declared.

"But it's an honest one," Andy replied. "You are **not** running away. You are **standing up for what you believe**, like Eugene Debs did."

"Yes, Andy, but jails are much more dangerous now than they were in Debs's day."

Andy pushed away his plate, left the table and headed for the staircase. "Let's not talk about this anymore tonight. I have a lot of homework."

As Andy thought more about resisting the draft, he thought about suing the government for conducting an illegal war and for deferring college students at the expense of those unable to attend college. Lisa Schiller, one of the organizers for Philadelphia Resistance, helped him think it through and devise a strategy. Lisa and Andy approached two Philadelphia progressive lawyers, Dave Kairys and David Rudovsky, who took antiwar protest cases, but they said they would not be able to raise the money required to develop a case based on the constitutional issues. Andy asked our friend Peter Weiss, a New York attorney connected with the Center for Constitutional Rights, and received the same answer. "Sorry, Andy, we don't have the funding for it."

In 1971, when Andy was about to become 18, a prominent Philadelphia lawyer, Harold Kohn, was seeking a volunteer, a potential draftee, to sue the Selective Service system. Kohn had just won a $29,000,000 settlement in a class-action suit against General Electric for price-fixing. He wanted to use his share of the money to fund a case against the government's use of a conscripted army to fight the war. He thought he might be able to convince the courts that this was involuntary servitude. When Kohn spread the word in the legal community, Lisa, the Resistance activist, flew into action and told Andy about it. Andy recruited his classmate, David Sitman, another seventeen year old who was also heading into the draft pool. Both boys were, with their fathers' permission (since they were still minors), anxious to enter the lawsuit. And thus began the saga of the class action suit, Rowland v. Tarr. (Andrew Rowland et al. vs. Curtis Tarr, the then Director of the Military Selective Service system.)

When Andy entered the kitchen on the evening he returned from the first visit to Harold Kohn's office, we all looked at him as he sat down.

"What happened?" Bud asked. "Will they take the case? How did it go?"

"The good news is that he is interested in taking the case. But the bad news is that he wants to challenge the draft because it deprives people of their private property! Can you believe that? I don't think I like this guy and his politics. He's so corporate." Andy reported. "You should see their office! It's way high in a building downtown, overlooking the whole city. It's huge." And he spread his arms wide.

A few weeks later Lisa introduced Andy to Frank Wagner, a high school student who would not be going to college. Frank was active in the Peace Movement in Kensington, a white, working class section of Philadelphia where he grew up. Andy and Frank set up a time to see Harold Kohn in his office. Andy described the encounter as we sat around the supper table the evening of his second visit to Kohn's office. Andy gestured for us to pass the meat as he told the story. "Frank, with his long hair in a pony tail, and he's wearing overalls, walks in and he rolls his eyes and he says: 'Youse sure have a fancy place here.' It was really funny. And the receptionist and the lawyers looked at him like he came from Mars."

A few weeks later Andy brought Frank home. A tall, blonde, gangly teenager who was one hundred percent working class, Frank charmed us with his astute comments about the social system, all done in a thick Philadelphia accent and using the grammar of the streets. The three of them, Andy, Steve and Frank, became close friends for many years. Frank was vociferously opposed to the war in Vietnam and had joined a collective of community organizers, mostly well-educated radicals from outside the community, who were putting out a revolutionary newsletter in a small building in the middle of Kensington, an all-white neighborhood, and one of the toughest in Philadelphia. The collective was engaged in an ongoing fight, mostly verbal at first, with a group of Vietnam War-supporters who called the collective "Commies." One night when Andy was at the collective, some local "patriots," drunk and frenzied, decided to go after the "Commies." Armed with baseball bats, the marauders systematically broke every window in the building and smashed the windows of all the cars with peace stickers that were parked in front of the building. The police were called multiple times in the hope that they would intervene. This was the time of the notorious police chief Frank Rizzo, the tough cop, who hated civil-rights protesters and anti-war demonstrators, and who once boasted to a reporter: "I am going to make Attilla the Hun look like a faggot." Rizzo targeted the collective as subversive. When the invaders finally succeeded in kicking in the front door, one of the collective members grabbed a shotgun and shouted: "One more step and I will shoot you. Who wants to die first?" The street thugs retreated. The collective disbanded and left the neighborhood the following day. Andy later described the incident as the scariest moment of his life.

When the lawyers realized that the case might go on for years, they asked Andy to recruit two sixteen year olds to join the roster of plaintiffs. Steve and his friend David Freudberg, (*now a prominent public radio producer and host)* were added to represent the class of potential registrants who were two years younger.

As David Weinstein, one of the younger lawyers in the firm was preparing the lawsuit, the boys were called in from time to time to sign documents, and to receive instructions. On one such occasion, Weinstein announced: "I'm sorry but we can't take a chance. Frank, we can't include you as a plaintiff in the case. You were in St. Gabriel's for a year and it's a reform school."

Frank and Andy were flabbergasted.

"What's that got to do with this?" Frank asked.

"I'm sorry Frank. But it's important to our case that all the appellants have a clean record. We can't afford to lose on these grounds."

Frank left the office and Andy ran after him.

At the dinner table that evening, Andy slid into his seat, placed his fists on the table, and told us the story. "I think these snobby lawyers just don't like to deal with working class kids, who talk funny. Frank is really pissed." Andy later regretted that he had not "told the lawyers to go to hell."

Andy's 18th birthday, May 20, 1971, was approaching. Filled with defiance and the examples of the large number of draft-resisters who had refused to register, Andy announced, "I refuse to do it."

"But you must or we don't have a case, Weinstein declared. "Look Andy. You cannot sue the government if you are a delinquent law breaker."

"I could sue the government for asking me to follow the rules of a law that's illegal."

"No, that's not the way it works."

So Andy swallowed his principles and registered, angry with Mr. Kohn and Mr. Weinstein for insisting that he do so, but believing at that time that the suit was worth it if there was any chance of ending the draft.

Andy and his co-plaintiffs thought they were initiating the case against the Selective Service system that was requiring them to lay their lives on the line to fight an illegal war that had not been declared. They believed that the draft was a form of involuntary servitude that was unconstitutional. They argued that the criteria for deferments used by the Selective Service were discriminatory because the upper middle class students who could afford to enroll in college were granted deferments until they graduated, whereas others were drafted when they reached their eighteenth birthday. They thought they were lucky to find a law firm that would support their cause.

Harold Kohn thought the boys' concerns were valid, but he also wanted to include his own, using arguments that he believed the judges would find more acceptable. He argued that the draft was illegal because it was a form of involuntary servitude and that it deprived the draftees of their property rights. He argued that the draft discriminated against some persons and favored others, not just putting students who were not attending college at higher risk, but putting all men at higher risk than women, who were, as a group, exempted from the draft. To win the case, he needed three or four potential draftees to serve as plaintiffs, and he reserved the right to keep them in line. He was the legal expert, not they. And neither Kohn nor Weinstein ever bothered to explain the intricacies of court procedure to the boys, such as why Frank's reform school background could have made him ineligible for the draft and thus not suitable as a plaintiff in this case and why Andy and the others had to register for the draft before they would be permitted to challenge that registration process.

Kohn and his associates were successful corporate lawyers and solid members of the establishment; nevertheless, they opposed the draft. Andy and his co-defendants were radical students who saw the draft and the war as an embodiment of everything that was wrong with society. They wanted to change things in a big way.

As the case slowly moved through the courts, the core arguments were dismissed, one by one. They had been dealt with as irrelevant in previous cases and thus not valid in this one (property, involuntary servitude). Or they were political questions (undeclared war). The question of International Law that had been raised was declared moot because, by the time it was argued, the war in Vietnam was over. Only the issue of gender discrimination remained, in the court's view, a valid reason for questioning the Selective Service procedure.

Andy, who had received a high lottery number, making it unlikely that he would be called, and then further relieved because the war had ended, arrived at our home one day as we sat in the kitchen. "Can you believe that after all that work, and all that time we spent, the only principle left is that women were being discriminated against?" he announced, as he turned on the faucet to fill his water glass. What a farce! I told Weinstein that I quit. I want to withdraw from the case. I don't want my name on a case that will get women drafted!"

At about the same time, Steve, who was still technically a plaintiff, and by then had turned 18, received a phone message to appear immediately at the law offices to speak to David Weinstein. Steve was escorted into the conference room by the receptionist and motioned to sit at a twenty-foot long, highly polished, mahogany conference table, facing Weinstein, who sat five feet away with a pack of loose leaf books laid out between them. Weinstein was agitated.

"Is it true, Steve, that you haven't registered?" Weinstein demanded.

"Yes, of course it's true," Steve replied; "I don't believe in the draft, remember?"

"But we sent you memos telling you that you had to register."

"I didn't get them. When did you send them?"

"Here's the first one," Weinstein said, turning to a page in the massive book he was holding. And he read aloud one letter and then another. Steve, not recalling any of the letters, stood up to see them. Weinstein quickly moved to close the book. Steve grabbed it from his hands and discovered that Weinstein was not actually reading any letters but making them up. Weinstein, now angry, said to Steve, "I am telling you this for your own good. You better register, immediately. The FBI was here a few weeks ago asking for our records. They know the plaintiffs' names. They're going to check to see if you have registered. How would you like to spend the next five years in jail?"

"I quit!" shouted Steve. "You people are a bunch of assholes. I knew that when you dumped Frank I should have quit then, but I believed the case was important. I quit now. Go find yourselves another sucker." He stormed out of the office and went directly to register for the draft.

*After Andy and Steve and David Freudberg had withdrawn from the case the only issue to be resolved was whether the draft violated the Fifth Amendment because only men were being drafted. By that time the name of the plaintiff had been changed from Rowland to Goldberg, and the defendant, the new Director of Selective Service, was Rostker. Eventually, the Supreme Court upheld the right of the Selective Service system to exclude women. So, the efforts to change the conscription process did not succeed. However, the case was responsible for at least a temporary suspension of the draft. The strength of the peace movement contributed significantly to the ending of the war. The dire predictions that all of Asia would turn communist and threaten the United States just fizzled away. And the United States has not used conscription in the wars in Iraq and in Afghanistan. However, now that women are permitted to engage in combat, they will be eligible to be called, should Congress ever reinstate the draft. Without conscription, the shortage of military personnel has led to multiple deployments of the troops, which in turn have led to severe mental health problems for the veterans of the new wars. Furthermore, the system in place continues to discriminate against the poor who sign up for military service, while most of the rich remain safe at home.*

# GOODBYE PHILADELPHIA

What a dilemma we faced. After six years at Penn, in 1973 Bud was offered the job as Chairman of Neurology at Columbia. He had built a great department in Philadelphia and worried that, if he left, his team would be faced with the difficult choice of staying at Penn or moving with him. This was especially true of the group of physician-scientists who had already made the move with Bud from New York to Philadelphia just six years before. They had settled in nicely; they had bought houses, found schools for their children, and seemed to be quite happy.

Bud met with each of his staff members, trying to hear from them what they would do if he left. Of the group that came with him from Columbia, all but two would be willing to return to New York, and a new staff member, from Italy, was enthusiastic about the move.

The conflicting pressure on Bud to leave and to stay was heavy. One day both Dean Paul Marks and Associate Dean Donald Tapley of Columbia's medical school showed up together in Philadelphia to persuade Bud to make the change. They talked about salary and space and even promised us an apartment, four bedrooms on Riverside Drive, near the Columbia downtown campus, with a subsidized rent. But at the same time, Bud had become a close friend and loyal advocate of Dean Alfred Gellhorn at Penn, who was having difficulties with the medical school Board of Trustees because of his proposed innovations. Bud did not want to desert his favorite Dean.

Two of our three children would no longer be living at home with us, so there was only Judy to be concerned with. It was true that she was happy in her current school, but that would end soon anyway. Judy did not complain about the move. She was willing to give up her new friends because, as she told me later, she was terrified to continue living in our neighborhood and in our large and vulnerable house.

Then, there was my job. I was getting tired of Wynnefield and all of its dangers. But I loved my job. I loved working. Bud decided that he would tell the people at Columbia that I needed a job in New York, similar to the one at Penn and that unless I found it before we were to move, we would not go. As luck would have it, the pre-medical advisor at Barnard College was about to take a leave of absence. Dean Marks spoke with the President of Barnard who then prevailed upon Barnard's Dean of Studies to interview me right away, which she did. I was offered the job at Barnard as premed and prelaw advisor.

With that taken care of, Bud was free to make his decision. Both of us wavered back and forth weighing the pulls from both places; they were my pulls as well. He made lists of the pros and cons of moving, a chart with two columns that somehow was going to help us decide. Finally, he chose to accept Columbia and I agreed.

Moving is in general a busy time for all families, but for the Rowland family it turned out to be chaotic, which just made the final goodbyes a lot easier. We sold Wynnestay shortly after it was put on the market. The man who bought it was a lover of antiques and old houses. The minute I met him I thought he was creepy. He was a traveling businessman who was moving to Philadelphia from a mansion in South Carolina, with beautiful antique furniture, a sporty Porsche, and a vicious German shepherd. Our arrangement with him was to allow him to buy the house a few months before we were ready to leave and then we would sublet it from him. He did not plan to live in the house until we moved, but he moved his furniture into an unused room, and his fancy sports car and his dog into the large detached garage. George was a scion of an old, established American family. His grandfather was one of the first American photographers, specializing in pictures of the old West. His uncle was a famous economist, but George was a person with a distorted sense of values. We were glad that he was white, buying into a neighborhood that was rapidly becoming mostly black. But we feared that he was not going to be a good neighbor to the friends we were leaving behind.

George took a liking to our seventeen-year old son Steve, whom he took for rides in the Porsche convertible, (and, we learned later, allowed him to drive on those few excursions). In return, he asked Steve to care for his dog, Laurie, who only understood commands in Finnish: "Tulla" (come) "Istua" (sit) "Antaa Menne" (let go) and "Alkaa syoda" (dinner time). Steve's instructions were to keep the dog tied up on a long tether and feed him once a day. He learned the Finnish words and would shout them to the dog much to our neighbor's puzzlement. Our own little poodle, Manfred, was scared to death of the shepherd and stayed away from the backyard for the entire time that Laurie boarded with us.

One day, George and Steve and I were in the house attending to the arrival of George's furniture. As he examined his Hepplewhite desk, George spotted a narrow scratch, perhaps six inches in length, whereupon he picked up a screwdriver and scraped it across the table with an earsplitting noise. "If I just left the scratch as it was they would have filled it with wood putty and polished it. This way they will redo the whole table top and the movers will pay for it!" he explained. Steve and I who were watching this performance were aghast.

Sometime in late April, after arranging our move but before we actually left Philadelphia, I was approached by a woman whom we had befriended because she was the mother of Steve's girl friend, Sharon, a Chinese-American he had met in high school. The mother, Pokow, was in great despair because her second husband, Jack Chun, had ordered Sharon and her sister Hsueh-Tse to leave his home, which was of course also their home. The girls, who were then 17 and 18 years old, both seniors in high school, were lively young feminists who resisted being ordered about, especially by their step-father Jack, whom they hated. One evening, after a bitter verbal confrontation, Jack shouted, "I want the two of you out of my house! You have a week to collect your belongings and leave!" Sharon told Steve, who asked me if she could stay at our house. "Of course Sharon can stay here," I replied. Hsueh-Tse went off to live with another friend. But after a few weeks Pokow was in despair because she had decided to leave Jack and to find a new home for herself, her two daughters, and Alex, the seven year-old son who was also Jack's child. She was tired of Jack's abusiveness. She missed her girls. Pokow called me. "Can we have lunch and talk?" We met the following day at a campus restaurant.

"Do you know of any rentals in your neighborhood?" she asked.

"Pokow, you know, we are leaving for New York in about two months. You could stay with us until we move and then find another place."

She looked surprised and also relieved.

"I've already talked to Bud about this and he agrees. Sharon has already moved in, and our house is big enough for all."

"Are you sure?" she asked.

"We'll be packing and moving, so a little more disruption hardly matters."

"You're amazing!"

"Let's try it."

She reached over to hug me. With Steve's help they moved in the following day while Jack was at work.

Our great big space was now getting filled: five children, four cars, three adults, and two dogs. One Sunday morning Bud and I woke to the sound of someone banging on our front door, screaming at the top of his voice:

"Where's my son? You kidnapped my son. I'll call the police."

Bud, leaning out of our bedroom window, shouted back, "Go to the police, and while you're there you can tell them that you threw your two daughters out of your house. Bring the police here and I'll tell them how we provided a home for your family at your wife's request."

Jack left.

Shortly after the Chun family moved in, Bud and I and our children went to New York for Mothers Day, to see Bud's mom and take her to lunch at the Stage Delicatessen, our favorite New York deli, just a few blocks from her apartment. As my sister-in-law and I, engrossed in deep conversation, crossed 57th Street, I stepped off the curb and one leg landed into a deep pothole. I ended up in the Roosevelt Hospital Emergency Room with one broken ankle and the other severely sprained. We returned to Philadelphia that evening, now grateful to have Pokow, who had turned out to be a fabulous Chinese cook, planning, cooking and serving our meals for the next six weeks—right up to moving day. Night after night we feasted, and for special occasions she even wrote out a menu, concocting names for her dishes such as "Dragon in the Snow" for a green gelatin dessert with an almond sauce.

Once it became clear to us that the Dean of the medical school at Columbia had promised the same apartment to us and also to another new recruit (an old Columbia recruiting trick, we later learned) and that the other family actually got it, Bud and I decided to buy a house next door to an old friend who was living in Piermont, New York and loving it. We too fell in love with the idea of living in a contemporary wooden house, with decks all around, on a cliff overlooking the Hudson River, and with room for all of our children, even the two who were now in college. We were happy to be living in what we hoped would be a safe environment. Judy was to be enrolled in Tappan Zee High, a fifteen-minute school-bus ride away. It was a large public suburban high school that she was eager to try.

On July 5th 1973, Bud and I drove from our new home in Piermont-on-the-Hudson down to New York City. I dropped him at his office at the Neurological Institute and proceeded downtown to the Barnard campus to report to my own job. It was a sunny day; my radio was tuned to WQXR and just as I arrived they were playing the "Triumphal March" from *Aida,* at the same moment as I found a parking place on Broadway right in front of the college gate. I got out of the car, popped six-hour's worth of quarters, and headed to the Dean of Studies Office in Milbank Hall, ready for a new beginning.

# MY FEMINIST BACKGROUND: MY MOTHER

My mother was a feminist from the time she was a teenager. Surrounded by Russian-Jewish men and women who were imbued with the ideals and the rhetoric of the Russian Revolution of 1905 as they worked in the sweatshops of New York, my mother decided that her sympathies were with the exploited workers. She often spoke about the Triangle Shirtwaist Factory fire in 1911, where 146 workers were killed, nearly all of them women, and mostly new young immigrants. The women were trapped inside rooms in which the doors were locked by the management to prevent theft. The fire escape collapsed, the fire truck ladders were too short, and safety nets were too flimsy to hold the jumping workers. The tragedy just confirmed how unjust the system was.

My mother loved her mother. At bedtime, when I asked my mom to tell me about Grandma, she would sigh and tell me how her mother worked an eighteen-hour day. "She woke up at five in the morning to pickle the herring, then she would clean the house, scrub the family laundry, hang it to dry on the roof lines, and press our dresses on an iron she heated on the stove. When we were at school, she would go downstairs to the store to wait on the customers. And on top of that, she cooked three sets of meals a day and 'kept kosher', with two sets of dishes and two sets of pots." As she said this, my mother would frown in despair, her eyes beginning to tear. But as she continued the story and described her father, her voice became strong again, this time with a bitter tone. My grandfather, with whom my grandmother supposedly shared the responsibilities of their jointly operated store, actually spent much less time there than she did, because "he was chanting and praying in the storefront shul just a few blocks away, coming home in time to demand his dinner and then taking his afternoon rest." My mother had become increasingly hostile to her father's tyrannical qualities, not the least of which was to deny his daughters the possibility of a college education. "Women are for getting married," he declared. "Going to college will ruin your chances of finding a decent, hard-working husband. Meanwhile, mein tochter, you can work to help support the family." So my mother left Washington Irving High School before graduation and went to work as a secretary and later as a bookkeeper in the fur trade. She met my father in 1917, when he stopped into her boss's place of business as a potential vendor. They fell in love and decided to get married in 1919 in a proper Jewish wedding. But one weekend in August of 1918, the young couple was driving to Boston to visit my father's sister when the car broke down in Connecticut. Deciding to share a hotel room, they managed to get a marriage license, to find a justice-of-the peace and to sign the papers. They were secretly married for eight months before the occasion of their proper wedding. No one in the two families knew about the elopement.

My father was a merchant who bought fur skins from farmers and from auction houses and sold them to coat manufacturers. After the wedding, my mother continued to work as a bookkeeper, only this time as a member of my father's company as well as the manager of the household. She was the one who was in charge of the family budget and who paid all the bills. She and my father decided how much money she would draw from the business each month for family matters and how much money he should take for his carfare, lunches and cigarettes. In those days the man of the house traditionally made household budget decisions by himself. Husbands gave their wives a weekly allowance, as did my father-in-law. When I married Bud, my mother's only specific advice to me was, "Darling, be sure that you are in charge of the checkbook."

As they settled into their new apartment in 1919, in Washington Heights, my mother bought herself a Steinway Grand piano, delivered this time through the front door. The invoice was made out in her name, Mrs. Ida Edelman. My father was doing well financially and he bought a black Auburn car, which both my mother and my father drove. My mother stopped driving in 1937 when the gearshift was moved from the floor to the steering wheel in the Chevy they bought that year. But she hung on to her driver's license for its ID value, proudly showing it even when she was in her eighties. None of her friends or her sisters drove. And although my mother-in-law, who was ten years younger than my mom, wanted to learn to drive, my father-in-law forbade her from doing so. He made sure that he was the one, the only one, in the driver's seat.

When we lived in the Bronx, my mom took the D Train each day at about 10 in the morning and returned home an hour or so before my father, to do last-minute errands and to supervise the housekeeper in the preparations for the evening. At first we had live-in housekeepers, later we had daytime helpers who left as soon as dinner was cleared. In those days of the Great Depression middle-class women could go to work or stay at home without being criticized. My friend Jane's mother was a single-mom and a public school teacher; they lived with Jane's grandma. I can't remember ever being resentful that my mom was not at home when I arrived from school; in fact in some ways it was a blessing. My friend Ruth's mom was a housewife. Ruth and I used to stop at her place first, on our way home from high school. Sometimes, as soon as we entered, Ruth's mom would yell at her daughter. "You forgot your lunch after I spent an hour preparing it." Or "Why are you so late?" She was lonely and depressed and Ruth became the target of her anger. Other times she was a sweet and loving mom. We never knew how she was going to receive us until after we got there.

Household help was affordable for many middle-class people, and mothers who stayed at home, such as Bud's, had live-in helpers just as we did.

My mother worked outside the home all of her adult life until she broke a hip at age 82. First, she worked as a bookkeeper, then as office manager for my father's business and later as office manager for my brother. She went to work five days a week until she retired. She died on March 8 1982, at the age of 88. It was International Women's Day.

# THE MAKING OF A FEMINIST: ME

As a little girl I loved to play with dolls, especially one called Betsy-Wetsy. You gave the doll water in a doll-size baby bottle and it peed and you changed the diaper. As a seven-year-old in Flushing there was no room for a full size doll carriage in our two-bedroom apartment. But when we moved to the Bronx, I begged my parents to buy me a carriage. "She's too old for a doll carriage," my brother told my parents. "She should be playing Monopoly with me." "I will play Monopoly, but what does that have to do with taking my dolls for a walk?" I continued to beg for a carriage. On my ninth birthday, the carriage arrived. I could store it in my room and take my new doll out in the street. One day I wrapped my doll in a blanket, placed her into the carriage and wheeled her into the elevator and down to the street. "Taking your baby out for a walk?" the elevator man asked. "Uh huh," I answered, pretending to look like a proud mother as I tucked her in. But once outside I realized that I was walking a doll, not a baby, into the park. For what? I raced back into the elevator, feeling my face redden as I hastily explained to the elevator man that I had forgotten something. That was the first and last time little Betsy got to go outside.

When I had to choose my high school, I followed my female class-mates to Walton, the neighborhood school. I chose it not because it was an all-girls' school, and not because I was afraid of public transportation. (I used the subway to go to my acting class in Greenwich Village and to my dentist in lower Manhattan.) I chose Walton because it was within walking distance of my home and it had a good reputation. My parents thought it was a wise choice. I briefly considered going to Evander Childs, a co-ed school, where my cousin Arthur was enrolled, but when I read that school's yearbook, it became clear that boys' sports was the focus of the school and I had no interest in becoming a cheerleader. I thrived at Walton, probably because it was an all-girls school; however, when senior prom time arrived, I had no one to invite to be my date. After high school, I chose to attend City College because it was co-ed, even though it did not have a liberal arts program for women. After three semesters at City, I transferred to the University of Wisconsin and after graduation I continued my education in the PhD program in Public Law and Government at Columbia. My idea was to become a professor and a wife, or even better, a wife and then a professor. I had a job as an instructor in Political Science at City College and then, in 1948, at Mt. Holyoke College for a year. I was awarded a Fulbright scholarship to study in London in 1950, an honor I decided to forgo in favor of remaining in New York and working with a psychotherapist to figure out my priorities.

Bud and I were married in the early fifties, that time in America when the heat was on middle-class women to stay at home and raise the children. And that is what my friends and I did, along with most other middle-class mothers. We became good suburban housewives, living first in the Riverdale section of the Bronx, and then in the nearby New Jersey suburbs, Leonia or Englewood. We spent our days cleaning the house, shopping for food, driving the children to wherever they had to go, making dinner for the family on weekdays and often for each other on Saturday nights, and feeling resentful of (and superior to) the few working mothers in our midst.

"What nerve they have," I said when two of us were discussing this, and Mona nodded in agreement. "They to go off to work, even if they don't have to work, and leave their three-year old kids with a baby-sitter and then expect us to supervise the playtimes between our children and theirs."

Or, if the playtime took place at the working mother's home, the supervisor would be a housekeeper, who, we surmised, might or might not be a person who shared our values. What if the babysitter was a rigid authoritarian like that Irish woman who made me pray forgiveness for talking back to her. Mona's daughter, Wendy, had made friends in nursery school with a little boy whose mom was a practicing physician. The little boy desperately wanted Wendy to come for lunch and playtime at his house. But Mona was reluctant to allow Wendy to go because the mom wasn't at home. We took pride in being the well-educated caretakers of our children and their playmates, even though many times in the late afternoons, when the kids were still playing outside, Sara, Mona and I would take out a bottle of Scotch and have a drink or two while we chatted. Driving the kids home after that was potentially dangerous, but we did it just the same.

But only a few years later I began to see things differently. On a spring evening in the early sixties, I drove into the city (New York) from Englewood to hear a talk sponsored by *Monthly Review*, a Marxist journal. It was there that I heard an economist, Anne Eaton, raise the possibility that a conspiracy against middle-class women had been perpetrated by the American industrialists who were busy converting from wartime to peacetime production. If the image of Rosy the Riveter worked during the war, how about substituting an idealized image of the good suburban housewife and mother, quitting her job, to stay at home to buy the goods, and to take care of the kids. Those who went to work were vilified. As she spoke I felt my heart beating faster. She was presenting ideas I could no longer bury because they were now making sense.

I left the lecture feeling giddy. As I was driving home over the George Washington Bridge I talked to myself. I repeated what she had said and kept agreeing with her and finding examples in my own life that confirmed her analysis. Sara had been trained as a psychologist; Mona was a scientist who had interrupted her training to get married and go to work as a lab assistant to support her husband who was studying for his PhD. The three of us had put our educations and our working lives on hold, to stay at home. At first it was hard to believe Anne Eaton's thesis that the "good stay-at-home mother" was not a directive from social psychologists, but from economists. How could such a conspiracy against us women come about? But the thesis was reinforced a year later when Betty Friedan's book, *The Feminine Mystique*, put a name to the phenomenon and described it in detail.

One evening, a short time after the lecture, Bud and I were talking about a niece and nephew, two "latch-key" children who were in deep trouble.

Bud said: "I'm so glad that you are staying at home and raising the children. Our kids are such great kids. I am sure that a lot is due to your presence."

"Thanks," I said, but I found myself feeling uneasy about his "compliment."

By this time our boys were in school all day and Judy was in nursery school in the mornings. I couldn't stop thinking over what he had said, but I was too unsure of myself to actually ask him why he assumed that children would be better off being taken care of by a mother who stayed at home with the kids but yearned for the day when she would be liberated from household duties and could pursue her own career? I wondered, when, if ever, should a middle class mother leave the household and go back to work. How important was it for children to have a mother at home all day? I never even once thought about substituting a father-at-home as an acceptable alternative. What were the other possible choices?

The move to Philadelphia gave me a fresh start. I was determined to find a part-time job just as soon as we were settled, and I did, as an instructor in the Political Science Department at Drexel University, teaching two sections of one course. A few months before the move, after I had told Eloise Davis, our part-time housekeeper in Englewood, that we were leaving, she arrived at work one day and announced; "Esther, I have been thinking it over. I hate the South Bronx. I worry about Jeff growing up there. I have friends in Philly who like it. I want to find a place there too." And that is what happened. She found a place to live, a school for Jeff, and worked for us on a ten-to-six schedule, five days a week. It was a perfect arrangement for me, and a good job for her. Eloise, a large woman with a ready smile, was a few years younger than I was. She had grown up on a farm in North Carolina picking cotton from the time she was ten. She moved north when she was sixteen, worked on a belt line in a chicken factory, and then as a housekeeper to escape the factory.

My children adored Eloise, who patiently listened to their complaints about the move. Possessed of a calm and steady disposition, she was never too busy to spend time with the children if they needed her advice. She helped the kids and she helped me in our enormous house. She made it possible for me to work outside the home by caring for my children when I was not there. Her own child, Jeff, was in school most of the day, but if he were sick or needed an adult, Eloise relied on her neighbors to help out, if they were available. So, my liberation depended on Eloise. That she did not have the same freedom from worry about Jeff was and still is a problem in our society. On the other hand, I paid for Eloise's social security (my share and hers) so that she would have a pension when she retired.

When I spoke at the Mrs. Club meeting, I was happy to say that being a doctor's wife was not enough. "What would it be like to be a doctor's wife, and a mother, and have a fulfilling career—all at once?" And then I got my shared job as pre-health professions advisor at Penn.

# FEMINISM IN ACTION: THE EARLY SEVENTIES AT PENN

Karen arrived at my office to tell me what had just happened at her medical school interview with the admissions director from Duke.

"I asked him," she said, talking loud and fast as she took her seat, "'Why does Duke's application ask whether we have diabetes or epilepsy?' He answered, 'Because that would tell us to be wary of accepting that person because of his shortened life span.' I couldn't believe what he was saying. And this guy is a doctor. And, get this--" she continued, slapping her hands on her knees-- "He goes on, 'as a woman, you have about the same chance of getting into medical school as an epileptic or a diabetic!'"

When I raised this issue with the interviewer a few days later, his response was, "Look, Mrs. Rowland, my job is to recruit students who will become doctors and stay in the profession. There is a shortage of doctors in this country. We cannot afford to train them and then lose them. You know," he continued, "when I graduated from Johns Hopkins Medical School in 1948, there were three women in my graduating class. *None* of them stayed in medicine. They got married, had kids, and disappeared."

As pre-med advisor, my goal was to advocate for every qualified applicant, male and female, to get into medical school. We had to get rid of the old quota system that limited the number of women to 10%, and even a smaller percentage for minority students. We had to convince students and faculty that women as well as non-whites could become great doctors and to inform them that many medical schools were coming around to believing this too. And we had to educate all those admissions officers who still held on to old prejudices and who were using the excuse that the small percentage of women and minorities who were accepted by medical schools reflected the small number of applicants.

The timing was perfect. A 1967 Executive Order from President Lyndon Johnson established a policy that forbade discrimination by government agencies in hiring and in educating women as well as minorities.

The order included all universities that accepted any federal funding. And in 1972, an amendment to the act (Title IX) enforced it, extended it, and rekindled direct action in the community to make it all happen.

To encourage more women to apply, one of the first tasks I assigned myself was to change the wording of the undergraduate catalog. The description of the pre-medical advising service was full of the so-called "generic he" words. For example: "When a student decides on a pre-med program he must take Chemistry 1 and then Biology 1. " "He must register in the pre-medical advisory office." "He must take the MCAT in his junior year." The solution was simple. I changed it all by using the second person. "If you are planning to go to medical school, you must take the following courses; you must register…" The idea that language had an impact on a student's decision to become a doctor or a lawyer sounded far-fetched at the time. Even some of my women friends were shocked that the "generic he" was being questioned and the usual argument against such change had to do with the absence of good alternatives. I argued that using even "he or she" was better than just "he." I was not yet ready to argue that alternating "he" and "she," or substituting "she" for "he" might be a good idea.

Old prejudices about "women's place" were still extant in the seventies. One freezing night in mid-winter, Bud and I were invited to a dinner honoring Dr. Jonathan Rhoads, the head of surgery at the University of Pennsylvania and former provost of the university. He was also a member of the Philadelphia Board of Education, President of the Philadelphia branch of the American Cancer Society and a prominent figure in Philadelphia civic life. The dinner was held at the Union League, a private all-male club on Broad Street in the center of the city. We parked our car a block away from the front entrance to the club and ascended the grand outdoor staircase, happy to be about to enter a warm place. At the doorway, waiting to be admitted were Dr. Rhoads and his wife, both also shivering. A doorman with a frowning face had just answered the bell.

"We are here for the Rhoads dinner," said Jonathan.

"I am so sorry," the doorman said, "but the entrance is on 15th Street. Just go back down the stairs, turn left and walk down Sansom Street to 15th. It's not far."

"But why can't we come in this door, as long as we are here?"

The doorman turned to Jonathan, "You," and pointing to Bud, "and the other gentleman could be admitted in this door," he said. "But I am afraid that the ladies can only enter on 15th Street."

At that, Mrs. Rhoads, a tall, patrician woman, dressed in a formal gown and a long evening coat, said in a steely voice, "I am Mrs. Jonathan Rhoads. My husband is being honored tonight. If you do not let us in this door, we will go home."

"One moment," the doorman was rattled. "Please step inside while I discuss the situation with my manager." And we four entered the forbidden door. Within moments we were escorted into a service elevator, taken downstairs, walked through a long corridor and found ourselves at the 15th Street entrance, the one reserved for women guests.

Some of the Penn students were quiet about the feminist movement but nevertheless felt their strength as independent women who could aspire to become doctors and to achieve their goals. But others were like Jan, a spunky psych major from Pittsburgh, who was the daughter of a doctor who worked with the coal miners' union. She preferred direct action. One day she ran into my office for her appointment. "Sorry I'm late. Mrs. Rowland." She gasped for breath. "But I was busy liberating the men's locker room!" She smiled. "You should have seen the guys, undressed and staring at us as we raced through, shouting, 'this place is now open to all of us.' It was amazing!"

Still others were such extreme feminists that they became separatists, having no room in their lives for men, whom they regarded as ipso facto oppressors, no matter how sympathetic those men were to feminist aspirations. It affected my two sons, who were feminists themselves but shunned by some of their women friends just because they were men. It was painful for me to watch the feminist separatists, just as it had been painful, as a white person, to experience the exclusionary black power phase of the civil rights movement. But as it turned out there was room for all of us. I became a participant in an evolving movement, the next phase at Barnard College.

# FEMINISM IN ACTION AT BARNARD: THE ATMOSPHERE WAS RIGHT

My job in the Dean of Studies Office at Barnard was to advise all the pre-professional students, this time at an all-women's college. The Barnard trustees had just voted to establish a Women's Center, which was fully funded and had a fulltime paid Director, Jane Gould, who was dedicated to the promotion of the feminist cause. Barnard also hosted a New York State Higher Education Opportunities Program (HEOP) that helped disadvantaged students with tuition and counseling. The atmosphere was right. We celebrated women, women of color, women aspiring to places that had been largely reserved to men. I worked closely with HEOP and Jane invited me to serve on the Women's Center Executive Committee. One of our tasks was to bring special women to the campus to talk and to mentor our students. The program (called the Reid Lecture) honored women who helped other women. Helen Rodriguez-Trias was one. She was a prominent progressive physician who grew up in Puerto Rico and was trained at Columbia. In subsequent years the writers, Alice Walker and June Jordan were honored, as was music scholar, Dr. Bernice Johnson Reagon of *Sweet Honey and the Rock*.

Ntozake Shange, who wrote the Broadway hit *For Colored Girls Who Have Considered Suicide When The Rainbow is Enuf* was a Barnard alumna. In 1978 the Women's Center reached out to name her as a Reid lecturer, and she was genuinely happy to accept. She invited Jane Gould and me to lunch to talk about her coming visit to the campus. Poking at her salad in a café she had chosen near her apartment on Central Park South, she told us that she had been having a difficult time in her personal life during the years she attended Barnard. She had not been an active alumna, so to be invited to Barnard as a Reid Lecturer was an unexpected pleasure. What could she do to make it a great event? In the two days she spent at the college, she not only gave a talk about her life as an African American and as a woman, but also spent an evening with the students, reading her poems, accompanied by two notable jazz saxophonists, Oliver Lake and Hammett Bluett. That night the campus was alive with jazz, and the rhythms of Ntosake's poetry.

To get non-traditional students to realize that they might have something more valuable than GPAs and MCAT scores to offer, I wrote a new manual for the Barnard pre-meds that included a section of vignettes. Using false names but true stories of accepted applicants, I told the stories about their challenges and their successful applications. A student whose parents were from Puerto Rico had no place to study quietly in her small and noisy home. Another, an African American, had a mom who was certain that if she became a doctor, no man would want to marry her. A white student had a dad who was an addicted gambler, placing the family in constant financial jeopardy. It was important for the schools to know what obstacles some of our students faced and how they handled them. And it was important for their fellow students to know that acceptances were based on more than scores and grades.

To prepare for the medical school interviews, I organized workshops with the help of the Career Services Office. We arranged for a videographer to tape a mock interview with the medical school applicant who then was able to review her performance before she got to the real thing. It helped.

Once interviewed, students would tell me about their encounters at medical schools, especially those that showed bias against women and minority students.

Joan applied to Johns Hopkins at the suggestion of an aunt and uncle who were both prominent physicians. The Director of Admissions interviewed her and said, "No one can do three things well. I know, because I have trouble handling research, clinical medicine and now this administrative job." She waited to hear what was coming next. "You," he said, looking straight at her, "you are a very pretty young woman. You will undoubtedly want to be married and have children. Those are two big jobs. Wouldn't it be better for you to get a master's degree in science and do something with that, rather than an MD?" (*She was accepted, and decided to go to Hopkins after consulting with her aunt and uncle. When I visited her there in her second year, she was unhappy but determined to stay. Now she is a prominent researcher in lung disease, a wife, and a mother.*)

One student had a woman doctor as her interviewer. When she was asked what branch of medicine she was thinking of choosing, the student said: "women's health." The interviewer went into a rage. "What are you talking about? There is only health, not men's health or women's health!"

When I thought it was appropriate, I would call the admissions director of the schools where such incidents took place to discuss them. Many admissions officers by then were women, and many agreed with me and did what they could to talk to the faculty interviewers. It was, however, a delicate situation. Medical school faculty members who offer their time to be interviewers do not like to have their knuckles rapped by the admissions office.

The 1980s was a difficult time for Asian-American students, who were applying to medical school in record numbers. For example, a medical school interviewer told a Barnard applicant of Korean ethnicity that the school had accepted a Vietnamese woman two years earlier, and now that she was in her clinical years, she was overly quiet and did not assert herself. "So, what does that have to do with me?" replied our applicant. Another Barnard student, a Korean-American, was scheduled for an interview at a prestigious medical school in Chicago. She called them to see about delaying the date of the interview and was told that she could arrive at the date she preferred. But when she appeared at the school at the newly designated time, she was told that her name was not on the roster. (Her last name was Lim. The day's roster also included a Columbia student named Kim. Even though they also had different first names, the secretary had eliminated our student, assuming that the two women were one and the same.) She was then accused of trying to get an interview without being invited and returned home humiliated and with a sizable financial loss of the money she had spent on travel and lodging. When I called the Dean of Admissions, who returned my call a month later, he agreed that a mistake had been made but refused to apologize and to compensate her for her expenses.

"It is so hard to get competent people to staff our office. You know how that is, I'm sure," he said.

"No. I do not know how that is." I replied. We have a first-rate office staff. Many of them are working here because they get free tuition for courses at Columbia. You should try that at your place."

My counterpart, the premedical Dean at Columbia, told me of a conversation she had with a Director of Admissions at a prestigious school in New York, who told her that the student whom she thought was exceptionally qualified, a Chinese-American, was "boring." He agreed that the student had excellent grades and scores, but "what can you expect? All they do is study." It reminded me of the pre-World War II prejudice against Jewish students who were considered too studious and too aggressive.

We premedical advisors were part of an active professional group that met annually and often jointly with medical school admissions officers. As a member of the Executive Committee for a few years, I created a place on our program devoted to women in medicine, an innovation that had been originally scoffed as "unnecessary" by one of the other women pre-med advisors. One year we invited Dr. Mary Howell, a well-known feminist physician whom Harvard Medical School had actually appointed as Associate Dean of Student Affairs, to talk about her book: *Why Would A Girl Go Into Medicine?* in which she documented the discriminatory practices that were used against women in medicine. At these annual get-togethers, we advisors from the women's colleges would gather at a special, unofficial breakfast meeting to swap stories about how our applicants were being treated and by whom. It was aggravating and also funny, but not surprising, to hear about the same insensitive reactions to the applicants from Barnard, Mt. Holyoke, and Smith.

By the 1980s, the idea of women becoming doctors and lawyers and entering the professions as full-fledged practitioners had become an acceptable reality, quite different from the fifties. Supreme Court Justice Ruth Bader Ginsberg, then a professor at Columbia Law School, told of her experience to the Barnard and Columbia pre-law students. As a first-year law student at Harvard in 1956, she spent an evening at the home of her law professor who had invited the class to dinner. The professor, who later became the model for the formidable character, played by John Houseman in the film, *One L*, asked each student to introduce himself (or herself in the case of Miss Bader, the only woman in the group). After she told her name and where she was from, he asked, "And how does it feel to be here, occupying the place of a deserving man?"

But even in the eighties, the language issue, the so-called "generic he" was still a problem. To solve it, some recruiters decided to simply say "she". This did not sit well with a number of male students who had no idea that the use of certain words could be prejudicial. One day, the admissions director of Stanford Law School came to the Columbia campus to recruit. "At Stanford," he said " a student can choose her own electives after her first year..." He went on and on using the pronouns "she" and "her" until one male Columbia student raised his hand and asked, "Is Stanford an all-women's law school?"

We had come a long way from the days when women were scorned for entering the man's world, but there were problems still to be solved at the undergraduate level and even more at the professional school level.

# FEMINISM IN ACTION:
## AN ONGOING STRUGGLE

One day in the mid seventies, I picked up the phone to make a call.

"Hi Bernie, It's Esther Rowland."

"Hello, Esther. What's up?" replied Dean Bernard Schoenberg, the Dean of Student Affairs at Columbia's medical school.

"Do you still have some stipends for first-year students who need summer jobs?"

"Yes, we have a few left. Who are you recommending? And what research are they interested in doing?"

"Mary Roman and Nancy Anderson; both in the class of '80. I just spoke to them and they are miserable at Columbia and have no plans for the summer, so I suggested that they apply for a fellowship. You must know, Bernie, they don't want traditional lab research; but if they could, they would like to document what they perceive as sexism and racism in the medical school. They are trained to do social-science research."

"Wow. That's fascinating. I know both of them. It sounds like a great idea! Tell them to call me."

With strong liberal arts backgrounds and a commitment to "serving the people," Mary and Nancy, two Barnard pre-meds, were enthusiastic when accepted by Columbia and could hardly wait to get started on their careers as doctors. But as soon as they arrived at the medical school, they found the environment to be hostile to women, unsupportive of minorities, and rigidly traditional. For example, first year women students discovered that the Anatomy Department did not teach women's anatomy because "learning about the anatomy of a male body was all that was needed." They discovered that the anatomy students were not treating their cadavers with respect. They suggested that the students be informed about them, who had they been, what had they died of. The response was that their questions and concerns were "inappropriate" and not to be taken seriously.

Dean Schoenberg funded Mary and Nancy from the same pool he was using for the lab researchers. He even found an office for them and they went to work.

The report was completed by the end of the summer and submitted to the office of the Dean of the Medical School, titled *The Double Image: Women and Minority Students at P&S*. The basic premise was that the educational experience at Columbia had been designed for traditional students: young white, mostly middle class men. Now there was a push from the federal government to add women, minority students, more poor students, and some who had been out of college for a while. Columbia was not making an effort to retain them. In fact, the old culture prevailed, the one that assumed that good physicians were white males who always had wanted to be doctors and who would flourish in a traditional curriculum. And that's the way it should be! Nancy and Mary documented the discrepancy between the new recruitment policy and the practices at Columbia. They interviewed students and faculty and cited articles about how other medical schools were solving the same problem. It was a 60-page document that presented the case clearly and provided helpful suggestions about how to improve the situation.

The Dean's office at the medical school responded to Mary and Nancy in a letter dated April 17, 1979, eighteen months after the report had been submitted. The administration agreed that they should work to remedy the situation of the minority students and make recruitment and retention of minorities a priority. The problem was recognized, but the solution they proposed at that time was minimal.

The same letter also expressed concern that women students were reporting instances of insensitive treatment, but concluded that, "there is no pattern of persistent institutional or departmental sexism. The Dean's Office has, in the past, reminded individuals of their responsibilities to teach in a nondiscriminatory manner... The Dean's office, the departmental Chairpersons and the Faculty Council (should) ...reinforce the established policy that there is to be no discrimination on any basis by the faculty." The letter did not address the harmful effects of an institutionalized culture that ignored the needs of the newly admitted women students. The action to be taken was merely a reminder to the faculty.

Unfortunately records about an old quota system that had been used to limit the number of women, blacks, and Jews, which people knew about but rarely mentioned, were missing from the Dean's office files. This made Mary and Nancy's task more difficult and they had to rely more on anecdotal evidence to backup some of their claims.

*(Not surprisingly, The Double Image has also disappeared from the Dean's Office files. Fortunately, Mary, Nancy and I have copies.)*

In 1978, Barnard provided more students to the entering class at Columbia's medical school than it had in any prior year and those women invited me to the first meeting of a woman's group they were forming. The meeting was held on the medical school campus in one of the lecture halls. When I arrived, the first thing I noticed was the presence of a half-dozen men, not the usual audience for a meeting advertised for women. And these men were hostile. As I took my seat behind him, a young man, dressed in a tweed jacket and wearing a tie, turned around and asked me, with a snarl in his voice, "What are you doing here? Are you somebody's mother?"

"Mother of them all," I snapped back. The Director of the Barnard Women's Center, Jane Gould, whom I had invited to accompany me that day, was sitting next to me. She beamed as she patted me on the back and said, "That should shut him up."

The meeting initiated an organization that would ultimately be taken seriously. But at that first session the hostility of the men was palpable. Even getting the publicity out had been a huge challenge; all the signs that had been posted on the bulletin boards throughout the school had been torn down as soon as they were put up. The organizers then decided to put the announcements in all of the women's bathrooms. It worked.

Not only were the medical schools lagging in sensitivity to women's issues, there were still problems on undergraduate campuses. One day, in 1991, my office phone rang. It was Julia Chase, my former co-worker at Penn who had joined the Barnard faculty just two years after my arrival there. Julia, now a tenured professor of Biology as well as a married woman with a child and a stepchild, had become one of the most well liked professors at Barnard. She took students on their winter break to study bat caves in Central America. She published articles in the physiology journals. She was an active member of the pre-med committee and, as a working wife and mother, became a role model for the young women who were applying to medical school and graduate programs. And she was also highly regarded by the Columbia Biology Department.

"Esther, I want to apply to medical school."

"You do?" I was shocked. "Wait a sec, while I shut my door," I told her. As I put my phone down and walked to the door, I wondered lf she was joking. "Are you serious?" I asked as I got back to my desk.

"You bet I am," she announced firmly. "I want to apply unless you think I'm too old and they won't consider me. I am 48, what do you think?"

"Well, I don't think you're too old. Everyday we hear about someone who has changed his or her mind in mid-career and the professional schools find them to be really interesting candidates. But you have tenure, why do you want to start the long haul of medical school?" I was really curious.

"Well," she replied, "You know there's always been this undercurrent of hostility toward me in my department, ever since I married and had kids. They have excluded me from meetings, given me the worst teaching times, put baby clothes on my desk after my miscarriage, all that stuff."

"They see you as a threat, Julia, because your course is so popular and because you are close to the biologists at Columbia."

"Yeah," she added, "or as a goof-off because I have a husband and two kids. But what happened yesterday is too much."

"What happened?" I asked.

"It was 9:00 at night and since the bathroom used by us faculty women is way down at the end of the hall, I slipped into the men's bathroom, and there was my name and an unflattering graffiti message, in big black letters right next to the urinal, and all splattered."

"What an incredible story! I can just see their jealous faces as you march out of Barnard into a medical career, earning twice as much as they do. But let me call Noreen at Einstein and ask her if your age will be a problem."

I called Noreen, the Director of Admissions at Einstein, and briefly described Julia's credentials. "I have no guarantees," said Noreen, "but Julia's age, itself, would not keep her out. Let me know when she is ready to apply. I will be looking for her application."

Julia took the MCAT, applied, was accepted at several schools, chose Einstein and became the oldest graduate they ever had.

By the time I retired from Barnard in 1995, the percentage of women entering medical school had grown from a third of the class when I arrived in 1973 to more than half in many schools, including some of the most prestigious ones like Harvard and Columbia. As for me, I cannot believe my luck. I happened on a career that embraced the promotion of feminism. I found myself in a job at a college that was proud to espouse the feminist cause (even if some students and some faculty members had problems with it.) I really loved to go to work each day at Barnard in the heyday of the second phase of the feminist movement.

# MORE ABOUT LANGUAGE

Dinner was over. I passed my plate to Bud who sat opposite me in the large kitchen in our apartment near Columbia, and he placed it on the counter just behind his chair. It was an evening sometime in the early nineties. The kids were grown and long since gone and we no longer had a daily household helper as we did in Philadelphia. After my day at work, I did the marketing and most of the cooking, except for steak, which was Bud's specialty, and Bud did all the washing up.

"Would you like to do the dishes?" I asked. Bud balked. Instead of saying: "In a minute." or "Of course." he just sat in his seat and asked:

"Why do you say it like that? Why don't you just say 'would you, or would you please, do the dishes?' It's my job and you know that I am happy to do it."

"If you don't want to do them, just say so." I snapped back.

"I'm only asking why you always skirt the question. What's wrong with saying 'It's time for you to do the dishes.' Why do you have to say 'Would you like to?'"

And that said, he stood up and piled the plates into the sink and turned on the faucet.

I thought it was an insulting question. If I wanted to make it possible for him to say he was not in the mood to do the dishes, what was wrong with me asking that way? But the more I thought about it, I realized that my own way of speaking did have that tentative quality. For example, if I was faced with an office deadline and needed my secretary to prepare a report that had been requested by the Dean, I would say "Jayma: I know how busy you are, but do you think we can get the report out on time?" Should I have said, "Jayma, Please tell the receptionist that you are too busy to see students this morning because you have to type the report." At home, I never told Irene, our housekeeper in New York, to please clean the silverware. Rather I would say, "If you can fit it in to your schedule this week or next, do you think you could polish the silverware?" Bud, a department head at a large medical center, and a physician dealing with life and death problems of great urgency, had a more direct approach. He was also a man and men have less trouble than women giving orders.

I thought about it for a few days and then decided to try to speak like a man. I practiced using direct language and learned to be comfortable with it, so comfortable that I began to become as impatient as Bud had been with me when I heard other women speak in what I now regarded as the old style, the slave style.

One morning I was shopping at D'Agostino's supermarket and got onto the checkout line with a large basketful of groceries. A woman with uncombed hair and a tattered leather jacket, toting a six-pack of beer, quietly addressed me by saying:

"I don't suppose you would let me get in front of you because all I have is this six-pack and you have a whole lot of groceries?"

My immediate reply was, "Of course you can, but why did you ask me in that way? Why didn't you simply say: 'May I go before you because all I have is this six-pack and you have a full cart?'"

The woman looked at me, at first startled, then hurt, and finally outraged. She immediately moved away from the opening I had made for her in my line, walked to another line, and shouted, "Who the hell do you think you are, telling me how to speak?"

# LUCIANO AND US

In September of 1983, at a dinner in a San Francisco restaurant with her parents and with Dr. Ernest Rosenberg, Giuliana Pavarotti, the teen-age daughter of the famous tenor, was choking on her food. After hearing her complaints of double vision and her slurred speech, and sensing that this might be neurologically related, Dr. Rosenberg telephoned his brother, a neuroradiologist at Johns Hopkins, and together they agreed that the seventeen–year-old Giuliana might be suffering from myasthenia gravis, which often affects eye muscles and the muscles involved in speaking and swallowing. Luciano Pavarotti and his wife Adua took their daughter to see Dr. Robert Layzer, the specialist in neuromuscular disease at the University of California San Francisco, who confirmed the diagnosis and suggested that the surgical removal of the thymus gland could be an effective treatment. Luciano was due to appear at the Metropolitan Opera in New York City in a few days and naturally wanted Giuliana to be close to him if surgery was in the offing. Dr. Layzer told Luciano that his mentor, Dr.Lewis Rowland, was a neuromuscular disease specialist as well as the Chairman of Neurology at Columbia. "Giuliana couldn't do better," Dr. Layzer assured him.

Billi DiMauro, an Italian in the Neurology Department at Columbia, provided Bud's home telephone number, and then told Bud to expect a phone call from Pavarotti at 8:00 PM that evening. I could barely wait until 8. After all, I loved opera and I was busy studying Italian on my lunch hours at Barnard. On the first ring, I grabbed the phone. "Buona sera," I said, using my best Italian pronunciation, which fooled no true Italian. There was a short pause, and the voice asked, in English, "Is Dr. Rowland at home? Mr. Pavarotti calling."

"Yes, he is here and ready to speak to you."

They spoke for about ten minutes. Bud listened to Pavarotti tell the story of Giuliana's choking episode and the events that followed. When Pavarotti described the visit to Dr. Robert Layzer at the UCSF medical center, Bud's face lit up. "Dr. Layzer trained here in our department. He is an excellent neurologist."

"We are coming to New York in two days. Would you be able to see her?" Luciano asked.

"Please call my office for the appointment," Bud replied. "I will tell them to fit you in as soon as you can get there."

"Mille grazie. Thank you Dottore."

Giuliana was examined, tested, the diagnosis confirmed. Bud, and Dr. Alfred Jaretzki, the chest surgeon he worked with, recommended immediate removal of the thymus gland, a procedure that had proved to be an effective treatment for patients with myasthenia. Pavarotti was a bit apprehensive at first, but after Dr. Jaretzki described the large number of successful operations he had performed, Luciano and Adua both agreed to schedule the procedure as soon as possible. The operation was performed and Giuliana's symptoms disappeared overnight. She recovered fully and immediately.

The grateful parents showered us with Pavarotti recordings and invited us to dinners, operas, and concerts. Bud and I soon became part of Luciano's inner circle of favored fans. One evening, he gave us tickets for a huge concert at Madison Square Garden, where we were ushered into his dressing room even before the concert began, a visit usually reserved for only the immediate family and for Herb Breslin, Pavarotti's manager. That performance at the Garden was a memorable one because there were thousands in the audience and no empty seats. The roars of approval from the crowd were deafening. They screamed for more after he sang "Nessun Dorma."

"Nessun Dorma"
https://www.youtube.com/watch?v=N6wFxG2q8-w

In the early days of our friendship, Pavarotti invited Bud and me to his New York apartment for drinks and then to one of his favorite Italian restaurants in New York: Nanni's on the upper East side, or Da Umberto's in

Chelsea, or Da Silvano's in the Village. At each place the onlookers treated us as celebrities too. They imagined that we were either family members or perhaps even famous performers. I enjoyed every minute of these experiences. What kind of serious person was I, I wondered, when I could be so carried away by celebrity hype? But it was true. One evening, Luciano sent Adua, Bud, and me ahead in a cab to Nanni's, asking us to wait for him there. We waited outside in the company of a small group of people who had been told that Il Tenore was arriving for dinner that night. "Pavarotti is coming," one of them told us. "Oh really?" I replied. And I was about to show off and say: "And that's his wife right there," when he arrived in his huge white limo, got out, ran over to Bud, me, and Adua with his big arms in an embrace, and escorted us into the restaurant to the astonishment of the crowd.

Adua Veroni, was, in our eyes, the perfect complement to her husband. They had been childhood sweethearts, were roughly the same age, and both grew up in Modena. She was blonde, chic, and theatrical looking, but also clever and practical. In New York, that fall and winter, she wore a leopard coat, stylish designer dresses, and high-heeled pumps. She took care of the business end of the partnership, and also the homes, and their children. She did not travel with him on all of his tours; there was too much to do at home. However, the year we met her, because of Giuliana's illness, she had come to San Francisco and then remained with her husband and her daughter in New York until all was well. Luciano loved women and there was a steady stream of what could best be called Executive Secretaries, all European, all beautiful and young, who closely monitored his fans at his performances, and took care of his many needs. It appears that Adua accepted these women as a staple of Italian male-celebrity life.

In November of 1984, a year after Giuliana's operation, Bud was invited to lecture at a meeting in Milan. Pavarotti, knowing this, asked us to stop in to see him, Adua, and Giuliana, in Modena. We planned our trip to spend a few days in Naples before going to Milan by way of Modena. The Pavarotti family had a copy of our schedule, and so did our friend, Giuliana

Galassi, a young neurologist in Modena whom we had recommended to the family as a local consultant.

Arriving in Bologna, the airport closest to Modena, Bud and I waited to see if any of the limo drivers was holding up a sign with our name. None were. Bud suggested that our next move should be the car rental desk, but just as we were searching for it, we heard "Estair! Bud!" It was Dr. Galassi accompanied by Adua Pavarotti. We hugged and they grabbed our luggage cart, speeding us through the exit where a huge black Masarati was waiting, with Luciano behind the wheel. He waved us in and took off like a fire engine, speeding to Modena on a highway that set no speed limit. We arrived safely at the Fini Hotel, where a room had been reserved for us.

"Unpack, rest a bit, and we'll come back in an hour," said Adua and they took off.

The Fini Hotel is a comfortable business style hotel, right on the main street in Modena, close to the center, and most important, close to the Ferrari Sales and Service Offices. As we waited for the elevator that morning, Bud and I chatted with another American who had also just checked in. "What brings you here?" he asked.

"Oh, we are just visiting a friend. And why are you in Modena?" I asked.

"I am here with my car," he replied.

"A new car you just bought in Italy?"

"No, my Ferrari that I bought three years ago. I bring it here to be serviced. It goes by ship and I come by plane. I do it once a year. It's the only way to treat a Ferrari."

And when I looked at him as if he were crazy, he quickly added, "The hotel is filled with Ferrari owners from all over Europe and the States. I thought you two were here for that reason."

Adua arrived as planned and drove us to their home, where Luciano and Giuliana awaited us. The family dwelling, a three story spacious villa protected by iron gates and surrounded by flowering bushes and trees and a huge private park is on Via Giardino not far from the town center. Luciano and Adua and their three daughters lived on the lower floors and Luciano's parents lived in their own apartment upstairs. We entered through a gate that opened and closed automatically. After parking the car, Adua led us into a large, comfortable room that was filled with antique furniture, a grand piano, and lots of sitting space including one extra-large chair, which was the Luciano's special seat. Giuliana was there looking radiant. She greeted us with a huge smile and a big hug.

Esther with Luciano, Giuliana, and Adua Pavarotti, Modena, Italy, November 1984

Bud asked her how she was feeling. "I feel great, full of energy and I am able to keep up with my gymnastics. Those horrible symptoms are gone." And Bud commented, "You know, when such a miraculous cure happens, we check the original diagnosis to see if it was reasonable." Luciano was listening intently. Bud continued, "But I remember your symptoms, and the test results. And you surely had myasthenia. No doubt about it."

We talked about our plans for the next two days before our departure for Milan. At one point we mentioned that a Chinese student was living with us in New York that year and Luciano grabbed the phone and asked us for our New York number. He dialed, and after a few rings, Yenren, our boarder, answered. Luciano said: "May I speak to Dr. Rowland?"

"He's not here."

"I know he's not there because he is here!" Luciano roared with laughter. "Would you like to speak with him?"

Bud got on the phone and tried to explain to Yenren, a serious and studious young man who was about thirty, that this was Pavarotti's idea of a very funny joke. (Years later, when Bud went down to Pavarotti's apartment to reassure him that his fatigue was not caused by myasthenia gravis, Luciano called me at home and asked for Bud. Before he could pull that same joke on me, I replied: "He's not here because he's with you!")

One evening the Pavarottis invited us to a special dinner that Luciano had arranged for us in his favorite local restaurant. It happened to be Thanksgiving Day and Luciano knew what an important holiday it was for Americans. He had therefore instructed the restaurateur to cook a turkey for us, but, when faced with the issue of whether or not that turkey should be the main course of our meal that evening, the answer was of course no. We were to have a proper Modenese meal: pasta, bollita mista (boiled meat) with zampone (pig's shank). Finally, after we were stuffed on great Modenese food and endless glasses of Lambrusco, the waiter wheeled in a turkey, which he carved for us at the table. Luciano beamed, looking back and forth at us and at the bird. He seemed so proud of himself for remembering Thanksgiving that we forced ourselves to eat, with outward signs of enthusiasm.

Luciano had to leave town early the next day, but Adua arrived at our hotel in the early afternoon, with gifts: a Valentino scarf for me, and tie for Bud. And then she drove us all the way to Milan. We were moved by the extraordinary care this famous couple extended to us. They were truly grateful to Bud for Giuliana's remarkable and complete recovery.

For the ensuing few years our relationship with Luciano continued to be a focal point in our lives, especially during opera season in New York. We became subscribers to the Met for the first time. Before we were married I was a fan of Mozart operas and had seen them many times at the Old Met on 38th Street. And after we were married in 1952, I remember dragging Bud to the opera occasionally, but never on a regular basis. But once Pavarotti entered our lives, we both were hooked. We bought season tickets, all of which contained at least one Pavarotti performance and, in addition, there were many times when the Maestro left house tickets for us at the stage door. Before each performance Bud insisted that we listen to the tapes or the CDs of the opera we were about to see. After each of the Pavarotti performances, we went backstage to greet our friend and bene-factor. At first, we would take our place at the end of an enormous line, but, once spotted by Herb Breslin, Luciano's ever present manager who took it upon himself to separate the friends from the autograph seekers, we were greeted enthusiastically and escorted down to the front of the line and right into the dressing room, feeling guilty, but a bit smug, as we passed the hordes of queued fans. Luciano, wearing his enormous red and black silk scarf over a black shirt, stretched out his arms in a welcoming gesture. Smiling and happy to see us, he would say, "Ah Dottore! And the lovely lady!" and he would put his arms around me in a great big embrace. We would tell him how much we loved the performance, and talk a bit about Giuliana, her health, and her activities. Then I would ask him to sign the program, which he would do with his thick black Sharpie. He would scrawl a huge "LUCIANO" and the year, and encircle it in a heart. Occasionally we would ask him for a greeting to someone else. Our daughter framed his birthday wishes to her, which he wrote on a picture of himself holding a cake, a prop I had spotted in our program. Each time we visited backstage, and it happened often, we walked away feeling special.

One evening he invited us to a concert he gave at the Met, in which he sang operatic arias and also Neopolitan songs. Bud and I had seats in the fourth row dead center, and sitting behind us were Joseph Volpe, the Met's General Manager and Donald Trump, whom Volpe had invited as his guest. Their conversation went like this as Luciano was completing an aria from Il Trovatore:

Volpe: "Just wait a bit, Donald. You might not like this one but you'll love the next piece." And Pavarotti sang "O Sole Mio."

"O Sole Mio"<br>https://www.youtube.com/watch?v=F5q7113ACWA

"Now wasn't that great?"

Trump: "Yeah. He's good. But I wanted to ask you something Joe. Are there any vacant buildings around here? Any empty lots?"

Volpe: "I don't know, Donald. Fordham Law School is looking to expand if something comes up."

Trump: "Do you think they would sell?'

Volpe: "He's going to sing an encore. I bet it'll be another popular song. You'll like it."

Luciano invited us to a Met Gala and special dinner on opening night; he invited us to the cast party at the end of the run of *L'Elisir D'Amore*. We had become part of a coterie that included Italian-Americans who lived in Queens or on Staten Island, and who had some family or friendship connections to him. We befriended Dr. Boeri, a friend of Luciano's from childhood in Modena, who was now a New York physician. We saw him at every Luciano performance that we attended. And then there was Clarisse, a tall, gangly schoolteacher in her forties, from Memphis, Tennessee. She was the most ardent groupie of the bunch. She wore a necklace with gold letters spaced along the bottom spelling out L U C I A N O. Luciano had a soft spot for her unbridled devotion and saw to it that she was invited to all the special celebrations. For Herb Breslin, she was "just a pain in the ass."

Luciano invited us to his fiftieth birthday party in 1985 and again to his sixtieth, and to his sixty-first. The latter celebration was presided over by Nicoletta Mantovani, his new lover who later became his wife. We sat with her parents and heard the story of the early courtship when Nicoletta was a university student and Luciano had hired her to be his assistant. The parents seemed to be of two minds about the relationship. They were dazzled by the celebrity status of their daughter but also cautionary about the thirty-five year age difference, and about whether or not the couple would ever be married.

In 1993 Luciano sent greetings to Bud, who was being honored on the 20<sup>th</sup> anniversary of his chairmanship of the Department of Neurology at Columbia. Guiliana Pavarotti arrived at the dinner, bearing a video that had been prepared by her father, which was played for all to hear at the celebration. "Dr. Rowland, my very dear friend, your name is the symbol of salvation for my family, especially Giuliana…I hope you stay with us for a long time, helping many other people."

In the last years of our friendship, the initial spark was gone and we were no longer a high priority on the guest list. At this time of his life, he was beset by marital problems with Adua, and huge problems with his health. His knees were collapsing under his enormous weight and he was barely able to move onstage. Nicoletta had entered his life seriously and tried to control his weight and to organize a potential new career in pop music for him, one that she was hoping would relieve him of opera performances and allow him to just sing from the podium. In fact, at the sixty-first birthday party, which was hosted by Nicoletta, Luciano was completely wrapped up in his honored guest, Sting, the pop singer, and he only waved hello to us.

In 1995, Lucian's memoir, *Pavarotti: My World*, written with a professional writer, was published. When the book came out, Bud and I rushed to buy it and turned immediately to the part about Giuliana's illness and her hospitalization in New York. To our astonishment, Pavarotti gave no credit to Bud or to Alfred Jaretzki, who had performed the surgical cure, but instead, he accused the doctors in New York of giving an unnecessary test (to which he had agreed), which put her into "shock." Luciano wrote: "To be honest, I was terrified, and this test going badly only reminded me of how serious her illness was and how vulnerable her condition." The reality was that she fainted during the veni-puncture, a minor procedure. The needle was immediately withdrawn; she rested and recovered within minutes. In other words, there was little of the drama that the anxious father had interjected into this incident. Brooding about it later, Bud and I conjectured that perhaps the professional writer had suggested that a crisis or near-crisis at this point would make the story more readable. The chapter, after all, was titled "Some Rain Must Fall." Nevertheless, when we asked Luciano to sign the book, he wrote his big "Luciano," and added "I Love You."

Pavarotti's appreciation for Bud and for the chest surgeon who performed that extraordinarily successful operation was bountiful when it happened, and it had lasted for nearly a decade. After the book was published, we continued to see Luciano backstage when he performed in New York. And at one point he even asked Bud for a medical consult about himself when he was feeling fatigued and thought that perhaps he had "caught" myasthenia gravis from his daughter. But it was clear that we were no longer on the highly favored list.

*Even more poignant were the end of Pavarotti's long marriage to Adua, the loss of his stellar voice, and his fading stature in the world of opera. His final illness, pancreatic cancer, ended his life in 2007 at the age of 72. Adua and Giuliana sent us the program of his funeral service in Modena and they keep in touch every Christmas with a warm greeting.*

The Wedding of the Week

In December of 2001, when the Sunday Times arrived at our door, I tossed away section after section until I reached the one labeled "Styles" and then turned page after page to land on the piece called "Vows" which featured the "Wedding of the Week." I was searching for the story about my daughter Judy, who had changed her name to Joy, and her new husband, Makanda McIntyre, who had changed his name from Ken.

*New York Times* photo published December 24, 2000

The most joyous of Joy's pictured there in her David's bridal dress, the model with a six foot train, was seated next to her husband, Makanda, in his African robes. They had crushed the wine glass and had jumped over the broom in the chapel next door where the marriage ceremony had taken place. We were all in the Great Hall of Union Theological Seminary, with platters of food from a Sunday brunch buffet that featured lox and bagels and rice and beans. When the picture was snapped, we were watching an African stilt man in his glorious feathers, with djembe drums beating and dancers flying.

Joy met Makanda when she was an undergraduate at Smith College and he was an adjunct professor of music, teaching a class in jazz. Joy loved the class and, for her, the teacher was a heroic figure, someone she would turn to many years later when she had personal problems, which her parents, by definition, would be unable to help her solve. At the time of their wedding, Makanda had retired from his academic career as Chairman of the Department of Performing Arts at SUNY College at Old Westbury, and had reentered the concert world as a performer and composer, with a specialty in all of the woodwind instruments and the saxophones.

Twenty years after the Smith class, Joy and Makanda were married, and their relationship was deemed interesting enough to be portrayed by two large photographs and an explanatory article, an article that no one had anticipated a month before the wedding. At that time I had asked Joy if she planned to submit an announcement to *The New York Times*, as I had done for my own wedding, 48 years before. She replied, "Of course not." But no sooner said, she realized that the publicity was exactly what Makanda needed in his quest for gigs. So Joy called the *Times* and they put her on to the "Vows" columnist, Lois Smith Brady, who was interested to hear the story of this unusual relationship between a sixty-nine year old African-American widower and his forty-two year old Jewish bride. Lois Brady excelled in her ability to tell an intimate and truthful story without harming her subjects or their families.

Behind the bride and groom in the *Times* photograph sat the bride's parents, a beaming dad and a slightly bewildered mom. Why bewildered? Because Brady had spent the past thirty minutes asking me questions as we greeted our guests, as we drank our toasts, as we ate our food, and as we met, for the first time, Makanda's family, and the lawyers and musicians who were friends of the couple.

"How did they meet? What kind of person is she? Is he? How long have they known each other? Tell me about the relationship. Tell me about the family." Not knowing what Joy herself had told Brady, her long period of alienation from all of us when she was in her twenties, what was I to say to this reporter with her notebook at the ready?

The day after the celebration, Bud and I returned to Bethesda, where we were living that year. A few days later a man called, identifying himself as a fact-checker from *The New York Times*.

"I'm calling to confirm the information in an article about your daughter's wedding."

"Ye-es," I said, as I felt my heart beat faster. "How can I help you?"

"We've noticed that your daughter has had many names: Judith, Joy, Shifrin, Rowland, Rosenthal. Could you please explain that?"

"O my God" I said to myself and then aloud I answered; "You know, I think your questions would be answered better by the bride herself. She is on her honeymoon in Jamaica but I have a number for her." I gave him the number, a bit surprised that the *Times* was willing to track her down in another country, but in a moment I realized that that's what newspapers do routinely. The guy thanked me and I hung up, proud of my quick thinking and praying that he would actually reach Joy, which he did.

I sweated out the week, sometimes thinking about the article, sometimes shoving it out of my mind. I dreaded the arrival of the following Sunday when the damned thing would be printed for the world to see. Knowing that the *Times* came out on Saturday night in New York, I called my niece Amy and asked her to get the early edition and read it to me. She agreed but told me that she had theater tickets and it might be quite late before she could call back. If there were no article, she would not call. The hours passed and I went to bed.

The phone rang in my deep sleep and Amy was the caller. "I'm just reading through the piece," she said.

"What does it say?" I begged.

"Oh it seems to be very nice," she replied. "There's one thing here I don't understand. The bride's mother said, 'It's not about Barnard, its not about Columbia, its about me.' What does that mean?" asked Amy. "That doesn't sound like something you would say. But the rest of the article is fine." And she hung up.

I was in a deep sweat. How could I wait until the next morning to read that babble? How could Brady have done that? What was the context? I was miserable. Then, out of the blue I had another thought. Bud was fast asleep next to me and I shook him awake: "Did you hear the phone ring a little while ago?"

"No."

"Are you sure? Didn't Amy call?"

"No he replied. No one called. Go back to sleep and let me sleep too." It was only a nightmare!

A week later the article appeared. It simply told the story of how Joy had turned to her former professor when she was trying to extract herself from an abusive relationship. She credited Makanda with saving her life.

Bud's statement was about Joy and her two brothers, all hard working in public law, public health, and public radio, and true to the tradition of public service in the United States, none of them were making money.

My statement would endear me to feminists all over and to Deborah Tannen whose book about mothers and daughters, published six years after the wedding, bears the title: *What! You Are Wearing That?* This is what I said: "She's getting back at all of us feminists by wanting a wonderful, traditional wedding gown, … She's retro-rebellious. … I think it's going to be a great working marriage. He was a very important mentor in her life. Now, he's a great house husband and she's a working lawyer."

We spent all day Sunday calling our friends all around the country making sure they had gotten *The New York Times*, and had read *Styles*, a section that most of them usually skipped.

Joy and Makanda lived happily for the next six months. Makanda, who had high blood pressure, type-2 diabetes, and a weak heart, prided himself on his devotion to a strict exercise regimen as well as a diet of grilled fish and fresh vegetables. He kept his doctor's appointments, all but the last one.

On June 13th, a Wednesday, I was at home in the late afternoon when the telephone rang. It was Joy.

"He's dead!" She was screaming and crying at once.

"Who's dead?"

"Makanda! I came home from the doctor's office where I was supposed to meet him and I found him on the floor next to the Nordic Track. He was lying there, hunched up like he was trying to get up. He was dead. The EMT is on the way. Call Dad and tell him."

"I'll be right there," I said, and I called Bud in his office and then ran for a cab and arrived uptown ten minutes later to see that an EMT ambulance was parked in front of her door. So it was true. It had really happened. I couldn't deny it. Bud arrived at about the same time and we went up together and found that the EMT team had confirmed the death and covered the body with a sheet. Makanda's sons arrived. Kaijee, the eldest, told Bud that he wanted to arrange for an autopsy, to which Bud readily agreed. Bud believes that everyone should have an autopsy.

A few years later, Lois Smith Brady had a follow-up column in *Styles*. This time she had contacted the "Wedding of the Week" people she had interviewed in the past to see where they were in their marriages at that point. One couple had bought a house and had a baby. One couple had gotten divorced. And a third story featured a photo of a desolate Joy, holding a framed picture of Makanda, and the sad story of his death.

Luckily, after a long grief period, Joy landed on her feet and was remarried to Darryl Alladice, a poet, and public school teacher, who arrived into her life with his vivacious and talented daughter, Zuri.

# MY MOTHER AND HER DAUGHTER

One day in the early eighties, shortly after my mother died, my mother-in-law and I were talking about my mom. "You know, Esther," Cele said, looking straight at me with a serious look on her face, "when I visited her in that last year of her life, your mother complained about you a lot. She told me how disappointed she was in you, how neglected she felt."

I was shocked. How could my mother talk about me that way? She was the mother who adored me. Was Cele telling me the truth? She had always been jealous of the close relationship I had with my mom. She wanted me to call her Mom, but I never did. She was always Cele. Was this her retaliation? The more I thought about it, the more I realized that my mother had a lot to complain about. My relationship to her could be characterized as typically mother-daughter, or love-hate, or you can charm everyone else, but we who live with you know you only too well.

Mostly I loved her very much and was proud to have her as my mom. She was tireless, never neglectful of giving her children important things: books, summer camp, music lessons, nice clothes, toys and games, and the display of love. When I was little, she tucked me in, said "Schma Yisroel" with me every night. And, if I begged hard enough, she would sing "Oyfn Pripetchik" and tell me a story about the song, describing the Hebrew School where the little boys were gathered around the fire and the little rabbi teaching them their alaf base (or ABCs).

"Oyfn Pripetchik"
www.youtube.com/watch?v=UUF-jHyEuNg

I loved that song and so did my children to whom she sang it thirty years later.

Her deep brown eyes beamed as she proudly talked to others about my brother and me as perfect children. She never showed favorites and we both knew that she loved us equally. So what was wrong?

Despite her successful Americanization, my mother was still an outsider. And, even though she loved to sing her little Yiddish song, she turned away from the culture of the old country and had no one to turn to except us, her small family. When her parents were still alive, she dutifully traveled to Brooklyn weekly or bi-weekly and on the Jewish holidays. But her youngest sister actually lived with them and took care of them. My father had many business friends; my mother had little in common with their wives. My father loved to play cards; she hated it for herself and for him, especially once the war began and a few women were added. One evening, my mother burst out crying. "What are you doing, playing poker with those prostitutes!" she shrieked. I was sixteen and thought they were going to get divorced. My mother's only confidantes besides me, were her sisters, whom she criticized for being too Jewish, too Brooklyn, and too willing to accept their lot in life, which she thought was meager at best.

My father died when he was 56 years old; my mother was then 55 and I was still single, living at home and attending graduate school. My brother Jack was also single and living with us. He and I were yearning to go out and to have dates and go to parties with our friends, and my mother was anxious for us to find the right person and to get married. Yet she also made it very clear to us that she was alone, and she needed us to spend time at home. But she was often "alone." Years before my father died, my brother, then a college student, and I would occasionally take the family car for an evening visit with close cousins and I remember my mother saying: "Why do you have to go to Lou's and leave Daddy and me alone?"

The year after my father died I took a job in South Hadley, Massachusetts, where I lived in a boarding house in a small room that contained a bed, bureau and desk. My mother insisted that I return home on weekends, which I agreed to do, feeling guilty about leaving New York so soon after my father had died. After a semester of this commute, I had the possibility of moving to an apartment with a new-found girl friend and I called my mother to ask her advice about the change and the small increase in my rent, which she was paying. "Don't do it," she said. "You come home on weekends. Why would you want to have a big place when you're not using it." I remember telling another faculty member in our department that I could not attend a faculty party on a Saturday evening because I went to New York every weekend. She asked why I had arranged such a schedule and I promptly answered, "My father died last year and my mother and my brother are alone." And then, with an incredulous look, she asked again, "But why are you going to New York *every* weekend?" I remember feeling trapped and resentful. Why was I so powerless in this relationship with my mother? I was 22 years old and acting like 12.

On the other hand I did go to Europe for the entire summer one year after my father died. My mother did not stand in the way of my accepting the job at Mt. Holyoke shortly after I returned from Europe. So she wasn't an unreasonable or selfish person. In fact, I believed that she really did want me to have the best life possible, to have opportunities for growth. But, at the same time, she held the leash tight. However, when Bud called me the first time, and I was away for the weekend, she had a long talk with him and could not wait to tell me how much she liked him from just that conversation. She really wanted me to get married--to the right guy.

A few years after our marriage, with an expanding family, Bud and I bought our first house in Englewood, New Jersey, a Dutch colonial that had four bedrooms, a space that was quite a bit larger than our apartment in Riverdale. One Saturday, when my mother was spending the weekend with us, she and I were sitting in the kitchen. I was talking loudly across the table to compensate for her significant hearing loss.

"What do you think of this one?" I asked as I showed her a picture of a dining room table we were considering.

She removed her glasses and said: "You know, Ketzie, I think I have a better idea. You know, I'm getting fed up with my apartment. The traffic noise is terrible, day and night, and that woman upstairs is sending me nasty notes. Here I'll show you the most recent." She walked to the front hall, fetched her purse and lifted out a sheet of paper torn from a spiral notebook. "This came yesterday." She handed it to me. I read: "Dear Whoever You Are in 10H. I can choose my own programs. I don't need to hear yours, blasting away. Please lower your radio and TV. Your Neighbor."

"I can't stand it anymore," Mom said. "I could move in with you and bring my furniture so you can have a lovely place and not get this over-priced rickety thing," rapping on the picture in front of us. She was working as a bookkeeper for my brother's company in Long Island City. "I could take the bus to Manhattan and then a subway to work; it would not be a bad commute."

I was taken aback. I had never imagined that she would become part of our household; we had never talked about it. Getting her high quality furniture, which she and I had chosen in Sloane's and in Lord and Taylor's when we moved out of the Bronx, would save a lot of money and a lot of shopping. We had reserved a bedroom for her in Englewood where she was to be a visitor every weekend anyway, so why not make it a full-time arrangement? The decision was made with very little examination of the cons. I was the one who worried about the potential invasion of our nuclear family life. But Bud, who has always preferred to include people rather than exclude them, seemed happy about the proposed move. The kids were delighted and I didn't dare reject my mom, although I was apprehensive.

Fortunately for me, the move turned out to be very difficult for her. The commute was exhausting. So she agreed that the best next step was to find a furnished studio apartment in New York and come to Englewood every weekend, which she did. Every Saturday and Sunday, she awoke at 6.00AM, made her pot of coffee, got breakfast on the table, swept the kitchen and was there to feed and to chat with whoever came downstairs first. The children adored her and my mom had the expanded family that she longed for, and we had her. For the next fifteen years Mama continued to work, to live in small quarters in New York City, and to visit us on week-ends, first in Englewood and then again in Philadelphia, and for a short time in Piermont, when we returned to New York.

One evening, in the mid seventies, when my mom was 82, Bud and I had ballet tickets for our two mothers and Judy. We arranged to meet in Manhattan, in a restaurant near my mother's apartment. Bud and I and Cele and Judy arrived first. When my mother entered she saw us in the distance and rushed to hug us without realizing there was a step between the entryway and the body of the restaurant. She fell hard. A waiter ran to help her, and Bud and I joined him. We got her into a chair, where she sat, stoically, insisting that we eat but unable to eat herself. She assured us that all would be better as soon as she calmed down. But her pain got worse and we called an ambulance that took her to Bud's hospital. It turned out to be a broken hip and her life changed, as did ours. After a short hospital stay and recovery in our house, she knew that she would never want to go back to work. She gave up her apartment and announced that she was living with us. But life in suburban Piermont was miserable for her. Bud and I were away from early morning until at least 7:00 at night. Only one child, Judy, was still at home and the school bus delivered her back home late in the afternoon. Judy and her beloved Nana were both abandoned. We lived on a highway, with no sidewalk and a steep drop behind the house. The place was a disaster for non-drivers.

Within a few months after my mother's arrival, Bud and I decided to move to the city as soon as possible. We bought a large apartment near Columbia, sold the house a few weeks after it was listed, and all was fine. My mother had regained her strength, ensconced herself in a nice bedroom in the new apartment, and spent the day waiting for us to return from work or school. Once I arrived home my mother was happy. But if Bud and I had been invited out or if there were a department function, as was often the case for a department chairman, she would say, "Not again. Don't you ever stay home? You work all day and then you run away at night."

On my way home from work one day I met an old friend, Helen Rodriguez-Trias, a physician and ardent feminist who had grown up in Puerto-Rico. I told Helen I was hurrying home to help cook dinner with my daughter, and my mother. Helen hugged me and flashing her huge smile, exclaimed, "What could be better than three generations of women under one roof!" "Uh huh," I replied aloud, and "Oh. God there has to be a better way," I said silently, thinking about my mother's complaints about our schedule.

A year later Judy was off to college and Bud and I were engaged in full-time work. We were gone all day, and out several evenings a week. My mother, who at least used to have Judy, whom she adored, to talk to about their shared feelings of abandonment, was now really alone and unable to control her circumstances.

"I am miserable," she declared. "I have no one to talk to all day and you don't even come home for supper." Not able to discuss this openly with each other, which had been our problem all along, we decided to make an appointment with a psychotherapist whom our son Steve was seeing. Mama, Steve and I together explained the situation and the therapist proposed that Mama move once again to a small, studio apartment, and she agreed. Bud and I would be close-by to visit. We found a place on Central Park West and it worked well for about five years. She read a lot, wrote a lot of letters, which she loved to do, took short walks in her neighborhood and entertained visitors including Bud and me and Steve and my cousin Lou, who came after work. Mama went to bed early, arose early, and fixed herself the frequent small meals that she preferred. It seemed to be working well until one morning she suffered a small stroke and, unable to walk, crawled across the room, almost literally at a snail's pace, to the telephone to seek help. In the hospital it was made clear that she could no longer live alone. She needed a larger place to accommodate her as well as a caretaker, and we found her a larger apartment in a nice neighborhood that was just a short walk from my mother-in-law. The two women finally became good friends. Before that, my mother was wary of Bud's mother, who was ten years younger, born in the United States, a self-confident woman, with loads of friends, and a busy social life. My mother-in-law visited my mom almost every other day. She helped my mother pay her bills, balance her check book, and often stayed for lunch or for tea. Unfortunately, my mother never liked any of her hired caretakers and she complained about them, even the ones that I had judged as warm, competent and caring. She did, however enjoy the friends and family who visited her, but when they left, she was unhappy again. "I don't like this apartment; it doesn't feel like home. I don't like having these strangers around me all the time," she said. "I don't know what to do with them, and they don't know what to do with me."

Things changed again when one day, my mother looking out of the window, saw me approaching the building. She started for the door without her walker and fell onto the floor. When I rang the bell, an alarmed nurse's aide and a moaning mother greeted me. We called an ambulance and she was transported to the emergency room at Bud's hospital and diagnosed with a broken shoulder and a broken wrist. The on-duty nurse sat by her side all night, slowly and carefully removing her wedding ring, to avoid having to cut it off. She proudly handed it to me, in tact, the next day. After the surgery my mother remained in the hospital for about two months while her bones healed. But she never wanted to walk again. She developed pneumonia, but her doctor treated her immediately and she recovered.

It was at that point that we realized that she might have been better off untreated, allowed to die from a disease (pneumonia) that had been called God's blessing to the aged. My daughter Judy who had just completed a course in medical ethics at the University of Massachusetts, sat on the edge of Mama's bed, took her hand and asked,

"Nana, are you afraid to die? Is dying good in some circumstances?"

"Oh, I don't know, darling," she said. "But your Dad will know what's best for me and how to take care of it. I trust him completely."

It was quite a remarkable conversation, which took place in a hospital room shared with three other patients. "Would you please shut up," one of the roommates shouted, as the conversation got into the "dying as a blessing" phase.

Once the bones were healed, Presbyterian Hospital was required to discharge my mother as soon as we found a suitable place. Briefly I thought that one such place could have been our apartment, with a staff of nurses, an option I decided would have been a huge intrusion on our home life and on our working lives. Instead, with the help of a geriatric social worker, we listed a series of nursing homes for her transfer. The first response was from the Jewish Home and Hospital, which was not far from our apartment. I accompanied my mother in the car from the hospital to the nursing home. First, she had an evaluation by the physical therapists, that cheerful breed of enthusiastic health care workers who believe that almost anything is possible with a will and good exercises. Two tall and strong young women entered the room where my mother was being admitted.

"Hello Ida," one said as she sat down in the chair next to us. "Welcome to JHH. We are here to teach you to walk again!"

Mama replied, with a snarl, "I cannot walk and I cannot learn to walk."

And she dismissed them with a wave of her hand and a shake of her head that seemed to say, "What are you thinking? Don't you see that I am old, and tired, and in great pain, and disgusted with the world, and furious with my darling daughter for bringing me here?" She curled her lips downward and directed her scornful look at the therapists, and then at me.

A bed was found on the floor that offered full nursing care, which was what she needed for her physical wellbeing. Unfortunately, her fellow patients were demented and she had no one to talk to except her visitors. Her roommate was constantly repeating unintelligible phrases. "Me Fors, Me Fors, Me Fors," she chanted all day long.

When I visited Mama, she often told me of her nightmares. And one day she told me, in a very low voice, that she had been touched, inappropriately, by the male attendant who had just left the room. "He grabbed me here," she whispered, pointing to her pelvis. I dismissed this as another nightmare, but wondered later whether it might have been true, since the nursing home itself was the equivalent of a nightmare. During the day all of the patients were wheeled to a central place in front of a nursing station and tied into their wheel chairs. As I stepped out of the elevator on my first visit, I was shocked to see this gaggle of wheelchairs, all in a circle like the covered wagons in hostile territory. Seeing me, my mother waved frantically. "Here, Esther, here I am." And when I went over to kiss her, she said, "I hate sitting here, tied up like an animal." I spoke to the nurse who said there was nothing she could do. They needed to keep an eye on the patients who were not ill in bed. And so my mother decided to become ill in bed. She refused to be placed in a chair and stayed in bed until she developed pneumonia, and, this time, Bud, knowing that she had given him permission to do so, had asked for a do-not-resuscitate order, which included taking no heroic measures to treat the patient, as long as she was kept comfortable.

March 7th, 1982 was a Sunday and it was my daughter-in law's birthday. The plan was for Steve and me to spend the afternoon in Philadelphia with Wendy and the evening back in New York with my mom. I called the nursing home at about 3:00 in the afternoon to find out how Mama was doing.

"She's got a high fever and is restless. But she is waiting for you. Come as soon as you can." The nurse's voice sounded different this time. Sensing the worst, I asked Steve if we could leave at that moment, and we did. The ride back to New York took three hours instead of two. There was heavy traffic all the way and every traffic tie-up seemed endless. We arrived at 6:30, raced to her room and found my mother in a deep coma. Steve and I waited and waited for her to wake up. We finally gave up and left to go home, to sleep, and to wake up to go back to her bedside the following day. But early the next morning the phone rang. It was a woman from the nursing home who said, "Your mother died during the night. She woke up from her coma briefly, and then slid back into it." She died alone.

Oh, Mama, what have I done to you?

At the funeral my children and I chose two songs: "Ofyn Pripetchik", and Pete Seeger, whom my mom loved, singing, "Turn, Turn, Turn."

"Turn, Turn, Turn"
http://www.youtube.com/watch?v=XisKfBDgBUI

# HOW I DID NOT GET MY PHD

At the time of my wedding to Bud, I had completed the course work for my PhD and had passed my oral exams. The only thing left was the dissertation on the one hand and having children on the other. Andy arrived just nine months after the wedding.

The new dissertation topic, suggested by Professor Neumann, centered on Ernest Jones, a British aristocrat whose family had connections to the royals. He was also a barrister, and a writer of poetry and prose. In the 1840s, Jones joined with the most militant group of Chartists, an English working class movement that was demanding not only the vote but also changes in the economic system that would benefit the poor. I was interested in learning more about the struggle and its failure, and especially about Jones, who seemed so out of place in their midst.

In the Special Collections section of the Columbia library, Neumann had found six large green boxes devoted to Ernest Jones, which, he suggested, could get me started. The boxes included a diary, letters, and even clips of baby curls, saved in glassine packets. Many of the items were notes that had been written by Jane Jones (Ernest's wife) to her mother or to her husband. In the style of the times, she wrote in parallel horizontal lines and then, instead of adding another page, she turned the single sheet ninety degrees and wrote another set of parallel horizontal lines right on top of the original. The net effect was a quadrille, all done very neatly and with great precision. And still another effect was to make these letters impossible to be read unless one could hold the original in one's hand. When I first encountered this material, it had not been catalogued and was pretty much untouched. I was working in virgin territory.

Jones was a friend of Karl Marx who was living in London from 1849 until the end of his life. In fact, when Ernest Jones died in 1869, Karl Marx wrote to Friedrich Engels. "Of all the Englishmen of our time, Jones is the only one who was completely on our side." Was Jones a Marxist? Was there a connection between the Chartist movement and Karl Marx? Was I on to something big? I worked intermittently as I was preparing for the wedding, and then again once we settled into our new Riverdale apartment. Less than a year later we had moved to Washington and Andy was born.

I was so proud of my new microfilm reader, even the librarian at NIH, who had arranged for me to get the reels from Columbia through inter-library loan, had congratulated me on my great purchase. "It's wonderful to see how motivated you are," he said. For $125 I had a reader at home that spared me the need to sit in a library. I could have my baby and take care of him, and do my research while he napped, or played safely in a secure playpen. Or could I? I was struggling.

My baby was crying, a screaming kind of cry, the kind that says, "I need your help right away, now, this second!" I dropped the microfilm container and ran. There was three-month-old Andy, screaming in his crib. I lifted him and held him tight and gradually he calmed down. If I tried to put him down, he started to scream again. Only holding him would work. Was it a tooth? Was it a bad dream? Was he hungry? Did he have a bellyache? How was I to be sure that it was not something to worry about? And if it was not, how was I going to get back to my work?

In 1956 our family, now of four, took a sabbatical in London for six months and I was able to do a lot more. A full time au pair for the little boys, a good nursery school for Andy, and desk space at the British Museum (where Marx himself had sat one hundred years before) gave me a new burst of energy and motivation. I met Dorothy Thompson, a British historian who was also working on Jones. She and I became friends; and after I returned home we helped each other find relevant material. I sent her Xerox copies of documents from the Columbia Library; she sent me material that she had gotten in a trip to Moscow. For the next several years, Dorothy and I shared information, but we were both losing interest in Jones and busying ourselves with other things, including enlarging our families and our household duties. Finally, she gave up on the Jones project, and concentrated on writing a history of the Chartist Movement, which she completed several years later. In a pre-publication version of the book, she included a remarkable acknowledgement: "I would like to thank my husband, Edward P. Thompson, and my three children, without whom this book would have been completed years earlier." And then she added: "but if it had been written without them it would have been a different and far lesser book." In the final published version, the jaunty acknowledgement was omitted.

As one delved into his story deeply, Jones seemed far less than a heroic figure. In fact, he was beginning to look like a charlatan who was using his well-born station in life, and his gifts as a writer, to further his own literary career. I felt betrayed when I came upon some letters from Jones's mother-in-law to her daughter, Jane, which referred to Ernest's affair with Catherine, one of their domestic servants. Ernest and Jane were quarreling a great deal and Jane had actually taken the baby and moved out of the house. Finally Jones was persuaded to dismiss Catherine and Jane returned. A few years later Jones wrote a serialized novel in his weekly magazine *Notes to the People* called "Women's Wrongs." Part I was a story of a domestic servant who was preyed upon by the master of the household. I had read the story before I noticed the reference to Catherine in the letters, and had been so impressed with Ernest Jones, the early feminist, who was sensitive to the power relationships between men and women, and between the rich and the poor. But, after reading Jane's mother's letters, I was disheartened. I began to lose interest in the whole project and I put it aside. It all ended in 1999, when a young English historian, Miles Taylor finally wrote a biography of Ernest Jones, crediting him for the work he did as a lawyer and as a reform politician in his later years in Manchester, but faulting him for that early romantic period in his life when he pretended to be a revolutionary. Unlike Dorothy and me, who were vainly seeking the selfless hero, Taylor told the story as it was. He visited me in New York just before he completed his book and I gave him some of my material and told him about the Catherine episode, which he had missed. When I asked him about Karl Marx's letter to Engels and the claim that Jones was the only Englishman who was on their side, Taylor immediately replied: "Of course. Jones had been schooled in Germany, spoke German fluently and shared their cultural biases. Period." A few weeks later he wrote to thank me. "It was a very helpful conversation we had, even if it means that the picture of Jones-the-rogue is now unavoidable." When his book was published, he acknowledged my contribution by saying, "I would like to thank Esther Rowlands (sic), who over tea and cake in New York City, helped me make sense of Jones' complicated personal life."

I had my third child in 1959 and, when she was in seventh grade, I embarked on a new career at Penn, and later at Barnard, as pre-medical adviser, a job I loved, and which did not depend on having a PhD. When my friend Pudge Landau heard me describe my working day, she burst out, "What a great job for a woman. You pry into people's lives, you retell their stories, and you make matches." As for the PhD, the Barnard administrative staff was not hierarchical. I was an Associate Dean with an M.A. and an M.Phil, (the degree offered by Columbia to those who have fulfilled all the requirements for the PhD except the dissertation.) My boss, Barbara Schmitter, the Vice-President for Student Affairs, had an M.A. degree. Her secretary had a PhD.

# OUR PARTNERSHIP

In 2008, Bud was honored for "lifetime achievement" by Project ALS, a group that raises funds for research in what is commonly known as Lou Gehrig's disease. This neuromuscular ailment has been Bud's primary interest for the past thirty years. In his short speech, which I had read the night before, he wrote that he wanted to pay homage to his wife, Esther, to whom he had been married for 56 years. On our way to the Waldorf-Astoria, the evening of the event, we talked about his talk, and I suggested that, in the part where he mentioned me, he add: "my wife, who has put up with me for 56 years, and vice-versa." But when he actually spoke he omitted "vice-versa" and just said that I had put up with him for that time and it wasn't easy. That comment was greeted with a round of applause by the audience and a request that I stand up and wave to the crowd, which I did.

In the early years of our marriage, when I was a stay-at-home wife, I had told Bud: "If you ever make a speech about your accomplishments, I hope you will never, but never, talk about how much you owe to the little lady, me, behind the great man, because the minute you say it I am going to walk out of the room."

For me, back then, the ode to the wife, was the standard remark expected of all men who received honors, and regarded by the speaker as the least he could do for his partner who made it possible for him to spend so much time at work while she took care of the home, the children, the meals, and the entertaining. Unfortunately that was true. But I found it to be patronizing and demeaning, just corroborating how much we wives were living through our husbands. I did not want to be the lady behind the throne, but on at least one of the thrones. I did not want to be the homebody if I had a choice. And if I did not have such a choice, it was just another sign of the inequity of the system and not to be glorified.

Esther and Bud At the Waldorf Celebration, 2008

But at the Waldorf that night in 2008, I found myself smiling when he said his piece. And throughout the round of applause I just nodded. I did not walk out. When a scientist at our table congratulated me for "being there" I did not hesitate to tell him that it was I who was responsible for Bud's initial link to Project ALS. Back in 1996, I was in a bioethics program at Columbia and one of my classmates, Naomi, was a physician who knew that I was married to Bud, the famous neurologist who specialized in neuromuscular disorders. One day she told me about her close friend, Marilyn Estess, whose daughter Jennifer had been diagnosed with amyotrophic lateral sclerosis (ALS). The family wished to get a second opinion and an appointment with Bud. Naomi asked if I could help. I spoke to Bud that evening, and he saw the patient a few days later. Unfortunately the diagnosis was confirmed. Project ALS grew out of Jennifer Estess's battle with ALS. She was a forty-year old energetic and enterprising theatrical producer with loads of friends in the acting community, including Billy and Alec Baldwin, Ben Stiller and his parents Jerry Stiller and Anne Meara, and Marisa Tomei. Shocked by her "death sentence," Jennifer's sisters, with the support of their many wealthy and influential friends, were determined to find the cure by raising millions of dollars to be used for research. They came to Bud for advice and help in identifying the most promising scientists and institutions that were doing ALS research at the time, and they honored him that night for his efforts.

At Barnard, in the eighties, The Women's Center and my office co-sponsored a talk by a psychiatrist who was a Barnard alumna. She talked about her experience as a premedical student in the sixties. She was married in her senior year and made the mistake of telling NYU medical school, where she had been accepted, that she was pregnant. The school withdrew her admission. Two years later she reapplied, was accepted, and purposely neglected to tell them that she was pregnant again. She graduated from medical school without a problem. She then proceeded to tell the group that she became a successful practitioner largely because she had used her husband's contacts in the field. He was also a psychiatrist and a few years ahead of her in his training. This talk angered my friend, Jane, the Director of the Women's Center. Jane was upset because the speaker did not show sufficient outrage at NYU for their actions: "She should not have quietly reapplied and lied." Jane was even more upset by the woman's proud announcement that she had used her husband's position to further her own career. At the time I found myself agreeing with Jane about the absence of outrage at the cancellation of the woman's admission to medical school. But I also knew that much of my own success in getting my job and doing my job well was because of my marriage to Bud. I relied on his contacts in the medical schools for information and for lab jobs for my students. In a world where connections are so important, to turn one's back on such opportunities seemed to be counter-productive.

I have always traveled with Bud who has been invited to give lectures, attend conferences, and receive honors all over the world and many of his friends have become my friends.

In turn, I have helped Bud recognize some of his old male prejudices. He used to tell me about the wonderful, talented, beautiful women he had met at the hospital, head nurses, doctors, who were still single. "What a loss to some deserving man," he would lament. And I would promptly reply:

315

"Maybe they preferred being single." And when he was about to hire a new secretary, he complained, "She is smart and young and I am sure that I will lose her in a couple of years because she will get married, so maybe I shouldn't hire her." And I replied: "You choose residents who are going to leave. Why don't you just hire that young woman and see what happens?" He thought about it and agreed.

So I have been happy to accept whatever Bud has done to help me, and whatever small things I have done to help him. Uneven as it is, it still has been a great partnership.

*(At a recent meeting of the American Neurological Association, a panel of women, all of whom now hold leadership positions in academic medicine and all of whom trained with Bud, gave him credit for the encouragement and advocacy he provided as they were entering what used to be an all male world. And one of them, a Barnard graduate, told the panel that she would not be a doctor today if it were not for me. So, as a team, Bud and I worked together to make sure that women and minorities found their rightful place in a profession that had excluded them in the past.)*

# THE IRENA TRILOGY:
## BEING JEWISH, POLAND 2002

In 1948 my friend Bob, who was from a classy German-Jewish family living in the Chicago suburbs, told me of the embarrassment he felt when he first encountered a man reading a Yiddish newspaper in a New York subway. I was shocked by his observation. After all, I was a Jewish New Yorker who had grandparents who read Yiddish newspapers. That was a given. Why was he ashamed?

But I do remember my own embarrassment when, riding the subway with my mom, I was sitting next to a bunch of Irish teenagers. They were just like the ones who lived near us on Creston Avenue, a block away from the Grand Concourse, who used to beat up Jewish kids with socks filled with flour as we walked into their streets on Halloween. There they were on the subway staring at and pointing to my mom in her mink coat, (a coat that had been given to her by my father's customers, and that she wore reluctantly and only because it was warm.) She was reading the stock-market page of *The New York Times*. They kept poking each other. "Wats she doin' takin' the subway?" I was sure that they were mocking her because she fit the anti-Semitic stereotype of the rich Jew.

Years later, on my first visit to Israel in the 1980s, I think I understood, for the first time, how it feels to be free from the enslaving phenomenon of "how do I appear to others." Even in New York City where Jews abound, I had experienced the negative side of being Jewish, i.e., as a victim of prejudice. And because my father was essentially an atheist and we did not belong to a synagogue, I missed out on the joys of being Jewish and the great cultural heritage of Judaism. On that trip to Israel I finally felt "at home." For there, in that section of Jerusalem where we stayed, practically all the people were Jewish. Some were loud and some were quiet. Some spoke English with an accent; some did not. Some were workers, others in business. Some were rich and some were poor. Some ate matzos during the Passover week and some ate the bread they had saved from the previous week. No one was being looked at as a Jew first and then as an individual. It was quite the other way around. It felt good. I was proud to be Jewish.

I was reminded of all of this during a trip to Poland in the summer of 2002, where Bud and I were the guests of Professor Irena Hausmanowa-Petrusewicz, the Chief of Neurology at the University of Warsaw. She had persuaded the Polish Neurological Society, which had only a few Jewish members, to have a joint meeting with the Israeli Neurological Society. The conference was held in Krakow, the site of an annual Jewish cultural festival that had been initiated in 1988 to remind the people of Poland and the rest of Europe of the great Jewish cultural heritage that had been prevalent in Poland before the Second World War.

The conference ended with a dinner in a restaurant in Casmiererz, the old Jewish section of town that was much like New York's lower East side. The conference coordinators had chosen Restaurant Ariel for the dinner. Bud and I were surprised that the people in charge had not read the local guide book which described it as follows: "Beyond a small tourist shop (consider this an omen), lies a room closely packed with tables and oil paintings of 19th century Jewish life. We've been warned by several readers before, and experienced it ourselves---the food is horrible."

"Maybe the guide book is wrong," I said to Bud as we walked in. But that was not the case.

The servers were Poles, not Jews. As we sat waiting for someone to take our order, Andrej Friedman, a feisty, red-haired neurologist who was the only Jew (besides Irena) in Irena's department, stood up. "We've been waiting a half an hour, just to give our order," he shouted to one of the waiters who was leaning against the bar and chatting with the bar tender. "What kind of place is this?" And, at the next table, Bud and I were sitting with Irena, our host, who had masterminded the meeting with the intention of fostering respect and admiration between the Polish and the Israeli doctors. She waved to Friedman, curling her finger into a "come here" motion. He came, shaking his hands in the air and moving his head from side to side. "Andrej," she said in a low, steady voice, "you must control yourself.

Your fussing will be taken as Jewish carping. You must stop this at once." Respecting her as his boss and mentor, he outwardly stopped complaining.

Irena, who was so concerned about Friedman's behavior, grew up in Warsaw, the daughter of prominent secular Jewish intellectuals. Her sister and she, both in medical school at the outbreak of the war in 1939, transferred from Warsaw University to the medical school in Lvov, in the Russian sector of the then divided Poland. They graduated as doctors and served in the Polish People's Army, which fought side by side with the Soviet Red Army until the end of the war. When Irena returned to Warsaw, she discovered that the Nazis had shot and killed her father in the street and her mother, a prominent dermatologist, had been gassed in a concentration camp. At the time of her return, the Polish Communist regime was in power and young Communists were replacing the elderly professors in the university who had been in their positions since the pre-war days. Under this policy, Irena rose to become the head of the Neurology Department. Life under the Communist regime, even for Party sympathizers, proved to be difficult for all but especially hard for those who were Jewish. There were bad years and worse years but Irena managed to survive as one of the great Polish neurologists. For a time, under the leadership of Wladyslaw Gomulka, the Party responded to popular demands for easing the repression. But in the late sixties, the hardliners forced Gomulka to deal harshly with the university students who were protesting against censorship in the theater, and to resume the campaign against the Jews. There was an organized drive to purge all Jews from the party and from professional positions. Irena was able to remain, but she was in a perpetual state of anxiety about losing her Jewish protégées and even her own job. After the downfall of the Communists in Poland, when things should have gotten much better, she found to her dismay that anti-Semitism was still firmly entrenched. Sitting in our kitchen on a visit to New York a year after the Krakow meeting, Irena told me a story.

"One day, not long after the collapse of the Soviet Union, when Solidarity was already in power in Poland, I called for a taxicab to take me to work. As I entered the cab the radio was on, broadcasting the proceedings of the Parliament, which was then dominated by the Left. I told the driver to take me to the Academy. He agreed and then turned off the radio.

'Just more of that Jewish liberal nonsense,' he said.

'Please turn the radio back on,' I said. 'I am interested in the discussion in Parliament.' He flipped the radio back on and did not look at me or talk again until we passed the Warsaw Ghetto Monument." And she leaned forward toward me, "And do you know what he said? He said: 'The Germans were right. It's too bad they didn't finish the job. There are too many left and they are up to their old tricks.'" She banged on my table as she continued. "I said 'Stop the car and let me out,'

'But we have not reached the Academy of Science!'

'I know, but I am Jewish and I can't stand the way you are talking.'

'Another one!' He threw up his hands as he groaned, and opened the door for me. So you see, Esther," she said, "It's not over."

# THE IRENA TRILOGY: KNOCK ON WOOD:
## CALABRIA 2010

"I knew it would happen because you arrived on the thirteenth," said Irena, the eminent member of the Polish Academy of Science, to me as we sat in a car on a hilltop in the small Calabrian village of Rende. "And my crazy daughter pays no attention and just keeps on doing crazy things."

Irena and I were in the back seat of the rented Fiat with the burned out clutch, waiting for the smoke to subside. Irena's daughter, Marta, a professor of History at Hunter College in New York and at the University of Calabria, was the driver, and Bud was sitting next to Marta in the front seat encouraging her to keep cool. Irena continued, in a half whisper, "My daughter—don't tell me how wonderful she is; I know that. She's a remarkable girl, with remarkable gifts but she is also suffers from hypomania." And as she leaned over to me, she used her professional voice to say: "It's a clinical diagnosis I am talking about, a serious condition."

"But Irena, in Italy they don't consider the thirteenth the unlucky day—here it's the seventeenth."

At that, Marta turned around in the driver's seat with a loud "SSH" to me.

I protested, "Marta, you were the one who told me about unlucky-seventeen in Italy."

"I know." She replied. "But we are driving to Naples on the seventeenth!"

When Bud and Irena were both invited to attend the conference of neurologists in Naples in the summer of 2010, we decided to begin our reunion in Marta's home in Calabria. Irena had been there for the preceding month, vacationing, resting, and catching up with her daughter, who lived mostly in New York City. Bud and I would also be Marta's guests for a few days, staying at the home of her next-door neighbor who was on vacation. The plan was to rent a car to drive around Calabria and then drive to Naples together.

On our last night in Calabria, before the trip to Naples, we were heading for a pizzeria, up a very steep hill atop of which sits the little town of Rende, just about 10 miles away from Marta's home in the village of Cosenza. We found the pizzeria, but it was located on a street that was too narrow for the six-gear Fiat to enter safely. So Marta had to back up a steep hill to be able to turn around. As she backed up, her clutch slipped and she used the emergency brake. We started again. The clutch slipped, we slid forward. She revved the motor; and the clutch started to burn. Smoke was pouring out from under the hood. Marta turned the motor off and we waited. Meanwhile a crowd gathered, and it included several young men who opened the hood but quickly backed off as the smoke gushed forth. They told Marta to wait ten minutes until the smoke died down.

While we sat in the smoke filled car, Marta called the rental car emergency number, which did not answer, and Irena, age 93, turned to me with her hand over her heart and said, with a deep sigh, "Esther, tonight I am going to die. I know it." And this was coming from someone who survived the Second World War, the Holocaust, the Polish People's Army battles against the Germans in which she served as a front line doctor, and the Soviet occupation of Poland. Irena still has beige-blond hair, the bottled version for proud elderly women who hate the look of silver gray. Her deep-set brown eyes still shine, and she dresses with impeccable good taste. Her face is expressive and sharp, with a small aquiline nose and fair skin that has remained relatively unwrinkled despite her age. Walking is very difficult for her, however, and she depends on hanging on tight to someone in order to go from here to there. Marta, of course, is the designated companion on this trip, and Marta never leaves her side, a fact that I tried to point out to Irena, only to be told "I know she is wonderful, but..." That evening Irena looked more worn than usual and her conversation was lacking the characteristic wry humor that so defines her.

"Irena, stop talking like that. If we have to, we'll call a cab and get home."

"Ach," she said, "and what about the Congress. I promised to be there for the opening ceremony."

"We'll be there. It's only 3 hours from here. We'll get another car." I tried to assure her.

"There are no other cars. I represent Poland at this Congress. I cannot be late. My crazy daughter has to climb a mountain the night before we leave, to get a pizza. I tell you she is a hypomaniac. She takes risks all the time. She does not think ahead. Her sister would never do this. Don't tell me how wonderful she is."

When the smoke died down, the onlookers checked the engine, and with a few probes they determined that the clutch was burned out but the brakes were okay. They advised Marta to descend the hill in second gear, which we did, stopping on the way at another pizzeria for a take-out. And, *mirabile dictu*, we made it all the way home! Practically starving, we attacked the pizza in Marta's kitchen. Irena, who had refused to eat at first, finally agreed to try a piece, since it had anchovies, which she loves. Marta at last got through to the rental car company by phone. They came to tow the car and, the next morning, they offered us a substitute, which carried us to Naples in plenty of time for the opening ceremony on the seventeenth.

# THE IRENA TRILOGY: IRENA, A TWENTIETH CENTURY EUROPEAN STORY AND TRIBUTE TO A REMARKABLE WOMAN

Marta was seated in my kitchen, pouring a glass of wine for me, one for herself, and fingering an Asian rice cracker.

"I hope my mother never sees your book if the stories only portray her as the superstitious control freak in the Calabria episode or the obsequious Jew in the Krakow story."

"I know that, Marta, and I also do not want her to be remembered that way. She is such a remarkable woman and you know how much I love her and I want her to know how much I love her." I drank a bit of my wine and then put my glass on the table as I continued to speak. "But then how should I write her story? How can I explain her complicated life?" Marta did not answer but just shook her head as I continued. "Did I ever tell you about the time in 1968, at a cocktail party at Penn, when Hilary Koprowski, as dapper and as brilliant as ever, introduced himself to Bud and me and said, 'I hear that you are close friends with Irena Hausmanowa. Did you know that she killed two husbands and is now married to a third? Did you know that she and her sister commandeered the chairmanships of two major departments in the medical school, toppling the existing chairmen who were both eminent specialists? With the blessing of the Communist government, these two upstarts arrived and took charge.'"

"So how did you respond?" Marta asked.

"We were stunned. We knew it was a bunch of lies or half-truths. But how do you say that to the Director of the Wistar Institute, which is one of Penn's most highly respected laboratories. So Bud just said, 'No I did not know. But I have invited Dr. Hausmanowa to be a visiting professor in our department. She should be coming in a few months. We are looking forward to having her here.'"

"And what happened when she came?" Marta asked.

"Well, when she came, about six months later, Hilary met her on the campus and immediately invited her to his home for dinner. After that, she and Hilary and Hilary's wife became close friends. They saw each other several times a week. Hilary played Chopin for her on his grand piano. They spoke in Polish, sharing stories of their childhoods and their schooling, as classmates, in the days before the war."

I was smiling as I described that friendship.

"And Hilary and Irena also shared a passion for science. She visited his lab and talked with him about the extraordinary accomplishments that made him the head of a major research center at the university. He was happy that she came to Penn and they have been in touch with each other since that visit."

Marta nodded as I spoke. "Yes, my mother has led a complicated life and she is an amazing and complicated person."

When Irena returned from Russia to Poland after the Germans were defeated, the Communist government was already in place and Party members such as Irena and her sister eventually replaced the prewar physicians whose ideologies had been deemed suspect. Irena's first husband, Janek Czerniakow, a Polish lawyer with whom she served as a fellow army officer in Russia, died of typhus during the war. (Janek was the son of Adam Czerniakow, the head of the Jewish Council, who committed suicide at the onset of the mass deportations by the Nazis). Irena's second husband, Dr. Artur Hausman, was a hematologist who developed a technique to preserve the crucial components of blood to be stored for later use in transfusions. One batch of that serum had been sent to the Communist forces in the Korean War and turned bad because it had become contaminated. Although it had never been used, Hausman was accused of committing sabotage and is reported to have taken his own life when he learned of the charges. Irena's version of the story is that he died of a heart attack when he learned of the charges.

Bud and I first met Irena in 1964 when she, the Chairman of the Department of Neurology at the University of Warsaw, came to the United

States to visit the New York Neurological Institute. Dr. Houston Merritt, the head of Neurology at Columbia, asked Bud, a junior member of the department, to entertain this prominent guest, which he did by showing her the hospital labs, introducing her to the neurology staff, and finally bringing her home to have dinner with our family. We knew no one who was still living in Eastern Europe and I was anxious to talk to someone about life in a Communist country. For, in those Cold War days, it was rare for people who lived in the Soviet bloc to be permitted to travel to the West. However, Irena had convinced her government that science was international and good science had no borders.

As Bud and Irena entered our home, the children and I rushed to greet her. A bit later, Andy, age 11 asked her "What is it like to live in Poland?" and I, who at that time was doing research on Ernest Jones, the British Chartist, asked her if she knew of Count Krasinski, a Polish aristocrat and writer who had befriended Jones. Irena, who had expected a boring evening in the suburbs, was impressed with our family and our questions, and Bud's invitation to have dinner in our home. And I found her to be a fascinating new person in my life. She was knowledgeable about world affairs, about European history, about European literature. She was attracted, as I was, to the ideals of the left but well acquainted with its problems. She spoke and read Russian, French and English and loved the arts as well as science. She was a Polish Jew and so was I, although our forebears had taken different routes. Even though her parents were intellectuals and she grew up in the capital city, and mine were small tradesmen who lived in small rural villages, we relished the stories of Sholem Aleichem and Isaac Bashevis Singer. We laughed at the same jokes and cried for the same reasons. I was surprised at how well we clicked, how well we seemed to know each other even after just meeting for the first time.

Knowing that neurological research was most advanced in Western Europe and in the United States, Irena had convinced the Polish authorities to invite prominent Western physician/scientists to Poland. She invited Bud (and me) to visit her group in Warsaw in 1969, again in the seventies, and again in the eighties. We have taken at least a dozen trips to Poland.

We have met her at another dozen international conferences, and got to know her really well during those three months in Philadelphia. And when her daughter, Marta, came to the United States for the first time in 1977, we became her American family, a closeness that has gotten stronger with time.

At about the same time as Dr. Koprowski was telling us his fanciful tale in Philadelphia, we learned that the students at the University of Warsaw were marching in the streets, denouncing their government for closing down a classic play by the nineteenth century Polish writer, Adam Mickiewicz. The Warsaw audience cheered whenever characters in the play, which was set in Poland in 1820, demanded that the Russians leave. The Russian occupiers of 1968 found this unnerving. They shut down the play, stopped the demonstration, and arrested the students, but then freed all but twelve; the twelve were all Jewish. Eleven of them had Jewish names and Marta, the twelfth, was identified as "Marta Petrusewicz, daughter of Irena Ginzburg."

Marta's non-Jewish step father, Kazimierz Petrusewicz, a partisan hero, and a Communist, wrote to the newspapers protesting the designation of Marta as only Irena's daughter. He had legally adopted her; her name was and still is Petrusewicz, and he stood by her. Irena soon thereafter was told to denounce her daughter or lose membership in the Party. She told us that she chose to lose her membership and thereby her remarkable career as the leading neurologist in Poland was threatened. Nevertheless, she maintained her authority.

In 1969, after Marta was tried, found guilty, and forced out of Poland, Bud and I visited Irena in Warsaw. Professor Fritz Buchthal, a mutual friend in Denmark, had already warned us not to discuss anything political in a Polish hotel room, which surely would be bugged. In fact, Buchthal told us two classic "debugging" stories. One had happened to a Danish friend of his, who, when visiting Warsaw, had noticed an assemblage of wires under a rug in his second floor hotel room. He managed to uncouple the wires from the large bolt to which they were attached, and a moment later, heard a thud and much commotion. It turned out that he had unscrewed the chandelier in the ballroom below.

The other debugging operation was Buchthal's own revenge. He had suspected that the listening device was in the radio in his hotel room. He carefully removed all the screws in the radio, removed the device, and put the radio back together without any screws in place.

Arriving at the Hotel Bristol, a hotel that had been known for its elegance before the war, Bud and I were brusquely assigned to our room by an unsmiling desk clerk who handed us the key. Upon entering, we put down our suitcases and began hunting for a sign of the listening device. When we opened the bathroom door we found the toilet broken and filled with feces. I told Bud that we had to complain and he reluctantly agreed. Together we returned to the front desk, where we waited on line to speak to a clerk. When someone was finally free to attend to us, I was livid. "Do you speak English?"

"Yes, Madam."

"Well then: You must change our room. We were given one with a broken toilet. It smells to high heaven. It's a disgrace."

"Sorry Madam the repair staff has gone home. There's a toilet down the hall. You can use that one."

"But we have been registered for a room with a private bath."

"Sorry, Madam. There is nothing we can do at this moment. Maybe tomorrow it will be fixed."

When we told the story to Irena later that day, she was shocked at my outspokenness. And I was taken aback by her shock, feeling so close to her that I forgot that we were living in two different worlds. But after a day in Communist Poland, I began to understand. We were warned by Irena not to speak against the authorities anywhere inside—not in our room, not in the hotel restaurant or lobby. It was okay to talk in her home and it was okay if we were walking in the park, away from others. After Marta's trial and conviction and Irena's choice not to denounce her, Irena's job was in jeopardy. Before we left Poland, she and we worked out an elaborate code for our future telephone conversations. For example, if she were to say: "I got a haircut," it meant that she was demoted in her department.

My first trip to a communist country had been in the summer of 1948, twenty years before the Poland visit. I was a graduate student at Columbia at the time, still hoping that the United States and Stalinist Russia could co-exist, that the dictatorship in the USSR might mellow, and that the anti-communist hysteria that was emerging in the United States would disappear. I had joined a World Study Tour, a travel group designed to visit, assess, and understand what was happening in post-war Europe. We were mostly university students, led by Professor Colstan Warne, Professor of Economics at Amherst College, and President of Consumers Union, a leading consumer advocacy organization. Our-next-to-last stop, after visiting London, Paris, and several cities in Italy was Vienna, a city that was then divided into four zones, the American, the British, the French, and the Russian. Our local guides warned us not to enter the Soviet zone on our own. But of course, in the evening, when we were enjoying our free time, a few of us decided to see for ourselves. As soon as we entered, we felt uncomfortable in that forbidden sphere. The streets were drab and mostly empty, monitored by young Russian soldiers carrying guns and patently unfriendly. We were pretty, young women, accustomed to making friends easily. But the serious young soldiers were suspicious, close mouthed, and hostile. We left after just a short walk, happy to be back with people who liked American college girls.

The last stop of the World Study Tour was Prague, beautiful Prague, which had been spared from the physical damage that we had seen in London and in Italy, but had just experienced a Communist takeover. The atmosphere was chilling. We arrived a few months after Jan Masaryk, the Foreign Minister (and one of my political heroes), had died in a fall from his office window. Masaryk's goal had been to form an alliance with the Western powers by signing on for Marshall Plan aid, and also to keep his ties to the Soviet Union. But his desperate attempts to do so had failed. The Communist coup in Czechoslovakia sealed his doom. The bureaucrats we met insisted on calling his death a suicide. The Czech people we met insisted it was murder; "defenestration" (throwing a person out of the window) was the word they used. When the tour was over and we returned to the United States, I found a recording of the great Czech opera star, Jarmila Novatna, singing a beloved Czech folk song, "Tece Voda Tece". The pianist accompanying her is Jan Masaryk. It had been recorded in 1942, six years before Masaryk's death. Just hearing him play made me cry.

"Tece Voda Tece"

http://www.youtube.com/watch?v=AABOpXip_wQ

As part of our studies, we listened to a talk from a high Party official. In the question period one of our members asked about the denial of civil liberties in Czechoslovakia and told him of the complaints that we had heard from private sources. "Now, who told you that?" the Party guy asked from the podium. "Just tell me his name and I will get in touch with him and explain to him why he is wrong. What is the name?" he demanded. We looked at each other, with eyes rolling. I wrote home to my mom and my brother: "Well, now I have felt what a police state feels like and it doesn't feel good."

In our second trip to Poland, Irena decided to skip the hotels and to house us in her own home. To do this we had to obtain an official permit. So Kazik, her husband, and I spent several hours at the District Hall for the neighborhood of Zoliborz, where they lived. Kazik, a biologist, had been a minister in the Gomulka government just after the war had ended. A heavy smoker, he had advanced emphysema. The morning after we arrived, Bud and Irena went to the hospital to work, and Kazik and I went to the town hall for the permit. Kazik was in his seventies, a small man, short and thin. He had a persistent cough, sometimes doubling him over until he caught his breath. His face was lined with illness, age, and the scars of years spent as a partisan fighting the Germans in the forest.

It was a sunny and warm day, and a level walk, and we made it with only a few momentary stops for Kazik to catch his breath. At the town hall we were told to ascend a huge flight of stairs to the permit desk. Slowly we walked up, Kazik hanging tight to the banister and breathing hard. At the top we made our way to the end of an inquiry desk line and waited a half hour for our turn, only to be then told that we had to get onto yet another line. When our new turn arrived, Kazik was given a paper to fill out and then told to return it to still another window, which he did. At the last window, there was a clerk, doing nothing, but she told Kazik that he had to deal with a different person who was not present. Meanwhile, the idle one sat on her perch, filed her nails, checked her makeup, tweezed her eyebrows, picked up a paper and put it down, picked up another and put it away. I was in a state of disbelief and asked Kazik: "Can't you ask her if she could help us since she has absolutely nothing to do?" "No," he replied. And so we waited. After another half hour, a new clerk appeared. She approved his form and told him to go downstairs to buy a stamp and bring it back to her so she could paste it onto the permit and we would be all done. So poor Kazik had to go down the big staircase, buy the stamp and climb back up. I worried that he would collapse from all the stair climbing, but, since everything was done in Polish, there was little I could do to help. When it was all done and we were walking home, I asked Kazik why that woman was filing her nails on the job and didn't it make him angry? "No, I don't get angry at the workers," he said. "Do you know how much they earn? Their salary is the equivalent of $30 a week and they have to work 6 days, Monday through Saturday."

Bud, Kazik, and Irena in front of the Warsaw Ghetto Monument

Bud and I were invited back to Poland in the mid 1980s. Conditions were already beginning to improve. An underground newspaper was widely circulated and with it a feeling of hopefulness that life could and would be better. And then in 1989, Solidarity, the Trade Union Movement, came to power, supported by the dissidents, the Catholic Church, and the majority of people in Poland. From then until now, the Poles have had a working Parliamentary system and a multiplicity of political parties. The government swings from liberal to rightwing, like most of Europe and the United States.

And just about the time that Marta was in my kitchen talking about her mother, the Polish government had awarded Irena the highest honor they give to an outstanding scientist.

*Now, in the new Poland, Irena, who was 97 in 2015, has retired from her post as head of Neurology in the hospital, but she still goes to her office at the National Academy of Sciences. She is a leading figure in Polish medical*

*science and a beloved "boss" to the huge number of women she has trained in a first rate Department of Neurology that is mostly female and has been so since the end of the war when she took over. She calls her young doctors "my girls," knows the ins and outs of their families' lives, and remembers their birthdays. She does no cooking and never did, but she never misses a day of work.*

Irena escorted by Prime Minister Donald Tusk receiving highest prize for science, 2012.

# JAYMA: A TRIBUTE TO A DEAR FRIEND AND COLLEAGUE

When Jayma came to my eightieth birthday party, in April 2006, I had no idea that she was ill. Characteristically, she never said a word about her back pain, which I later discovered had already been plaguing her for a month—and getting worse. A week after the party, she and I had our annual birthday lunch together. (We were both born in April and always exchanged gifts at a special lunch we arranged for just the two of us.) She never mentioned the pain and she managed to hide her discomfort. In mid-May, a month later, I called her.

"Jayma, I guess I'll be seeing you on Saturday. Bud and I are going to see the documentary at Lincoln Center. We're excited." It was a film about the Camden 28, a group of anti-war activists that Jayma had been a part of in the 70s.

She replied: "Maybe. But I would rather spend my free Saturday afternoon playing with the children. And, besides, I heard that the film was focused too much on religious motivation for the action and that was not why I was part of it."

She never came, and she died of breast cancer that had metastasized to her spine and to her stomach on August 20th.

I met Jayma Abdoo in the mid-eighties when the Dean of Studies, Vilma Bornemann, a friend of the Abdoo family, suggested that I hire her as my assistant after my previous secretary had given notice. I interviewed Jayma and could not believe my luck. She was highly intelligent, well qualified, enthusiastic about taking the job, pro-union and anxious to join the clerical workers local. Best of all she knew my children from her Philadelphia days when she worked as a paralegal in the law firm that advised the members of Resistance, a group of activists who opposed the war in Vietnam, two of whom were my sons, Andy and Steve. My enthusiastic response to her just deepened as time went on. In addition to every thing else that was remarkable about her, she worked demonically, and took responsibility for finishing her work always well within the deadlines that were so important in our office. She was kind and attentive to the students, always mindful of their needs and their anxieties. I was able to breathe easy for the time she was with us. She left after a year to go back to school and, as much as we would miss her, I was excited for her and completely supported her decision to continue her education. About six years later she returned to our office, armed with a B.A. degree, summa cum laude, from Columbia's General Studies College, some experience in the pre-professional office in the General Studies program, and a master's degree in history from the University of Virginia. Dean Bornemann had heard that Jayma was back in New York and looking for a job. I called Jayma to see if I could help her locate something that would use her new educational achievements.

"Dean Rowland," she said, "I hear that you are looking for someone right now. I would really like to have my old job back."

I was astounded. "Jayma, you have a master's degree. Why would you want to be a secretary?"

"I need a job and the sooner the better," she replied.

"What other jobs are you considering?"

"Department store clerk or super-market cashier."

I realized that she really wanted to be a worker, and not part of management at that time in her life. I hired her at once.

In the summer of 2006 I was in Woods Hole with Bud when I learned from my former colleagues at Barnard that Jayma was in the hospital, and dying, I called Jayma's sister Lynda, to ask if I could come down to New York to visit. Lynda, an executive at the designer company, Ferragamo, had taken leave from her job to serve as Jayma's 24-hour nurse at Roosevelt Hospital. Jayma, a tall, large-boned woman who normally had a full complement of thick, straight black hair crowning her head, had, until then, not wanted to allow her friends to see her in pain, gaunt, bald, and unable to concentrate on anything but her miserable condition. She had asked Lynda to keep us all away until she felt better. But after the doctor told the family that they had done all they could at Roosevelt and that hospice was the next step, Lynda, in shock over the implication of hospice, encouraged her to allow visitors. "Yes, Dean Rowland," she said, "you may come. Jayma has finally agreed to accept visitors outside of the immediate family." Jayma, too, had heard the doctor's recommendation for hospice care. She reacted by declaring that she had to be around for the seven-year old twins, Lucy and Wyatt. "Dying is not an option," she said. The doctor then suggested "hospice-with-treatment," which made it easier for the family to accept.

I arrived at Roosevelt Hospital the day before Jayma was to be discharged and, with Lynda's permission, sat by Jayma's side, holding her hand as she sought a comfortable position in bed. On the other side was Lynda, fixing Jayma's pillows, stroking her forehead, offering her a wet cloth to moisten her lips, whispering into her ear that going home the next day would be the right thing to do. I wanted to repeat Lynda's words, "It will be okay" but I could not say it. I wanted to tell Jayma how much I loved her, how valuable her friendship was to me. But I could not say it. I just sat there, feeling useless and helpless and agonizing as I watched her suffer. Finally, the floor nurse walked in to make the evening preparations. "Please step outside," she said. "You can return later." I decided that it was time for me to leave and I did, feeling empty, and depressed as I said goodnight to Jayma. "Take care," I said stupidly. "You'll be home soon." I tried to figure out why it was so hard for me to communicate with Jayma that awful day in the hospital, and realized that even though I thought I knew her so well, she was still preferring to call me Dean Rowland instead of Esther. Despite our birthday celebrations, and our monthly lunches after I retired from my job, she seemed more comfortable with certain formalities, even if our relationship was warm, and caring, and filled with conversations about our families, office gossip, and national politics, on which we shared almost identical perspectives. Lynda later assured me that Jayma always referred to me at home as Esther and that calling me Dean Rowland in the office and in the company of others, was done out of deep respect. So it was not distance after all but a different kind of closeness.

At Jayma's memorial tribute, at Barnard College in early October, two hundred and fifty people who thought they knew her, sat in a large meeting room in Barnard Hall, with tearful eyes and wide open mouths, surprised by the many sides of Jayma Abdoo that they had never known until that very day. Present were devoted Barnard students and colleagues. There was a contingent from Wall Street, associates of her brother Brian who worked in the financial industry. Seated among them were members of the Camden draft-board break-in whom I had met at the film showing in May. There were co-workers from Philadelphia, as well as her godchildren, her family and her personal friends. Her family knew her well, and I was lucky enough to know many of the pieces of Jayma's life—but not all. The sentiment after the meeting was, "Oh, I thought she was completely focused on me. When did she find time for all those other things?" Or, even more prevalent: "Oh my God, I wish that I had known more about her. I would have loved to talk to her about so many things. And now it is too late!!"

When I arrived at Barnard in 1973, my goals for our office were to increase the percentage of women and minority students in medical and law schools and to encourage all of our students to look into public interest service at the end of their training. When Jayma arrived as my assistant, she worked hard at assembling panels of alumnae to serve as mentors to our student clients. When I retired in 1995 she was one of the candidates for my job, but the Search Committee questioned her qualifications because she was "only" an administrative assistant. She remained in the same position as administrative assistant, but gradually, under her new boss who could only work part-time, she took on more responsibility: advising students, and writing letters of recommendation. By that time the number of women entering professional schools was up to 50% but the number of minorities still lagged. Jayma continued to create support groups among alumnae professionals who were minorities and those who were working in public interest careers.

At one of our monthly lunches, a ritual we had established after I retired in 1995, just as we were leaving the West End Café, she said, "Oh by the way, they changed my title to Assistant Dean." She grabbed her coat and mine and seemed to want to change the subject as I said, "Well, it's about time! What great news! Congratulations!" I was elated by her announcement because elevating an administrative assistant to a deanship was almost never done. "Hurray for Barnard," I added. Jayma always had a hard time talking about herself and this last minute blurting out of an undeniable recognition of her competence and her dedication clearly illustrated why so many people at her memorial service were amazed to hear about her accomplishments

Jayma was born in 1951 in Oradell, a New Jersey suburb of New York City. Her father, a graduate and prominent alumnus of Columbia College and Columbia Law School, was Catholic, of Lebanese descent. Her mother, a Barnard alumna, and also Catholic, was the daughter of a professor of Italian at Columbia and of Italian descent. The family members were close and loving, but politics divided them. The younger brother remembered heated arguments at the dinner table with the mother and the two girls (Jayma and her older sister Lynda) lined up against the Republican father. By the time she was ready for college, in 1969, Jayma followed the path of many contemporaries who were outspoken critics of the war in Vietnam and the political and social system that had taken us into that war. She spent a year at Trinity College in Washington D.C. and dropped out to become a full time anti-war activist. She joined the anti-war protesters in Camden, a city in southern New Jersey, just across the Delaware River from Philadelphia. The group was later called the Camden 28.

Jayma age 20

The story of this event is not well known, but it marks a major turnabout in the history of the Vietnam War and also the history of civil disobedience in the United States. Camden was, and still is, a poor city with a large population of impoverished minorities and no money for improving schools, prisons, health care, or housing. The discontent that was aroused throughout the nation after the murder of Martin Luther King was still seething in Camden in the 1970s. A local Catholic priest, Father Mick Doyle, was keenly aware of the lack of funds required to make the city livable for most of its residents, while the federal government was spending billions on the war in Vietnam. He decided to protest the continuation of the war by an act of civil disobedience: raiding the draft board and destroying the files. He was joined in his mission by twenty-six others: three priests, one Lutheran minister, several social workers, social activists, and students, who shared his commitment to respect human life. At age 20, Jayma was the youngest. At that time the Catholic Left had already established itself as a powerful voice in the anti-war movement that was sweeping the country, spearheaded by the Berrigan brothers, one of whom was a Catholic priest, who were repeatedly imprisoned for their peace activism.

The story of the raid on the Camden draft board has been told in that remarkable film Jayma never saw, called *The Camden 28,* directed and produced by Anthony Giacchino, a young documentary filmmaker who grew up in a neighboring town in New Jersey and wondered why neither he nor any of his friends had heard of "such an important event that had happened so close by."

The participants had planned the raid for months. Their object was to sneak into the draft board in the middle of the night on August 22, 1971, destroy as many files as possible, and then run for cover into pre-arranged safe houses. Preparation involved knowing when the guards had completed their rounds, climbing a ladder to an upper floor of the United States Post Office building where the draft files were held, disengaging an alarm system and finally breaking into locked file cabinets and destroying the files. It was a difficult operation for a bunch of amateurs, but fortunately, or so they thought, a friend of a member of the group gave them the much-needed expertise.

The new man, Bob Hardy, a construction engineer, joined the group in the middle of their planning stage and actually came to their rescue by providing sophisticated tools to quell the alarms and to break the locks, and walkie-talkies, hand-held radios to keep the raiders in contact with each other. Without him, they would have had to call off the operation. With him, however, they entered successfully, destroyed many files, and were promptly arrested at the scene by a swarm of FBI agents. Bob Hardy had secretly contacted the FBI the very first day he became a part of the scheme. He reported to the FBI daily. He claimed later that the FBI had assured him that the group would have been stopped before the act took place and that no arrests would be made because nothing illegal would have happened.

Instead, however, the FBI waited until the draft board had been entered and the files obtained and destroyed. They arrested those they caught on the spot and then rounded up the others who had been present in Camden that night. By a fluke, Jayma had never made it to the scene of the crime because there had been riots in Camden that day and all buses, including the one Jayma had boarded earlier, had been diverted away from the city. She escaped arrest and was declared to be a fugitive until she decided to turn herself in. Shortly thereafter she was freed of the charges and not indicted or tried. However, she moved to Camden for the length of the trial, attended it daily, and served as an eloquent witness for the defense.

The trial took place in the Camden Court House two years after the break-in and lasted over three months. A remarkable judge, Clarkson Fisher, presided. Unlike his predecessors in similar trials, he was open-minded and obviously impressed by the sincerity of the group. He listened to the arguments of the defense that the draft was skewed against the poor, that the money spent on the war should have been put to use to save Camden, a city of poverty and squalor. He allowed the defendants to show pictures of both Vietnam and Camden burning and, although he instructed the jury not to put the war on trial, he was obviously sympathetic to the rationale of the defendants. He also allowed the defense to call the renowned left historian and author of *The People's History of the United States,* Howard Zinn, to testify and to describe the origins of the war and the history of civil disobedience in the United States. He allowed the mother of one of the defendants, Mary (Betty) Good, a conservative Catholic, to tell the tragic story of another of her sons who was killed in Vietnam. "To take that lovely boy and tell him: 'You are fighting for your country'-- how stupid can you get? Can anybody here tell me how he was fighting for his country?"

Judge Fisher allowed Jayma, as a witness for the defense, to describe in great detail how she had become an anti-war activist by watching David Brinkley on public television in her Catholic high school history class, and seeing American soldiers and Vietnamese soldiers and civilians being killed. She became an avid supporter of Eugene McCarthy, dismayed at his loss of the Democratic primary in 1968, and horrified at the brutal treatment of the student anti-war demonstrators by the Chicago police. As she and her best friend watched the riots in Chicago, they sang "The Great Mandala" a Peter, Paul and Mary hit song. "It's basically about whether we want to…just keep watching evil go on, or do we have to do something about it?" Jayma testified.

Judge Fisher insisted on hearing about the motivation of the defendants, but primarily, he was appalled at the role of Bob Hardy, the informer, and of the FBI who had essentially turned the informer into a provocateur, and had allowed files to be destroyed. In the end, the jury acquitted everyone, primarily because the FBI, which not only did not prevent the break-in from happening, but also provided the tools and the expertise to make it happen, and could have aborted the action. It was an unprecedented verdict, received with cheering and weeping in the courtroom, and culminating in the singing of "Amazing Grace" by the defendants, the spectators, the marshal, and the jurors.

After the trial, Jayma was offered a position as paralegal in the Philadelphia law firm that had handled the case, Kairys, Rudovsky,

Messing and Feinberg, a firm that focused on civil rights and civil liberties litigation. Philadelphia in 1971 was a city run with an iron hand by the former police chief, Frank Rizzo, who was elected Mayor and did his best to suppress every demonstration that had to do with either civil rights or anti-war activity. Jayma joined the National Lawyers' Guild and, as part of the Guild agenda, worked as a leader in the campaigns to "Stop Rizzo," to stop police brutality, to get the Philadelphia City Council to sponsor an anti-apartheid resolution in support of the movement in South Africa, and to support Gay and Lesbian Rights in Philadelphia. She worked diligently and was highly effective. In the early eighties she moved back to New York and that is when I met her and hired her to be my assistant.

At our annual birthday lunch at the Interchurch Center in 2002, Jayma described the remarkable thirtieth reunion that was held in commemoration of the trial. "It was really preposterous." She had just returned from Camden. "Imagine calling it a 'reunion' as if it were the gathering of a high school class," she added as she shook her head in disbelief. "And guess who was there? The FBI and Bob Harding, all in the same room with us!" She smiled at how ironic it was, but her face became serious again as she recalled the pathos it engendered. The defense lawyers and the prosecuting attorneys, the FBI informant and the defendants, relived the experience, three decades after the trial. It came about because the Historical Society of the U.S. District Court of New Jersey, recognizing the significance of the trial and its outcome, cooperated with filmmaker Giacchino to present an oral and visual history exhibit in the courthouse. They arranged for as many as possible of the original participants to gather back at the courthouse and recount the events. Several of the principles, including the judge, had died. But among those who attended were fifteen of the original defendants: Jayma, the lawyer who had been Judge Fisher's clerk at the time, one of the FBI agents who had since retired, several of the witnesses, including Howard Zinn and Mary Good, one juror, and Bob Hardy, the FBI informer. Hardy at first had decided to stay away but at the last minute he changed his mind and came. Several members of the group were infuriated by his presence, but others were more forgiving. He had, after all, testified for the defense and denounced the FBI. The remarkable trial, which Supreme Court Justice William Brennan, referred to, as "one of the great trials of the twentieth century," and the remarkable reunion, are now part of the history of Camden and a source of pride for the community.

But at that birthday lunch when Jayma described the reunion, just as we were putting on our coats to leave the restaurant, she turned to me and said: "You know, I am no longer so sure that any of us has the right to take the law in our own hands, even for a just cause." I was stunned to hear her say this. It was a subject we had no time to explore further that day and unfortunately it never came up again. But when she did not show up at the filming, I wondered if that newfound feeling had something to do with her absence.

While working for the law firm in Philadelphia, Jayma had become the godparent of Noah and Jeannie Rudovsky, the two children of one of the partners. For nearly thirty years she threw herself into the role of auxiliary parent. She attended every school-parent activity; every performance, every birthday party and she called both of them, wherever they were, every Sunday night. Noah and Jeannie both came up from Bolivia for Jayma's Memorial Service and spoke of their love for her and hers for them. Noah, who was working at that time as the personal photographer for the first democratically elected president of Bolivia of indigenous origin, Evo Morales, told the audience that one of Jayma's last wishes was to meet President Morales. "Ironically," Noah noted, "President Morales is on the Columbia campus at a Summit Meeting this very moment, but unfortunately it is too late for him to meet Jayma."

Jayma's love for children and her ability to relate to them as an added parent and a devoted friend extended beyond the Rudovsky children to her own nieces and nephew, who came along later, and finally to a friend's twin children who lost their father in the 9/11 attack. Jayma visited the twins, Lucy and Wyatt, every Sunday, arriving by 9:00AM and staying for a good part of the day. At the Memorial, the mother of the children described the weekly visits. "Jayma's coming, Jayma's coming!" they would shout. And then they would run to the door as they heard her approaching. She would spend hours with them, playing games, telling stories, and pitching balls to the little boy. Now there is another huge emptiness in their lives in addition to the absence of their father, the absence of Jayma.

Jayma was, for me, always the serious, responsible adult. She was such a classy looking woman in her thirties and forties, who wore simple but elegant clothes, mid-calf length skirts, and mostly black. She never talked about herself, but rather about her nieces and nephew and Noah and Jeannie and Lucy and Wyatt. I had not known Jayma when she was growing up. However, at her memorial service, one of her oldest friends talked about their childhood. She described how she and Jayma, who were classmates in elementary school, would dress up in costumes. "Jayma always had to be the brave queen throwing herself into the line of fire to save the people in distress. Wearing her robes, with a crown on her head, she would wave her toy sword and slay the phantom interlopers." The audience laughed in recognition, as the speaker told the story.

*I think of Jayma every April, when our birthdays arrive. I would want to talk to her about the latest political absurdity that we could laugh about together. But she is gone. Yet she lives on as a memorable example of the many rewarding but unexpected people and places that have touched my life.*

# THE GREAT WALL: CHINA 1981

Flying with our friends from the 1981 World Neurology Conference in Kyoto, we landed into the choking smog of the Beijing airport. Our friends spotted their tour company's banner and Bud and I were saying good-bye to them just as a small, poker-faced man approached us. "Are you Dr. and Mrs. Rowland?" he asked. He was dressed in a drab grey suit, looking as stiff as the Mao collar that hugged his neck. Bud nodded his head said "Yes" and I was about to add: "But how did you know?" But he grabbed our carry-on bags and just said, "My name is Liu. I work for the Foreign Affairs Branch of the Nanjing Health Department and I will be your guide for the next three weeks. Please follow me." He helped us with our checked luggage and led us to an outer waiting room where we were further greeted by a delegation from the Capital Hospital and Ms. Hsieng, the official Beijing guide. They led us to a black, square-shaped sedan, (made in the Soviet Union as were most of the cars in China at that time). It was waiting for us outside the terminal door. Our guides helped put our luggage in the trunk and we sped away on a forty-minute ride to the Peking Hotel in the heart of the city. The road was lined with thin trees on either side but no grass to hold down the dust. We were surrounded by bicycles, the number multiplying a hundred-fold as we got closer to the city, at which point the driver announced our presence, and our priority status, by leaning on the horn of the car throughout the remainder of ride. The few other cars on the road did the same, resulting in noise pollution that almost matched the concentration of dust in the air.

Mr. Liu and Ms Hsieng and the Russian Car

Our invitation to spend three weeks in China had come from the Health Department of the City of Nanjing. My brother Jack's friend from the war years, Reverend K.H. Ting, had arranged the trip. Our itinerary included visits to Beijing, Jinan, and a final stop in Nanjing, where the Ting family lived on the grounds of the Nanjing Theological Seminary, of which K.H. was the Director.

We arrived at the hotel and a bellman, accompanied by Mr. Liu and Ms. Hsieng, escorted us to a gloomy room that was filled with heavy mahogany furniture, dark red curtains, and almost no natural light. Our suitcases contained our clothes and two 60 watt bulbs that a friend had suggested we bring to replace the 20 watt versions in our bedside lamps. It was a good move that allowed us to read at bedtime. We ate in the hotel dining room in a room reserved for foreign guests only. Nearby, in a smaller dining room, Mr. Liu ate, accompanied by other Chinese guides. So, he was never far from us.

Bud and I spent our first morning in China on the Great Wall, the ancient structure that meanders through the mountains of North China, crumbling in some places, but sturdy in the segment near

Esther and Bud on the Great Wall

Beijing. We climbed up the uneven steps to the crowded walkway, a narrow path that had room for people going in two different directions, and enclosed by balustrades of solid stone. Among the myriad of tourists who were walking that morning were several neurologists who had been with Bud in Kyoto. So we were not surprised to bump into friends from various parts of the United States and even one from Italy. But Daniel Nathans, the Nobel Laureate and geneticist from Johns Hopkins in Baltimore, was also there that morning. He was on a sightseeing break from his lecture tour, half-seated in a niche in the wall and reading a guidebook. He had known Bud in the late 50s when both were residents at Presbyterian Hospital in New York. Bud recognized him.

"Dan Nathans? Is that you?" asked Bud. Dan looked up at us. "I'm Bud Rowland from Columbia. Remember me? And this is Esther, my wife."

"Oh my God," said Dan. "Bud Rowland." And the words tumbled out of his mouth: "I cannot believe my luck. You are just the person I want to see. What are you doing in China?"

"We are here for a three-week visit arranged by the Health Departments in Jinan and Nanjing and also a bit of sightseeing. But why am I just the person you were hoping to meet?"

Dan Nathans explained, "Yesterday I got a call from Guy McKhann [then the Chairman of Neurology at Hopkins]. A prominent Washington lawyer, a real big shot by the name of Philip Zeidman, had called Guy in desperate need of a neurologist in Beijing. Zeidman's son is in a Beijing Hospital with encephalitis. The father is frantic." Dan's voice got louder as he said "frantic." He then continued, "And out of the blue you appear. How long will you be in Beijing?"

"We're here for a couple of days. How old is the patient and what is he doing in Beijing?" Bud asked.

"He's an exchange student at Beijing University. He's twenty."

As he was talking, Dan pulled a piece of paper out of his pocket and handed it to Bud. "The kid's name is John Zeidman and he's in Beijing Hospital #1. Do you have time to see him?"

"I'll try to get there this afternoon," Bud replied as he took the paper.

Dan shook both of our hands very hard. Turning to me he said: "I hate to ruin your vacation time with Bud, Esther, but this is a matter of life and death-- literally. The kid is in a coma and has no family here."

We descended the stairs from the Wall to the parking lot and found Mr. Liu, waiting in the car. Bud told him of the new mission, and Mr. Liu responded. "But you are on a tour. We have an itinerary. We must do the things we set out to do." Bud replied: "Just direct me to Beijing Hospital #1 and let me see the patient and talk briefly to his doctor. It should not take long."

As much as I understood how important it was for the poor kid to see an American neurologist, I was a bit apprehensive about my workaholic husband's new mission, fearing that it would take more of his time than he announced. I knew how much he loved to feel morally useful when on vacation. I knew that he, and many of his doctor friends, believed that their primary goal was doctoring, even off-duty, and often at the expense of all other obligations, but I said nothing. And Mr. Liu, seeing how serious Bud was, agreed to help,

Shortly thereafter, Bud managed to see the boy, meet his caretakers, and talk with the State Department representatives who were already deeply involved in the case. Bud was satisfied that the boy, who was still comatose, was being treated by competent doctors, even though the cultural revolution in China had eradicated an entire generation of medical students by closing down all the medical schools for fifteen years. Beijing Hospital #1 was clean and had a good nursing staff, but the intravenous apparatus was ancient, and the mechanical ventilators that would help the unconscious patient breathe were primitive. So Bud recommended that John be transferred back to the United States as soon as possible. Arrangements were made for a transfer to a U.S. Army Hospital in Manila by military plane.

U.S. Military plane sent to Beijing to evacuate John Zeidman

For the next few days Bud was free to see all the sights in Beijing that had been on our agenda: the Forbidden City, the Ming Tombs, Tiananmen Square, and the Peking Opera. We both had a great time seeing the treasures of the Royal Palace, the Tatami Mat, woven of ivory, and the Emperor's Gown, woven of bronze and embroidered in silk. I marveled at the huge carved statues of camels and elephants and lions that lined the road to the Ming Tombs, and Bud agreed. As an opera lover of the western tradition, I thought I would hate the Chinese opera, which I had heard was traditional, heavily stylized, and cacophonous. But I found myself completely engaged in the form, once I realized that, unlike the opera I was accustomed to, this drama combined song, speech, gymnastics, dance, fabulous costumes and elaborate stage sets. Bud liked it too, and we even decided to go a second time. In our free time, Bud and I took walks in the neighboring parks where we became the object of staring Chinese who had not seen many Westerners before. We too did some staring, especially impressed by how the Chinese squat rather than sit on benches. We also stared at the toddlers who squat to urinate and to defecate, right through a slit in their pants. Sometimes we walked from our hotel to Tiananmen Square, looking at the gigantic portrait of Mao and, in preparation for the National holiday, October 1, the additional gigantic portraits of Marx, Engels, Lenin and Stalin. I wondered what Marx and Engels would have thought of the Cultural Revolution. Would they have seen it as a necessary step on the road to a socialist society? Or was it an aberration?

In 1981 Chinese men and women were still dressed alike, in Mao suits. The goal seemed to be to look as drab as possible. Long, fitted, colorful silk dresses with side slits, the typical favorite of Chinese woman of the pre-revolutionary era, were regarded as decadent and no longer acceptable, and high heels were gone. The night before we left Beijing, our official hosts invited us to a banquet in a good restaurant, a seemingly endless meal of delicious food. I sat near some young Chinese women who were employees of the Beijing Health Department. Between courses we chatted. I asked them whether they liked wearing the Mao uniform. The one sitting next to me turned to look at her friend on the other side who said, "We love the summer when we shed the jackets and wear colorful light cotton blouses." Both young women were smiling at what they considered to be a satisfactory answer. Although the Cultural Revolution was technically over by 1981, fear of saying or doing the "wrong" thing still prevailed. The object of the Cultural Revolution had been to create a new human being, devoid of class privilege or class differentiation. The attack had been focused on China's cultural institutions, its traditions, and the intelligentsia.

There was not much for Bud to do at the hospital, but he insisted that he be present at the patient's side on the day of the transfer. That was just the day we were leaving Beijing for Jinan. Hearing about this new addition to our itinerary, Mr. Liu, who had been helpful in accommodating Bud's wishes, finally lost his patience. We were sitting at breakfast and Mr. Liu had just come by with papers in his hand to tell us about the day's schedule. But instead, Bud told him about going to the airfield with the American student. "There are others who can help this boy," Mr. Liu said. "There are State Department representatives; there are the Chinese doctors. Beijing

Hospital #1 is the best in the country." Mr. Liu grabbed a chair to sit next to Bud, placing his papers on the table.

"Why do you think this is your responsibility when we have reservations on the train to Jinan, your host city, where you are the guests of the Department of Health. Do you not owe them the courtesy of arriving on time?"

Bud replied firmly: "'This is a matter of life and death of a critically ill boy whom I agreed to help. It looks like the case will be out of my purview in a few hours, but until the transfer is completed, I am the American doctor on call. We can take a later train to Jinan."

And Mr. Liu hastily replied, "We cannot take a later train. We have reservations on this one and this one only."

At eleven o'clock, Bud left the hotel in a car sent by the American consulate. An hour later, Mr. Liu arrived at the hotel room to take me to the train station, where he and I waited—for the train and for the missing Bud.

I asked, "What if he does not get here in time and we miss the train?"

And, clenching his teeth, Mr. Liu replied, "We cannot miss the train."

He said nothing more. I was surprised that he had not worked out an alternate strategy. He was not checking for a later train. He was not calling his boss to make apologies. He just sat there with me, looking at his watch from time to time, saying nothing.

The train arrived and so did Bud, within minutes of each other. Mr. Liu nodded as he saw Bud running toward us. He signaled to both of us to follow him onto the train and led us to a comfortable sleeper compartment that was decorated like a Victorian living room.

Mr. Liu and Esther on train

We collapsed onto the tasseled red cushions on soft couches that were turned into beds at night, and Bud told me what had happened at the airport. "When the Army plane arrived, the doctor on board refused to accept the patient. He took one look and said that John was too ill to be transferred. There was nothing to do then but return him to the Beijing Hospital, so the ambulance just turned around. Luckily, his parents are arriving tonight." Bud looked disappointed as he stretched out on the red cushions. He continued: "I guess the doctor was afraid that John would die in the plane, so he had to protect himself. But I still think the kid would have been better off at the American Army Hospital in Manila. Anyway, I am now out of the loop. I just hope they do the right thing."

We ate well on the train, and between meals, attendants brought us tea in porcelain cups that had their own matching covers to keep the tea hot. We read and slept and looked out of the windows to see water buffalos in the nearby rice paddies and tall mountains in the distance.

The train was completely full. I found out later that China has a few designated national holidays when workers who had been sent to far-off places were permitted to return to their families in the cities for a few days. We were in the middle of such a holiday at that moment. Thus the possibility of exchanging our train reservation for another time might well have been impossible. Mr. Liu must have pictured this potential disaster as he sat with me in the station, but he never said a word about it. His persistent frown changed into a relieved smile (one of the first I saw) when Bud finally appeared.

In Jinan, Bud's job was that of consultant. He saw patients in the morning and discussed them with the Chinese staff doctors. The afternoons were kept free for us to see the sights in the neighboring countryside. Jinan had been famous for its Mountain of a Thousand Buddhas. When we visited, half of these carved statuettes had been destroyed as symbols of a decadent culture. The huge park, which once had been a great source of pride, now looked neglected. There were empty spaces where Buddha statues had stood, and bare pedestals from which the Buddha statues had been lopped off. One of our guides suggested that the name of the park be changed to the Mountain of 500 Buddhas. Mr. Liu was our interpreter but we also joined tours for English speaking tourists. On one occasion we were taken to a People's Commune, a collective farm that reminded us of the kibbutzim we had visited in Israel. On this one in China, families lived in individual houses but shared the workload of the farm, the lumber mill, and the bakery. We were told that the participants shared 75% of the profits of each of the enterprises. As we onlookers gathered for a question and answer session with the Brigade Chief, one of the other Americans, knowing that homosexuals were denounced and hounded in China, asked, "How are gays treated on the collective farm?" The official looked puzzled for a moment, but then broke into a smile. "All of our people are happy and gay," he replied

One day Bud and I and our guides took a two-hour trip to the nearby mountains to see what we later deemed as the best sight in Shantung Province, the Linyan Temple. To get there we drove along acres of cultivated fields. Oxen were pulling a rectangular piece of wood, the plow, upon which stood a man, holding the reins and guiding the animals as he threw the seeds into the furrow. On the way we passed women washing clothes in the streams. When we arrived, we used the "bathroom," an open ditch topped by a wooden bench with holes carved into it. We had been in China for two weeks and I had by then gotten accustomed to, and proud (and relieved) to use, the open-air, community toilets. The main Temple was magnificent. What I liked the most were the huge wall cases, each containing a larger than life clay figure of a Buddhist monk. There were about 30 of these on display, each different from the others. The clay clothes they wore hung like real fabric and every figure had been molded from real humans and wore expressions that captured emotions such as happiness, anger and grief. The faces of the statues were done in beige clay and the robes in soft pastel colors. It all dated back to the Tang Dynasty of the 600s.

The last week of our trip was in Nanjing where we stayed in a hotel near the home of our friends, the Tings. They were my brother's closest friends in China, a couple he had met in Shanghai just as the war was ending and China's intellectuals were moving back from inland to the great coastal cities. The Americans were making plans to leave China, but there was still work to do. Jack spent his days in the office at the Air Force base doing the unit's statistical reports, and preparing for the transition. Each day he was free in the late afternoons and evenings to visit the Tings. He studied Chinese with Siu-May, a slim, bubbly woman with a twinkle in her eye and lots to say in perfect English, and he often stayed for dinner with Siu-May and her husband K.H., a bishop in the Episcopalian Church. In contrast to his wife, K.H. was a serious man, who spoke English softly and carefully, as if he were afraid that he might be misunderstood.

Jack met the Tings through Chinese friends he had made in Kunming and in Chungking, where he had been stationed for most of his tour of duty in the Second World War. Chungking was the place where the historic meeting between Chiang Kai-shek and Mao Tse-tung took place in September 1945. The day before that meeting, Jack and two of his fellow GIs, Ed Bell and Howard Hyman, spent an hour with General

Mao, a meeting that had been arranged by Kung Peng, one of their Chinese friends. She was Chou En-Lai's secretary and had asked Mao if he would like to meet some friendly American soldiers. It was a brief but pleasant meeting. The three soldiers gave Mao, who was a heavy smoker, a few cartons of American cigarettes and he asked them what they thought the American public knew about the political situation in China. Before the meeting ended they posed for a photograph that is now housed in the museum in Chungking.

Jack, Mao, Kung Peng, Ed Bell, Kung Peng's husband, Qiao Guan-hua, wearing eyeglasses, behind Ed; and Howard Hyman kneeling in front

A copy of the picture was reproduced in the guidebook that Bud was carrying as he boarded the plane at JFK to the Kyoto meeting and found himself sitting next to a man who was leading a China-bound tour. As they were making themselves comfortable, Bud's book dropped to the floor and he bent down to pick it up, saying to his seat mate: "You know, my brother-in-law's picture is in this guidebook. Let me show you," and he opened it to the famous snapshot of Mao and Jack and the other GIs. "How interesting!" the seatmate exclaimed. "And that guy on the other side of Mao just happens to be me." It was Ed Bell.

We arrived in Nanjing on the morning of October 6th at about 11:00AM, on a train that had been scheduled to arrive at 6:00AM. Our official greeters, Dr. Zhang-zho and his wife had come to meet us at 6:00 and then again at 10:00; finally we arrived at 11:00. They took us to the Nanjing Hotel, where we had lunch together and discussed our plans. After lunch, Siu-May Ting and her son Yenren appeared in the lobby, waiting to welcome us to their home city. I had not seen Siu-May since 1949, when she returned home to China after two years in New York City. As recipients of YMCA fellowships, she had worked for a master's degree at Teachers College and her husband had studied at the neighboring Union Theological Seminary. In 1948, their first son, Yenren was born in Women's Hospital at 110th St. and Amsterdam Avenue. Now, thirty-two years later, she was a victim of rheumatoid arthritis, using a walker. I had bought her a gift at the airport in Japan, a beautiful fountain pen, not realizing that her hands were crippled and her fingers gnarled. It was a happy and a sad reunion.

Mr. Liu and a local tour guide delivered us to the Tings's home later that afternoon. It was a spacious two-story house on the grounds of the Nanjing Theological Seminary, a home designated for the Director and his family. As we entered the grounds and approached the house, Mr. Liu appeared to be astonished. He also looked like we had ruined his day. We were not sure whether he was astonished that a single Chinese family was living in such a fancy place, or whether he was astonished that Bud and I had such important friends. Or perhaps he, like Bud and me, could not understand why, in Communist China, there was such an institution as a Theological Seminary, sitting on a grassy campus, with no students in sight. All we knew was that K.H., who was then also a member of the National People's Congress, China's legislative body, had the title of Bishop in the worldwide Anglican Church. One of his jobs was to show the western world that religion was tolerated in China, but that it had its own national characteristics, which fit the Communist ideology.

That evening Bud and I talked with the Tings about the Cultural Revolution and I was surprised and disheartened to learn that Siu-May and K.H., who had been active supporters of Mao's revolution in 1949, had been placed under surveillance because they had lived in the West and were fluent in English. The Red Guards had ransacked their home, destroyed their papers, their photographs, and their clothes.

At the onset of the Cultural Revolution, their oldest son, Yenren, had just started high school when the schools were closed down. Most students, including Yenren, joined the Red Guards, a mass youth movement, which supported Mao's plan to get rid of capitalists, landlords, feudal relics, religious trappings and capitalist ideology. The teenagers were also encouraged to spy on their parents and to denounce them if they were intellectuals. No one ever suggested that Yenren, or his younger brother, had done such a thing to their parents. But the Tings were well known intellectuals in the community and thus subject to persecution. Fortunately, in their case, it had been relatively mild. Other intellectuals had been beaten and publicly humiliated, and some had been imprisoned. On the train from Jinan to Nanjing, Bud and I had met an elderly man, dressed in Western clothes and smoking a pipe. He knew some English and we talked to him and to the woman with whom he was sitting. The man, Du Xua was a playwright, and the President of the Shanghai Writer's Association. The woman was a famous opera singer, Ren Gua Zhen. They told us that during the Cultural Revolution, she was out of a job and the opera company was closed. "In fact," she told us "there were only 8 approved operas that could be performed in China, all carefully selected by the ruling powers." Mr. Du, who had been imprisoned for four years, did not hesitate to say, "The Cultural Revolution was a fascist dictatorship."

Yenren in middle of back row with wife, baby and brother Siu-May and Esther in front

At dinner that evening Yenren talked about his experience in the countryside, hundreds of miles away from home where he worked as a farm hand in the rice fields and later in a steel mill. I asked him: "Was that a good thing for you, a city boy, to work side by side with the peasants?" "No." he replied, "The peasants hated us because we just got in the way. They could not understand what we were doing there."

When it was all over, and he returned home to his family in the late seventies, he and his younger brother studied on their own to pass the qualifying tests for admission to the university. They both passed. The brother was admitted, but because Yenren was more than thirty years old at that time, (he was 31), he was too old to be offered a place. My brother

Jack helped Yenren enroll in a junior college in Oakland, California, where he maintained a perfect record. Then he was admitted to Columbia, and I invited him to live with us, which he gladly did. He started by taking classes in the summer of 1981, just before Bud and I went to China. Preparing me for my trip, Yenren taught me the words to "Chee Lai," the Chinese national anthem, and together we listened to Paul Robeson's recorded version.

"Chee Lai"
www.**youtube**.com/watch?v=GYGYvQICcks

In return for the free room and board, Yenren happily walked our dog in midday and took charge of cleaning up after meals. Otherwise he remained in his room studying hour after hour, and going out only to his classes and to the library. To save time at the lunch break, he chose a daily diet of ramen noodles because they were inexpensive and because they took the least time to prepare.

I relished the opportunity to meet again with Siu-May and to have a private talk with her, just the two of us. And we met for a final time the following day when Bud was lecturing at the medical school. I knew I could find out what she really thought. She was smart, and caring, and wise, and she fit into American culture so well, when she lived in the United States between 1947 and 1949, that it was hard to believe that she grew up in a country as different from ours as China. We had had many long talks back then and I almost felt like she was a big sister. So I asked her: "How was the Cultural Revolution permitted to thrive when so many people were so adversely affected by it? Who were the perpetrators and how were they permitted to do so much harm?" She answered. "Young people like Yenren were the Red Guards. In the beginning they were completely caught up in the movement and we parents neither encouraged nor discouraged them. Later, as the network of victims became an ever-widening circle, the Red Guards themselves got caught up in their own destruction and bitterly fought each other. The whole movement had the approval, and probably the instigation of the highest officials, especially Chairman Mao." As she spoke, her voice was tinged with both anger and sadness. "As time went on, the pattern of the Cultural Revolution became more vindictive. Our friend,

Kung Peng (Chou En-lai's secretary) was ill with cancer and she was denied treatment. No doctors, no hospital, no chemotherapy. She died-- an early death. Her husband, Qiao Guanhua, was one of the high officials, (Foreign Minister), who supported the Cultural Revolution. He had a brilliant mind, but you must know, Esther," and she looked at me with an expression on her face that was serious and also sad, "that intellect is not everything."

"Is he still alive? Do you see him?" I asked.

"He is remarried and we no longer have any contact with him," Siu-May replied, making it clear that she preferred not to discuss him further. I was taken aback to hear about the persecution of the Tings the day before, and then again about the treatment of Kung Peng, that beautiful young woman in Jack's picture. I was reminded of something my friend Leo Huberman, the socialist writer and editor, once said: "Even though I would be a strong supporter of 'the revolution', I know I shall be among the first to be thrown into prison by the new revolutionary government."

When we returned to New York, Bud and I described our experiences to a non-Communist, leftist friend, a social scientist from Italy, who assessed the Chinese situation with an air of academic objectivity. "Ah," said Giovanni, "the Chinese have found a way to eliminate the burdens of the old traditional bureaucracy, the army, and the institutions that needed to be by-passed, to make way for the new society." It was a sociological analysis, with no approval or disapproval stated. I was impressed with this way of dealing with an historical development, especially since I have always wondered how a society could get rid of the inequality between the worker and the intellectual, between the rich and the poor. I would automatically have agreed that drastic steps should have to be taken. And I was almost ready to say to Giovanni, "Perhaps this was a necessary step." But, having seen how it affected the Tings and Kung Peng, all ardent supporters of the Chinese Revolution, made me ask, "At what price?" For Bud, seeing the near-destruction of scientific and medical progress and the sacrifice of an entire generation of medical students, the Cultural Revolution was an abomination.

A few days after our return, eager to get news of the American student, Bud called Dan Nathans and found out that the young man had eventually made it back to Johns Hopkins, but never recovered consciousness. He died three months later in January.

*Yenren returned to New York in 1984, became an outstanding student, and went back to China with both a bachelor's degree from Columbia College and a master's from Teachers College to become Professor of Teaching Of English as a Foreign Language in Nanjing Normal University. His mother died many years ago and his father died recently. Yenren writes to Jack and to me every Christmas.*

# RIVER RAFTING ON THE SAN JUAN: 1985

In May 1985 Bud had just accepted an invitation to be a visiting professor for a few days at the University of Colorado Medical School in Denver, when our phone rang. It was Bill Landau, the Chief of Neurology at Washington University, calling us from St. Louis.

"Can you believe," he asked, "that I've managed to get four other neurologists and their wives to take a rafting trip on the San Juan River in southern Utah? If a few more come, like you and Esther for instance, we can have a whole boat to ourselves." Bud and I were both on the phone.

"What are the dates?" I asked.

"The week before Memorial Day. It's a five day trip on the river and a day to get there and a day to return."

"We'll talk it over and call you back," said Bud.

As it happened, the opening day of the raft trip was the day after the Denver job was to end. The timing was perfect. We could make the short trip from Denver to Bluff, Utah, and join the group just as they were assembling. "Let's go!" I was excited, and Bud agreed. We called Billy back and signed on.

When I told our office staff at Barnard the next day, I became the envy of all those smart young clerical workers who were an especially athletic, and outdoorsy bunch. They volunteered, not only to cover me in my absence, but also to supply me with loans of their best down sleeping bags, and lots of advice about camping in the wilderness.

The Sunday we left for Denver was also Bud's annual department picnic and baseball game. The plan was to go directly to the airport from the picnic, which we did, even though the last slide, onto the plastic garbage bag that was serving as a makeshift third base, left Bud with a knee that continued to swell for the next six hours. By the time we arrived in Denver, he required a wheel chair to get from the gate to the cab. "It'll be better tomorrow," he said. But it got worse and he spent the next days lecturing and making rounds in a borrowed wheel chair. Fortunately his lectures took place in a hospital so, between sessions, he saw orthopedists and x-ray technicians, none of whom could explain the ever-swollen knee. Nothing was broken, that was certain. And despite his temporary disability, Bud was enjoying the challenge. On the morning of the day of the raft trip I was in the hotel room packing and Bud was on the phone with me just before delivering his final lecture, still in the wheel chair.

"I'm able to work from a wheel chair, but that's not a way to go camping. So let's find out if we can cancel the trip—we'll go another time-- so find out about the direct flights to New York instead of the flight to Cortez," he said.

I called the Wild River Outfitters, and told them about Bud's condition.

"Oh I am so sorry to hear that," the trip organizer said, and he sounded really sorry. "You know it's too late for a refund, we have already bought all the supplies. Can you get your husband at least as far as Bluff, where we are to launch? He could rest in the motel the first day, if necessary, and be delivered by car to join the group the following day at Mexican Hat. That would be just before we enter the inaccessible part of the river."

I said, "I don't think that will work, but I'll ask him."

By that time I knew that Bud had already decided to go home. He had been away from his office long enough. There were patients to see and a department to run—even from a wheelchair. So I called Dawn, my secretary, who had been planning the trip with me as if she herself were going.

"Guess what?" I said, "I'll be back at work tomorrow." And I explained why. "Bud has been having leg pain all week and even though he is getting better, he wants to get back to New York, and to work."

Hearing my disappointment, Dawn asked, "Can't you go by yourself? Does he need you on his trip back to New York?"

Bud called me back an hour later to hear about the new arrangements.

I asked, "Bud, tell me the truth, if I get you a direct flight to New York and we order you a wheelchair in both airports, do you need me to be there to help you?"

"Of course not," he said. "Why do you ask?"

"Because I decided I'm going on the trip, without you." And I added, "Unless you really need me."

"Oh no you're not!" he shouted. "You go and I go too!"

Then I told him of the alternative offered by the rafting company and he was happy to give it a try. In the end, he was better enough by the time we launched to be reasonably comfortable on the raft and better and better each day thereafter. He had self-diagnosed his ailment as gout, for which he had already started the medication.

For five days we rode the San Juan River, surrounded on all sides by the browns and the yellows and purples of the Southwest's low striated mountains with flat mesa tops. We bobbed on the rapids: mostly classified as mild twos and threes, and an occasional dangerous four or five. We stopped for walks into the wilderness where we saw almost intact Anasazi ruins, ruins that had not been looted because they were inaccessible to the potential thieves who would have had to come by way of the river and its rapids, or by helicopter landing on the mesa. We slept under the stars, with no tents blocking the view of the sky. The meals were simple, fresh and tasty: grilled meat and vegetables and lots of fresh fruit and salads. One of our boats was filled with the supplies of fresh meat and produce that would be needed for a five-day trip. Our cooks were the crew, a half-dozen caring young men and women, all in love with the serenity and beauty of the wilderness that they knew was on its way to oblivion no matter how much they taught us to respect its sanctity. We learned to pick up everything we dropped, some to be carried back with us on the boats, some organic material such as food and excrement to be buried properly in the sandy terrain. There were no toilets. We just found places behind rocks to evacuate. After dinner we gathered for stories and song, with the flowing San Juan River as our backdrop. Dan Murphy, our guide, sang a beautiful

*Una Furtiva Lacrima*, a Donizetti aria. He told us he used to sing it down near the Hudson River when he was a graduate student at Columbia. The evenings, lit by the stars and filled with the sounds of the river, ended with an early bedtime.

On the fifth day, we arrived at Lake Powell, the end of the river. After landing, we were returned by truck, to Bluff, to the Recapture Lodge, our original gathering place. Bud and I had arranged transport to Cortez Colorado on a four-seat Cessna run by a small outfit that serves rafters, hikers, and sightseers. At the Lodge, a friendly couple that owned a station wagon offered us a ride to a field of wheat where the little plane was awaiting us. When we arrived at the field, the plane was parked with the motor idling and the pilot signaled us to hop aboard as he sat there with his hands on the controls. I asked him if he would get out to help us with our duffel bag, since Bud was still using a cane. "I guess so," he said reluctantly, and he cut the motor, limped out, dragging his paralyzed left leg, and gave us a hand. (Later that day we learned that the hemiplegia was the result of an emergency landing he had made while piloting a similar plane.)

All seated and ready to go, he instructed us on how to unlatch the door in case of emergency and then he turned the key to the motor. It sounded like our old Peugeot, which we got rid of because it was so hard to start. One try, another, another and then the carburetor flooded, the sparks were flying, and all of a sudden there was smoke and the smell of burning, and then the flames appeared. The pilot reached for the fire extinguisher. "Oh damn," he said. "It's empty!" The fire got larger each second and he shouted, "Get out!" I was glad that I had paid attention to his door-opening instructions, and I thought about trying to retrieve our duffle containing $400 worth of borrowed sleeping bags, but decided not to risk it. Bud, in the front seat, I in the back, and the pilot, all got out at the same time. Bud and I held hands and together ran and hobbled as far away as possible from the burning craft. We watched the fire as it began to consume the entire plane, but left when the fire department arrived. We gladly accepted a ride back to town from the same couple who drove us to the airport, and who had decided to wait until the plane took off. I am sure they entertained their friends for weeks after, telling the story of offering strangers a ride to the airport and watching in horror the blaze instead of the take-off. The pilot was with us in the car. Using a wireless phone he had taken with him from the plane, he called his company. Bud and I were busy telling our driver to drop us off at the café in town rather than at the Lodge, when we heard the pilot say to his boss, "the passengers are an elderly couple from New York." (I had just turned 59 and Bud was 60.) As we told our story to our fellow rafters who were gathered in the cafe, we became the center of attention. One of them drove us back to the field to see the charred remains. The fire fighters had been unable to save anything.

Back in the café, we had to address the issue of how to get out of there to meet our scheduled flight from Cortez early the next morning. We decided that the airplane company owed us a safe trip to Cortez, and not in another one of their crummy planes. Two men from the company finally arrived to talk to us.

"We'll be happy to provide you with a car to get from Bluff to Cortez," one of them said as he unfolded a map and pointed to where we were. "You should drive fifty miles north to Blanding, Utah, another hour across over into Colorado, and then another fifty miles south, and finally another two hours to Cortez, due east."

Because Bud's knee was still swollen, I was the designated driver. It was already getting dark and the thought of a five- hour drive in unknown territory was making me nervous. "Why the fifty miles north and then again south, wasn't there a direct road from Bluff to Cortez?"

The answer was: "Yes there is, but you've got to ford the river."

I remembered living in Bethesda and driving through Rock Creek Park where we enjoyed the river ford on that road, especially in the spring when we had to drive through six inches of water.

"Can't we do that?" I asked, "rather than drive the extra hundred miles? Show us on the map just which road to take."

While they were puzzling over the correct response to that question, a young guy, kind of short with reddish hair, who had been sitting at the next table, walked over and greeted the plane company men by name, to which one replied: "Hi Fred! Nice to see you."

"I was listening to your conversation," Fred told us, as he joined our table, "and although I was planning to spend the night in Bluff, I would be happy to drive you to Cortez. I live there and would be going back there early tomorrow morning anyway, but tonight is okay."

Fred Blackburn had saved us. We felt a little funny allowing a perfect stranger to make such a generous offer, but the atmosphere in this small café in the middle of nowhere fostered that kind of comradeship. Fred knew everybody there and he acted as if we too were his buddies. He escorted us to his VW beetle, no baggage this time, and off we went. The road was a two-lane, country highway, which became less and less occupied by cars the further we drove. After an hour or so Fred stopped the car, for no discernible reason I thought. There was no sign that said: "Stop! River Ahead!" or "Caution, Road Disappearing!" no warning at all, but the sound of a river was unmistakable. Fred jumped out, rolled up his pants knee high, and walked into the river until he got to the middle of it, the deepest part. When he returned he knew just how deep it was, actually just below his knee. He revved up the engine and with perfect concentration, drove the car through it at a steady pace. When we got to the other side of the river Fred told us how many cars get stuck because the drivers lose their nerve and stop in the middle. Once that happens, the car stalls and that's the end of it. So this was a real ford, not a Rock Creek Park less-than-one-footer. Had I been the driver, I knew that I would have driven into the river and stopped in the middle, or even more likely driven up to the river, turned around, and headed back to Bluff in tears.

During the easy part of the drive Fred told us a bit about his life. He was born in Cortez and knew everything about the land, the mountains, and the indigenous people who lived there. He was an anthropologist who taught at Southern Utah State University, specializing in leading field trips into the wilderness and serving as expert guide to the Anasazi culture. He was known in the world of anthropology for his concept of a living museum, meaning that the artifacts belonged where they had been found, not removed to safe storage within the walls of a building. (*The Smithsonian magazine, several years after our meeting, hailed Fred as a pioneer in his field.*)

But getting back to our ride. Everything went smoothly until we approached a well-lit tavern on the highway, just outside of Cortez. Fred slowed the car and it was clear that he was nervous. It was Memorial Day Weekend; the bar was filled to capacity with locals who would be driving dead drunk as they left the bar to return to their homes. Fred knew how many deaths there had been each year on this very evening. We got through the flaming plane, we got through the ford, but who would ever dream that a tavern on the road could be another, equally dangerous hazard? Fred drove us safely to the motel in Cortez and the next day we got safely home. After telling Bud that I would go without him, I was really happy that he had been with me every step of the way. And he agreed, but added, with a big smile on his face: "This is an example of how your feminist antics nearly got us both killed."

*A few years later Fred, who ran a workshop in Colorado that trained volunteers to understand and appreciate American Indian cultures, helped Pearl, one of my Barnard premeds, find a summer placement with the Southern Ute Tribe, after she successfully completed his training program. It turned out to be an invaluable experience for her and for the Ute family she lived with, who "adopted" her. Pearl, a Korean American had straight black hair and almond-shaped eyes, much like her hosts. They adored her and she in turn set up a recreational program to occupy the young people of the tribe during the long summer months when they were not in school.*

# A SURREAL STORY: MARSEILLE 1986

In the spring of 1986 Bud was told that he had been selected to receive an honorary degree from the University of Aix-Marseilles, but the date had not yet been set. He was also told that at the ceremony-to-be, he would have to make an acceptance speech and speak in French, a language he had never studied. "Well," he said to me, "at least I have lots of time to write a speech, and maybe get a French tutor."

"Will you talk about something neurological?" I asked.

"Oh, no," he answered. "It'll probably take place at a general commencement ceremony. I think I'll talk about New York and Marseille. They are both huge port cities with lots of immigrants. It will be fun to look for the similarities and differences." And with that noble sentiment, he promptly forgot about the degree and the speech, hoping to discuss it further with our friends in Marseille at a neurological meeting we were to attend there in May.

On May 16 we went off to Japan for a meeting in Kumamoto, which was to last for five days. After that we were due in Marseille at a special congress on neuromuscular disease (Bud's specialty). When we arrived in the hotel on the bustling Vieux Port in the center of Marseille, the registration clerk handed Bud an envelope. He opened it as we were checking in. I read it with him. It was from our French hosts and it said:

"Hoping to save you the wear and tear of an extra trip to Marseille for the commencement, we have managed to arrange the honorary degree ceremony to take place on May 30th, at the conclusion of this Marseille meeting. The degree can be offered without a full commencement ceremony, and the Rector of the University has scheduled it to coincide with the closing ceremony of our Neurological Congress."

"Oh my God!" said Bud, sliding the paper into his pocket, as we followed the porter to our room. Instead of a few months, he had three days to prepare his talk.

Without unpacking we ran from the hotel to a large bookstore on the Canabière, the long wide street that ran through the center of town. We knew the store because we had bought English language books there on a previous visit. Bud thought we could surely get a history of Marseille in English and that he could come up with some interesting connections to New York.

"What do you have about Marseille in English?" Bud asked.

"This entire table, Monsieur," the clerk replied and, walking around the table, he picked up and showed us every tourist guide they carried: Marseille museums, monuments, hotels, restaurants, things-to-do, and so on and on. Not one book was going to help and we were crestfallen. Suddenly, the clerk remembered something. He escorted us to the Art section and produced a large, recent arrival, a book on Surrealism, which was written in both French and English. Just glancing through it convinced us that this would be the source Bud needed.

Back in the hotel, the young French neurologist who had been delegated to become Bud's language tutor came to our room.

"You know," said Bud, "I don't know a word of French. I studied German and Latin in school."

Jean-Claude replied, "Don't worry. You will only have to say about three sentences in French and then you can switch to English." He smiled as he continued: "You know how we Frenchmen are. We love our language. We want people to speak French when they are in France. But we also cannot bear to hear it spoken incorrectly." Then he took out his agenda and asked Bud when he would be free. "I can come to you for about an hour each day for the next two days and more on the last day—as needed. Just write the greeting: something like 'Ladies and Gentlemen, thank you for coming. I am honored to be here.' I'll translate it into French and we'll practice the pronunciation. Then you can declare that your aim is to spare their ears from further pain and switch into English for the remainder of the talk." It was wise advice. Four hours of practice was barely enough for even those few sentences.

Bud and I read through the book and learned about a crucial period in the history of Marseille, when it was under Vichy rule. In 1940, an order had been delivered to Occupied France by their German conquerors that all German and Austrian citizens who were living in France had to be deported back to the Third Reich immediately. By cooperating with this demand, the Vichy regime was making it clear that the designated refugees and even French citizens who were "enemies" of the Third Reich were no longer protected from the Germans. Word of this had reached the United States where powerful and concerned Americans spontaneously formed an Emergency Rescue Committee. Its goal was to save as many as possible of the great artists and intellectuals, by transporting them to the United States, arranging for exit visas as well as U.S. visas, forging documents when necessary, and leading them over the mountains to Spain and then to neutral Portugal to find a ship to New York City.

The person hired for the job of sorting out the people who would be saved in this way was a young American Quaker and Harvard graduate by the name of Varian Fry. He had seen the Nazis at work as a journalist in Berlin in the mid thirties and he knew that Hitler's goal was to murder the people he considered his enemies. Fry turned out to be extraordinary: courageous, hard working, and dedicated to his mission. He threw himself into the job with total commitment. He embarked immediately to Marseille, worked from a hotel room near the Vieux Port, right on the Canabière, and proceeded to do his job with the help of a few trusted men and women, who were already living in France. Within this group was a twenty-five year old German refugee with a French passport, whom he nicknamed "Beamish" because of the way his eyes lit up each time another seemingly impossible task was presented to him. Working day and night to sort through the thousands of refugees who had found their way to Marseille, to select the ones to whom the precious American visas would be issued, Fry and his team were ultimately credited with saving the lives of as many as 2000 artists, poets, writers, musicians and other intellectuals, including Marc Chagall, Hannah Arendt, Jacques Lipschitz, Franz Werfel, and his wife, Alma Mahler, and several of the founders of Surrealism.

The remarkable story of the Rescue Committee is now better known. Fry himself wrote a book, *Surrender on Demand*, published in 1945. There have been a few books written after our visit in 1986, and an exhibit about the mission was shown in the nineties at the Holocaust Museum in Washington and then transported to the Jewish Museum in New York. But at the time of Bud's commencement address, the only reference we knew of this life-saving adventure, which happened to link Marseille to New York, was our art book which described the experience of Andre Breton, the poet and author of the first Surrealist Manifesto, Andre Masson, Wilfredo Lam, and Max Ernst, the painters, among others, as they awaited documents that would take them out of France and rescue them from certain death. Bud went on to describe how Fry, tired of his hectic but lonely life in the Hotel Splendide in the center of Marseille, discovered an empty mansion on the outskirts of the city. Excited over the prospect of living on an estate, away from the crowded city, he rented the property for himself and his staff, as well as for a number of clients. The artists and writers, Breton, Masson and their associates, created a Surrealist salon and residence at the Villa Air-Bel, also called "Chateau Espère-Visa" by Victor Serge, the Russian revolutionary writer and activist who was one of the dwellers. They passed their time at communal meals, discussions, and lots of games. One of the games, "Le Cadavre Exquis" (Exquisite Corpse), required the players to draw a part of a figure (head, torso, or legs), fold it over, and pass it on to the next player who had no idea of what had been done before. When all the players had completed their contributions, the large paper would be unfolded to reveal an amazing body. Eventually most of the members of the group ended up in New York. Bud concluded his talk by describing how this Marseille-New York connection saved the lives of so many great European contributors to world culture and thereby enriched American culture a thousand-fold. Judging from the compliments he received after the talk was over, the audience was fascinated and pleasantly surprised. Expecting a speech about science and neurology, they got one about art and the nail-biting escapades used to evade the Nazis, a little known piece of the history of the Second World War that linked the two great cities.

Bud, reading his talk, after receiving his honorary degree from the
University of Aix-Marseille

Back home a few weeks later, I told our story to Flora Schiminovitch,
a professor of Spanish at Barnard College, who had written her doctoral
dissertation on Macedonio Fernandez, an Argentinean surrealist writer.
"But that is the essence of Surrealism," she declared, excitedly, sounding like
a professor sounds when her student finally is able to see the connections.
"Surrealism is the expression of the totally unexpected, the unplanned, the
irrational or perhaps the mystical experiences in our life on this earth. You
lived it by finding that book. They, the Surrealists, lived it by the unantic-
ipated appearance of Varian Fry. Chance is the glue-point of all Surrealist
connections."

Now, many years later we are still flabbergasted by such things as
finding Varian Fry's original papers, which had been deposited at the
Columbia University library, just two blocks from our home, and by
the International Rescue Committee, which was led by George Rupp,
Columbia's former President, with whom we had a personal connection.
Even more astonishing, in 1996 Albert Hirschman, a famous Professor of
Economics at Princeton's Institute of Advanced Study, came to our home
to attend a party we held for our friend, Marta, who had been his col-
league. A few weeks after that party, I visited an exhibit of Varian Fry's

rescue work at the Jewish Museum in New York. That exhibit identified the historic "Beamish" as Albert Hirschman, "now Professor of Economics at Princeton University," the man sitting in our living room the day of the party.

Flora Schiminovitch, my friend in the Spanish Department, also entered our lives unexpectedly, surrealistically. In the early sixties Bud and I and the children were living in Englewood and summering in Woods Hole, Massachusetts. One August day at Stony Beach in Woods Hole, I met a young, vivacious woman with dark curly hair, a broad friendly smile and a "Hola. how are you?" to everyone in a charming Spanish accent. As we explored each other's lives, I discovered that Flora was born in Argentina and came to the United States when she was in her twenties seeking a better life than she and her university compatriots were experiencing under the government of Juan Peron. I also discovered that Flora and her husband Sam, a physicist, lived in Englewood, just a block away from us. On the beach that day, we agreed that we would look for each other in Englewood once we returned in the fall. Early in October, Flora called and announced that she was walking over with her baby for a visit. They came, and my mother, who was also visiting that day, made tea and we chatted. In the course of the conversation, Flora mentioned that she had a brother in Hollywood who wrote film music and had written, with much acclaim, the theme song for *Mission Impossible*, the most popular TV show at that time.

"What's your brother's name?" I asked.

"Lalo Schifrin," she replied.

My mother and I looked at each other in astonishment.

"Shifrin is my mother's family name. Could we be related?"

Flora replied, "I don't know. But I am related to a large Shifrin family in New York. When I first arrived here from Argentina, they found me an apartment. They gave me clothes, including an old mink coat, which I still have. I know Bella Shifrin and David Shifrin and ..."

My mother ran over to Flora and hugged her tight. "We are cousins! Now sit here and tell us," my mother said while pouring tea into a cup and handing it to Flora, "How did those Shifrins get to Argentina?"

"When my grandfather left Russia to go to New York," Flora said, "his boat was stopped in Liverpool. The passengers had to evacuate because of a typhus epidemic. They got on the next ship to America, but this one went to South America." She laughed as she moved her arm from high to low. "So he landed in Buenos Aires, where he met and married my grandmother. They had a son, my father, who studied classical violin and became the first violinist at the Teatro Colon. You know," she explained, "that's the great opera house in Buenos Aires. It's a beauty." She continued as she reached for her tea, "Lalo and I were born in Buenos Aires but we are both now in the United States. Did you know that when Lalo arrived here, the Shifrins arranged for him to live with our American cousin David Shifrin, who became one of the world's greatest clarinetists. What a wonderful experience that was for two budding musicians." Flora put her cup down, leaned her elbow on the table and her hand onto her forehead as she was thinking about the Shifrin family and all of its branches. "Isn't our chance meeting a strange coincidence?" she asked.

"You might say it was surreal!" I said with a big smile.

# INDIA, 1986

As I reached into the drawer to find the one sari I owned and had never worn, a dark green silk, trimmed in what looked like real gold, I could not help wondering if this visit to India that Bud had so quickly accepted was a mistake. We had never wanted to travel to India because of the extreme poverty we dreaded seeing. But Bud reasoned that this trip was different. He was to be the first American neurologist to give the annual Oration sponsored by the T.S. Srinivasan Foundation in Madras. The Oration was to be given in November 1986, and the trip itself was to be a three-week tour of India, with lectures in and visits to the north and the south. I was included in the invitation and we were to be housed, fed and given access to a car and driver in each of four major cities. How could we turn down such an alluring offer? A few weeks after Bud accepted, we received our tickets, packed our bags, and read as much as we could about Indian history.

Doctor (Professor) and Doctor (Mrs.) Barucha met us in the Bombay airport at midnight, when the plane landed. He was the Professor of Neurology at the University Hospital in Bombay where Bud had been asked to visit. The Baruchas were both physicians, both in their eighties. He, a tall man, was wearing an open collared shirt and lightweight slacks, western style. She, a slim woman with her grey hair tied in a ponytail, was wearing a rumpled cotton sari with rubber flip-flops on her feet. They seemed relieved to have spotted us as we entered the waiting room, greeted us warmly, and directed us to a large black sedan parked near the front door. Mrs. B was the driver. I had thought Indian professionals would have servants and drivers and ironed clothes and leather shoes. Obviously this was not the case with this woman, who, I soon discovered, prided herself on her involvement with the important things in life, like teaching her grandchildren to speak Maharati, the language of Bombay. She had no interest in clothes. With our luggage safely packed in the trunk, she drove us to our hotel and, later that week, in heavy traffic, to see the sights. I soon discovered that her driving style was to push the pedal and go, and then deal with the police, most of whom knew her well and gently cautioned her to please observe the rules, not ride in the oncoming traffic lane, and not ride the wrong way on a one way street, even for a short distance.

From the Bombay airport to the Taj Mahal Hotel, where we were staying, the road was lined with huge concrete pipes, cut open at both ends, in which hundreds of Indian families were living. When we arrived in the heart of the city, the pipes ended and we passed shantytowns, filled with people who were chatting, or selling goods to one another, or eating and drinking, as if it were midday. When we reached the Taj, a grand hotel facing the sea, the people were sleeping in the doorways of the nearby shops, their belongings encased in cotton bags, their beds unfolded. When we emerged from the hotel later that morning, they and their bundles were gone.

The Taj, a hotel that caters to royalty and Bollywood stars, is just a block away from the Salvation Army residence, the Red Shield House, where my friend Carmel was living. Carmel had moved to Bombay from New York soon after her divorce in the early seventies. In India she could live cheaply and undertake a new career as art-historian, photographer, and later, sculptor working in bronze. She had studied sculpture in the

United States and had put her training to good use as an artist and as a connoisseur of Indian art. Since arriving in India, she had become an authority on Indian cave sculptures and Hindu myths and legends.

Carmel arrived in the hotel lobby just after Bud had left to visit the hospital with Dr. Barucha. Her hand was partially covering a swollen mouth. "Forgive the way I look," she said as we hugged each other. "It's the penalty for living in a room without a fridge. I grabbed a cookie from a package on the shelf and bit into it without looking. It was full of ants that bit me back. Anyway it's so great to see you. Let's go."

We had arranged to spend the morning at Elephanta, one of the great rock-carved sculpture sites in India, this one just an hour away by boat. Carmel knew the story of every cave, pointed out the intricacies of the carvings, the placement of the figures, the meaning of the symbols. I was deeply impressed with the craftsmanship, by the beauty of the sculptures, by the monumental effort to depict the stories of the Hindu Gods that had been carved into those rocks more than a thousand years ago.

The following day, Bud was free and the Baruchas spent the morning with us. They were of the Parsi religion, which does not believe in burying the dead; rather they prefer recycling. That day, they took us to the Parsi graveyard, an enormous park where the vultures feed on the bodies laid out above the ground in a special closed off area. Fortunately, no funerals were being held on the day we were there and we did not witness any vulture luncheons. For our own lunch, the Baruchas took us to their club, originally a British Club, "No Indians Allowed," in the days of the Empire, but now catering to Indians, like the Baruchas, who seemed to thoroughly enjoy belonging to this beautiful establishment. We sat in a huge outdoor dining room that had a roof, but no walls, and crows lined up on the wooden rafters, swooping down to pick morsels off the trays carried by the waiters. No one minded when the birds retrieved scraps from the trays of those who had completed their meals. The more challenging experience, for waiters and diners alike, was when the birds picked off morsels from the food about to be served.

We learned quickly that begging was pervasive and the beggars were persistent. Many times on that trip we were confronted by pleading women carrying sickly, sometimes deformed children. And often, the deformed children, some still toddlers, were also begging. The problem was that if the tourist offered one beggar some rupees, that became a signal to all the nearby others to gather, soliciting by using the most pathetic gestures, with their hands held together as in prayer, and sometimes on their knees. If I wished to back off, I could sense a mounting hostility. It was a fearsome moment, with no easy solution. Later I asked Carmel what she did as she walked in the street. "The alternative is to give to a responsible charity that helps the Indian homeless. That's what I do," she said. "But, I agree" she added "that when you are on the street it's not easy to just avert their pleas, even if you know that you are helping in a different way." One day I hurried past a small group of women who were begging and as I passed them, with my eyes turned away, one of them shot out her foot to trip me. I caught my balance and hastened on angrily. They were laughing as I ran from them.

From Bombay we stopped briefly in Hyderbad and then spent a week in Madras, participating in all the ceremonies that preceded and followed the Oration that Bud had been invited to deliver. The wealthy endowers of the lectureship, the Srinivasan family, attended the lecture and the reception afterward. I wore my green and gold sari. Maithili, the Indian woman tour guide who had taken me all over Madras in a three-wheeler that morning, came to the hotel room to teach me the art of sari draping and even pinned me up for safety. The rash act of wearing a sari endeared me to our host family, and, perhaps because of that, we became great friends thereafter.

Prema Srinivasan, front row second from left, her family, and Esther

Prema Srinivasan invited Bud and me to dinner in her home that night. Her house is part of a compound of several buildings, the largest of which is the home of her eldest son. There are also garages, and homes for the servants. The water in India is contaminated and although the local population has developed a tolerance for it, foreigners are warned to avoid drinking anything but bottled water. The Srinivasans purify their own water and pipe it into the many buildings so foreign guests (as well as the family) can drink from the tap. Prema's home is decorated in Italian contemporary style with large 20th century Western paintings on the walls and good Italian modern furniture. One of her closest friends is an Italian architect whom she has hired as a consultant. He helped remodel her home and has become something between a member of her household staff and a member of the family. One of the rooms in Prema's house is reserved for daily prayer with a guru, a Hindu priest who would come each morning to offer spiritual guidance. Together they would meditate, surrounded by large pictures and sculptures of the gods and goddesses, with wreathes and vases filled with fresh flowers.

Our hosts insisted we see all the important sights that were within a two-hour drive from Madras. We visited the great sculptures at Mahabalipuram. They took us to the sea, to bathe and to spend a few hours resting in a cabana. One afternoon we went to the Madras Snake Park—but not alone. On the way we stopped at the home of the Srinivasans' friend, Harry Miller, who was an active member of the Park directorate and who took us on a personally guided tour of the center for the study of herpetology. He found me to be a willing disciple as he handed me one after another snake to examine. "May I?" he asked as he reached over my head, draping a bunch of snakes, as one would place a long scarf, over my shoulders, all the while assuring me that none would harm me.

I am not certain that I actually liked wearing live animals around my neck, but I managed to go along with the novelty of the experience, much as I had enthusiastically eaten fugu (raw blowfish) in Tokyo, knowing that if it had not been prepared properly I would die within an hour. I trust people who I believe are knowledgeable, and so far it has worked. It is also called "being a good sport".

One day our guide drove us to a shrine in the countryside, a huge, Hindu church that housed many paintings and sculptures. It was crowded with worshippers. As we prepared to enter the building, a small calf came up to me, his owner hoping that, for a few rupees, I might like to have a picture of myself with the calf. As I reached over to pet the animal, it put its head down, butted me in the stomach, and started to repeat the attack to the dismay of the owner who quickly used his stick to keep the calf away. It was a shock and a revelation to me. Having experienced the friendly snakes, and the ever-present smiling monkeys who loved us tourists, especially if we tossed them peanuts, here was a hostile animal letting me know how it really felt.

After Madras, Bud and I were on tour, with only one more lecture in his schedule. It was in Trivandrum, where our hosts housed us in a resort hotel, right on the sea. Each morning, we could watch the fishermen pushing their long fishing boats off the land and into the water and then climbing in, dragging their hand woven nets. The boats carried about twenty men and were shaped like long American Indian war canoes but with the bow and the stern ends pointing upward, and a series of oarlocks on each side.

Trivandrum -- fishermen launching boat

As we returned from the beach to the hotel on the day of Bud's lecture, we noticed the chambermaid, wearing her colorful red and yellow cotton sari, smiling and humming as she filled the drinking water bottles with the garden hose. So that accounted for Bud's sudden-onset bellyache! A few hours later a car arrived to take him to the university where he lectured, carrying his manuscript in one compartment of his brief case and a roll of toilet paper in the other.

From Trivandrum we went to the North to Delhi and Agra, before returning home. The day after our arrival in Delhi, Bud and I tuned into the portable short wave radio we had purchased during our stopover at Heathrow, to get the day's news. We had been preparing to meet our driver for the trip to Agra, when an announcement came about a curfew in New Delhi. A flare-up of violence that characterized the ongoing Hindu-Moslem conflict (in this case a conflict over the proposed conversion of a mosque into a Hindu Temple), made it unsafe for people to wander the streets, especially foreigners like us who would be easy targets. We checked with the hotel staff to find out that the curfew was serious and being enforced. Fortunately, the hotel was large and had restaurants and comfortable lounges. To keep entertained, since there was no television, we listened to our portable radio. We had a choice of two English language programs: the US Army station, with local news about happenings on the base, or Radio Moscow, which was featuring songs by Pete Seeger. We chose to listen to Pete.

"If I Had a Hammer"
https://www.youtube.com/watch?v=Rl-yszPdRTk

Our confinement was relieved on the second day of the curfew by having tea with the Jains, who had been visiting professors at the Harvard Divinity School where our daughter Judy studied a few years earlier. Since we, as tourists were unable to move safely about the city, Lakshmi and Devaki Jain came to the hotel. They were Indian intellectuals: Devaki, the wife, was an economist, and Lakshmi, a public servant. In his youth he had been an active follower and disciple of Gandhi. Devaki wore the traditional silk sari. Lakshmi, was dressed in a hand woven suit. He told us of his mission to restore the small craft industries in India. As a political statement, a Gandhian concept, he never wore anything synthetic, only cotton, silk, or wool and always hand woven.

On the third day the curfew lifted and our driver took us to Agra, on a four lane two-way road packed with cars and trucks and buses, some straight up and several overturned, and cows and donkeys, and people walking. We did not witness the accidents that resulted in the overturned vehicles; some of them may have been newly disabled and some may have been there for weeks. As we drove, we also passed concessions where tourists were offered elephant rides and food from outdoor stands. The closer we got to Agra, the more tourist-lures there were. And suddenly, in the distance we finally saw what we had been waiting to see. The gleaming–in-the-sunlight-white marble Taj Mahal was as beautiful as we had been told. Walking from the car park to the buildings, Bud and I were surrounded by young Indian boys selling post cards— not of the Taj Mahal, as I had expected, but rather of the nude and provocatively seductive statues at Khajuraho, the so-called Indian Temple of Love that was 250 miles away.

Esther and Bud at the Taj Mahal, December 1986

After the solidly packed three weeks, our appreciation of India was far different from what we had expected. We had seen the bronzes in the museums, those graceful statues of the gods, who appear to be twirling as their many sets of arms stretch out and form graceful curves of rare beauty. We were enchanted by the colors, especially in the south, where the women were dressed in saris: cotton, silk, and hand dyed, in vivid reds and yellows and greens. We had seen cows standing and grazing in tiny patches of vegetation in the narrow medians of major traffic arteries, surrounded on both sides by trucks, cars, three-wheeler vehicles, donkey carts, motor cycles and bicycles, as well as masses of people walking on the roads. We had seen the poor sleeping in the streets at night and begging during the day. We had entered the homes of well-to-do and extremely wealthy Indian families who, in some ways were much like us, as they spoke in perfect English about current affairs and world events. But they were also very different; deeply religious, proud products of a rich ancient culture, and conscious heirs of the victims of British colonial rule.

# CUBA: 2003

At last we arrived in Cuba at 3:00AM on a Sunday morning in mid-September 2003. Bud was to give a paper at a conference of neurologists, and, because of the travel restrictions that prevailed in 2003, I was told that since I was a "health professional" I could be a speaker at an "auxiliary meeting." "We'll put you on the program. You can talk about undergraduate preparation in neuroscience," the conference organizer said. He had sounded so convincing that, before we left New York, I decided to bone up on my "assignment" by interviewing my friend Rae, a neuropsychologist who taught undergraduate premeds. Of course, when we arrived in Havana there was no such auxiliary program. Furthermore, although I could have been deemed a "health professional," I was retired and not eligible to be granted a license. The alternative to having a license of my own was to be called an "accompanying person." This category permitted one to travel in Cuba, but forbade me from spending any money there.

Bud and I had dreamed of going to Cuba ever since the early sixties when we read C.Wright Mills *Listen Yankee* and heard glowing reports about their visit to Cuba, shortly after the revolution, from our friends, Leo Huberman and Paul Sweezy. We knew that a lot had changed since the first days of the revolution. We knew that dissidents were not tolerated, that Yankee had not listened, and that the U.S. embargo had seriously damaged the Cuban economy, which, now that the Soviet allies were gone, was in shambles. We were not comfortable going to a "police state," where we knew we would only be shown the things the government of Cuba wanted us to see. Our friend Marta suggested we get in touch with the nearest branch of Human Rights Watch, which we did. Once we told them that we were going to Cuba, they asked us to please deliver books and papers to several dissidents who were jailed in Havana. They would provide us with the names of the prisoners and the addresses of the jails. Both Bud and I were apprehensive about this suggestion, fearful that it would jeopardize our hosts as well as us. We decided to write to Paul Farmer, a friend of a friend, whom we admire for his important medical work all over the developing world. His reply to us was that when he goes to Cuba he steers clear of politics: it's all too complicated and it interferes with the reason he is going there in the first place. We accepted his model and decided not to deliver anything to the dissidents. We would just be guests and see what we could see.

After a half-hour wait on line for the immigration and passport check, we were waved into the Havana Airport baggage claim and then into the waiting room. Joel Guttierez, our young Cuban host, spotted us immediately even though our only contact with him had been through e-mail, 25 pages of which we had accumulated over a period of six months. He looked and acted exactly as I had expected from his correspondence: a slim man in his late thirties, earnest, energetic and smiling as he lifted our bags onto the trolley. He was there with Veronica, his wife, an engineer; serious, pretty, and totally devoted to Joel and his extraordinary efforts to host an international conference on neuromuscular disorders. By the time we met them on that hot September night, I felt as though we had known them for years.

While waiting for Joel to get his car, we talked to Veronica about their family. They have one eight-year old daughter and Veronica teaches at an engineering school. Bud asked: "Can academic workers like you and Joel afford to own cars in Cuba?" Veronica looked puzzled and replied, "I'm sorry but I do not understand the question. My English is not so good. When Joel returns, perhaps you can ask him?"

I scowled when Bud asked his question. It sounded so patronizing. But when Joel drove up in a 1950s Chevy, painted in thick layers of what looked like dark green house paint, with misaligned doors and a broken trunk lock, I realized that the question was not really out of line. However, after their apologies for the difficulties they were having closing the trunk, I remarked: "Wow, this is a real vintage car!" It was the right thing to say. Joel beamed with pride, smiled, and nodded his head in agreement, and off we went to our hotel. We learned later that this car actually belonged to Joel's father, borrowed that night because Joel's own car, a small Russian sub-compact, a bit newer than the Chevy, did not have the trunk room to accommodate the luggage that Americans usually carry, even on short trips. He was right.

The road from the airport to the center of Havana was dark and empty at that hour of the morning. The Chevy skirted potholes and bumped on the uneven pavement. The billboards, however, were fantastic: quotes from Jose Marti: "Ideas are more powerful than guns," exhortations about the building of a great socialist society, and homage to Salvatore Allende: "Allende Lives!" For me, an old socialist, it was thrilling to recall how different this was from our experience when we entered London from Heathrow more than forty years before. The road from the airport in England had been lined with billboards advertising American washing machines and dryers and cars and razors and toothpaste, with pictures of smiling consumers. Finally we got to Havana center, had a quick tour of Revolutionary Square and the marble statue of Jose Marti. Most remarkable of all, the face of Che Guevara, about ten stories high, was etched into the side of a tall building on the edge of the square.

Our accommodation was in a guesthouse run by the Ministry of Higher Education. It turned out to be the former home of the cigar manufacturer, Don Jaime Partagas. Our room the first night originally must have been a maid's quarters: small, crooked and without natural light. But it was air conditioned and cool after a long hot day and evening. We were promised a move the very next morning and were thereupon elevated from the worst room to the best. In fact it had been Senor Partagas's master bedroom with its own terrace, a huge bathroom that was dimly lit, with a stall shower that had such low pressure, the water only trickled out. The bedroom and anteroom were furnished in simple wicker pieces. There was a good closet and mercifully a good safe in which we stored our stash of dollar bills since the ATMs in Cuba did not accept U.S. bankcards and U.S. based credit cards were unusable. There also was a giant Carrier air conditioner in the wall. We slept well in Cuba, awakened however each dawn by a half dozen crowing roosters in the back yard of the house next door.

The first day we were on our own. The meeting had not yet begun and we taxied into the old town to see the Museum of the Revolution, a unique historical collection of pictures and documents of Cuban struggles for independence, starting with the struggles of the Taino peoples against the explorers and early colonizers. (The Tainos were defeated, slaughtered, and died of smallpox that had been introduced by the European conquerors.) Then there was the struggle for Cuban independence against the Spanish rulers, and after that, the struggle against the United States, and against United Fruit and all the other foreign companies that owned Cuban resources and agriculture. It ended with the Cuban revolution of 1959. History, from the point of view of the poor and the exploited, is rarely displayed in the museums in the United States, so it was a refreshing, and even an exhilarating opportunity to have this experience. The gift shop postcards included pictures of the vintage cars as a proud monument to Cuban ingenuity. They were making the best of a bad economic reality, the restrictive U.S. embargo. In the process, they were also thumbing their noses at the wasteful technology of capitalism. Bud quoted an old saying: "The best thing to do when you get a lemon is to make lemonade," and he grinned.

My secret pastime, as the neurologists attended their meeting, was swimming in the Hotel Nacional, a Batista-built luxury hotel, right in the center of town, and just around the corner from the site of the conference. The Nacional is one of Cuba's commercial assets. It caters to well-heeled tourists, has good restaurants, a grand lobby, and most of all an outdoor swimming area, where one could spend the hot days on lounge chairs, reading, sunning, cooling off in a huge kidney shaped pool (or a second lap pool) and sipping Cuba Libre. I did all but the sipping that glorious day while the experts were dealing with the world of neurological disorders.

The big tourist hotels in Havana all have displays of Cuban history and politics in a section of the lobby or sometimes in a separate room. Huge photographs of Fidel and Che, dressed in army fatigues and carrying rifles, are hung in the lobby at the Havana Libre (formerly the Havana Hilton), taken when they stayed there as guests for several months immediately after the revolution was won. The Seville had a wall of pictures of the Cubans who were then prisoners in the United States, with brief biographies of each of them. The Nacional had a large room devoted to painted murals of its own guests in the 40s, 50s 60s and beyond. They start with Meyer Lansky, the Jewish gangster and king of the gambling casinos, and move up to recent guests such as Harry Belafonte and Nelson Mandela.

In our last evening in Havana our hosts took us to a Workers Social Club on the seaside, which was formerly a Yacht Club for the rich. There we were in a grand outdoor space, partly covered by a high wooden roof, listening to and watching the waves hit the sandy beach in front of us as we ate a buffet meal of rice and beans and chicken. Dancing was the activity of choice for the Cubans especially, but the foreigners were lured onto the dance floor and getting looser and better by the minute. In the course of the evening, I noticed that my wrist was hurting, probably the result of a fall I had taken earlier that day in the pool. Dreading the thought of lugging bags the next day with a sprained wrist, I asked Joel where I could get an Ace bandage. I am not sure that he was familiar with Ace bandages, but he certainly knew that no pharmacies were open that night in Havana. "I might be able to get you some gauze if the Yacht Club has a first-aid room." He made a few inquiries and the reply was that it would be very difficult for me to get a bandage at that hour. When we returned to our room I tried to treat my wound the Cuban way. I found an old rag, two rubber bands, and made myself a bandage/splint, wrapped tightly around my palm and wrist. I slept well and was mostly healed the next morning. We left Cuba knowing that, unfortunately, it will take more than an Ace bandage to fix the U.S. and to fix Cuba. *Listen Yankee* was too simple and the cold war "solution" too harsh.

Once we boarded the plane, I became increasingly nervous about our re-entry to the United States. When we booked our tickets, we chose to travel on a two-legged itinerary: New York to Cancun, Mexico; Cancun to Havana. No one had questioned us when we departed from JFK. We were just going to Mexico. From Mexico to Havana there is no problem; there are no restrictions. But now we were to face the immigration police on our flight from Cancun to New York.

After landing in Cancun, we had a four-hour wait between planes. We picked up our luggage and fortunately there was a checkroom at the airport, and also a café with comfortable booths that was going to become our lounge, and our rehearsal site. As soon as we were seated and had placed our brunch order, I turned to Bud and said: "We've got to practice what we are going to tell the immigration police at Kennedy, and make sure that we tell them the same story. So you are the cop and I am me. Ask me what I was doing in Havana."

"OK," said Bud, and he put on a serious face. "So, Mrs. Esther Rowland. Your husband has told me that he was invited to give a lecture at this meeting. What were you doing there in Havana?"

"Sir, I was accompanying him. Where he went, I went."

"How much money did you spend in the seven days that you were there?"

"Oh, Sir, I spent nothing. The Congress paid for our hotel and meals. We have a letter verifying that. And I only walked to places, or went in the taxi with my husband. He bought all the gifts, using the daily amount allowed by the US government."

"Mrs. Esther Rowland, I don't believe a word you are saying. You will have to leave your husband now and come with me. I am putting you in jail." And Bud let out a huge laugh.

"It's not funny," I snapped. "People have been fined thousands of dollars for going to Cuba without a license."

We boarded the plane to New York and I tried not to think about what was going to happen. After we landed at JFK, we made our way to the US citizens' section of the passport checkpoint and waited our turn. I busied myself putting our documents in order. When we reached the booth, Bud handed the passport control agent, a young Chinese-American, both passports and our customs declaration.

"And what were you doing in Cancun?"

"We were returning from Havana where I lectured at a medical conference," Bud declared.

"Oh, that's interesting." The agent looked impressed. As he stamped both passports and handed them back to us, he smiled and said, "Welcome home!"

# EPILOGUE

So, Gerta, has it been a "normal life?" Yes and No. Could I have done things better? Yes. Has it been a "good life?" Yes.

As I look back there were many moral decisions I had to make, which at the time may have seemed to be the right thing to do, but in retrospect, I am not so sure. Bud and I were so certain that buying Wynnestay and living in Wynnefield, an integrated community, was the right thing to do. We recognized our privileged position, with choices available to us that others did not have, and we chose to stay and fight rather than turn our backs and run. But it was dangerous. We were devotees of public school but some of those schools did not serve our children well.

Even though I regarded the mandate to stay at home to raise my children as a conspiracy against women, I am not sure that the alternative— both parents going to work —is better when the society has not solved the problems of day-care, job sharing, part-time work, and generous leaves of absence.

As much as I did not want another baby after the three healthy ones already in my life, the comment by the doctor who did the procedure has haunted me since the moment he said it. I think we must rethink "reproductive rights" and push harder for day-care facilities that would make it easier for women in my position to return to work and keep the baby.

I regret that we did not encourage our children to talk to us more about their day-to-day problems. I do not know why we did not talk things out? Were we too busy? Were we too "laissez-faire," allowing the kids to be "independent" when they were too young to make good decisions.

I deeply regret the way I handled my mother's situation in the last year of her life. We did not know how bad a choice it was to put her in a nursing home in those days, five years before the Nursing Home Reform Act of 1987, which only slightly improved the situation but at least addressed nursing home abuses like tying patients to their chairs. Even today, the nursing home option may not be a wise choice for someone with her cognitive skills intact. The alternative of keeping my mother in our large home, with around-the-clock care, would have been the right thing to do.

Now for the good things: I am proud of the protest marches we joined and I am proud of my sons who went a step further and landed in jail briefly. Had something bad happened to any of us because we stood up for what we believed, I would have been deeply saddened. But I am still not in doubt about the importance of non-violent action in the battles for civil rights and civil liberties and solving international problems without resorting to war. I was glad that my sons participated in a class action law suit that challenged the draft and that the Vietnam war ended before Andy or Steve had to decide whether or not to choose a long jail-term in protest. I am proud of my daughter, Joy, who has been a life-long feminist, a people's lawyer, and the most caring daughter anyone could wish for. I never doubted that Bud had done the right thing by joining AIMS, serving as its President, and defending the organization and what it stood for. His answers to the "charges" against him during the McCarthy period were honest and principled. The people who "charged" him were not.

I recognize that I have been extremely fortunate in many ways—by being born to parents who loved me and who encouraged me to pursue my goals. I was so lucky to meet and fall in love with Bud, who shared my beliefs and who is a great neurologist and a great human being. Our children are healthy and happy and smart, and they are all contributors to society. Growing up in an interracial community has made them comfortable with people of different races, and two of them have had interracial marriages. All of our grandchildren are passionate about examining issues of race and working for social justice. Being an interracial family has helped us, through love, understanding, and genuine appreciation of "the other." Our children and their partners, and our grandchildren and their partners are all amazing people. We have inspired them and they have inspired us.

What a stroke of luck it was to find my job. I loved the challenge of figuring out new ways to convince professional schools to enlarge their vision of what makes a good doctor or lawyer and I encouraged my students to believe in themselves and to pursue their goals. As a feminist, I loved working at Barnard, a women's college that embraced the feminist cause. And now my former pre-medical students have honored me with a scholarship in my name.

My journey with Bud, my "fellow traveler," has been an amazing sixty-plus years of marriage that has only gotten better with time. I am proud that he and I share the same values and that we have worked together to put them into practice. As political "fellow travelers" we have been able to enthusiastically support the good causes and not care about whether or not communists supported those things too. As a traveling "fellow traveler" I had been able to arrange my work schedule to accompany Bud who has been invited to conferences and to give lectures all over the world. Our sojourns into far-off places have broadened our consciousness, enlarged our friendships, and made us better people.

It has been a rich life, filled with love, and laughter, and adventure, and its share of sorrow and challenges.

When I was thinking about how to publish this book, I asked a neighbor who is a literary agent what she thought. Her answer was that since I was not a celebrity, and since my story was not about something horrible or lurid, but rather, as she put it, "quotidian", it would not be a good choice for a commercial publisher. So here it is—a self-published collection of stories about how members of a particular family interacted with the historical events of Twentieth Century America. It may be "quotidian" but I hope it's not humdrum.